This is a very important book. It not only makes a distinctive and original contribution to Marxism, it is also important for philosophers of science and moral theory. Marx's dialectical materialism fits into neither of the prevailing conceptions of inquiry: reductionist, ahistorical, atheoretical positivism or postmodernist constructivism. Engelskirchen articulates on Marx's behalf a sophisticated non-reductionist materialism grounded in the contemporary philosophy of science, philosophy of language and the metaphysics of natural kinds. The question of Marx aside, Engelskirchen's realist conception of social science is a fundamental contribution to the literature of the philosophy of science and will be of interest to anyone who, in pursuing the study of complex phenomena, seeks to avoid a forced choice between positivism and postmodernism.

The book will be equally important for philosophers interested in moral theory. Marx is a deep critic of bourgeois moral and legal values but his normative concerns are also in some sense continuous with the values he criticizes. This is the classic question of commensurability/incommensurability in the sense of Kuhn. Engelskirchen's treatment is a marvel of dialectical sophistication. He brilliantly extends his non-reductionist approach to the epistemology and semantics of natural kinds to illuminate the respects of continuity and difference between bourgeois and Marxist normative conceptions. Here too the results will be important to those who until now may have paid little attention to Marx. Anyone interested in how normative conceptions change over time will find in Engelskirchen's approach a convincing alternative to relativist conceptions.

Dr. Richard Boyd, *Susan Linn Sage Professor of Philosophy at Cornell University, USA.*

Capital as a Social Kind

Capital as a Social Kind provides an introduction to social kinds in social theory. Thinking about kinds, the way we sort the things of the world into categories – water, for example, is a natural kind – has made an important contribution to our understanding of science in the last half century, but these advances have been largely applicable to the natural, rather than the social sciences. Drawing on the rich examples offered by Marx's analysis of capital and exploring a methodology that will be of interest to both Marxist and non-Marxist social theorists alike, *Capital as a Social Kind* extends this approach to the study of social life.

The book argues that, provoked by his study of Aristotle, Marx's attentions foreshadowed contemporary themes in the realist philosophy of science. Importantly, social kind analysis is relevant not only to understanding his critique of political economy but illuminates also a materialist study of law, justice, morality and the transition to socialism. Social kind analysis also opens a path for the development of today's moral realism by suggesting the need for a systematic study of the causal structures of social life. In this respect the importance of normative themes in Marxism is defended against claims that the Marxist tradition lacks the resources to call capitalism unjust or to defend morality and human rights.

The origin of capital, Marx suggests, can be found in the rupture of an original unity between the laborer and the means of labor, and the book explores the way a structure of separations best characterizes capital as a social kind. This uncovers a little developed emphasis in Marx's work – his focus on the phenomena of separation that define our lives and also on forms of association required to transcend them. Given that capitalism has made the instruments of labor instruments of social labor, forms of association that would recover worker control over them must be democratic. The transition to socialism, the book concludes, *just is* winning the battle of democracy. This book will be of interest to students and researchers of economics, philosophy and indeed any social science subject.

Howard Engelskirchen is a lawyer and a philosopher who has previously taught at the University of Santa Clara, Western State University College of Law, the University of Hawaii, Iowa State University and Union College, USA.

Routledge frontiers of political economy

Capital as a Social Kind

Definitions and transformations in the critique of political economy

Howard Engelskirchen

Routledge
Taylor & Francis Group

LONDON AND NEW YORK

First published 2011
by Routledge
2 Park Square, Milton Park, Abingdon, Oxon OX14 4RN

Simultaneously published in the USA and Canada
by Routledge
711 Third Avenue, New York, NY 10017

Routledge is an imprint of the Taylor & Francis Group, an informa business

First issued in paperback 2014

British Library Cataloguing in Publication Data
A catalogue record for this book is available from the British Library

Library of Congress Cataloging in Publication Data
Engelskirchen, Howard.
The political economy of capital : definitions and transformations / by Howard Engelskirchen.
p. cm.
Includes bibliographical references and index.
1. Capitalism. 2. Marxian economics. I. Title.
HB501.E574 2010
335.4'12–dc22

2010038948

ISBN: 978-0-415-77691-2 (hbk)
ISBN: 978-1-138-01311-7 (pbk)
ISBN: 978-0-203-82874-8 (ebk)

Typeset in Times
by Wearset Ltd, Boldon, Tyne and Wear

For Gwenaël

Contents

Coda 174

Preface

The impetus for this project reaches back a number of years. Originally I set out to investigate the proposition announced in Marx's "Preface" to the *Critique of Political Economy* that property relations are the legal expression of relations of production:

> In the social production of their existence, men inevitably enter into definite relations, which are independent of their will, namely relations of production appropriate to a given stage in the development of their material forces of production. The totality of these relations of production constitutes the economic structure of society, the real foundation on which arises a legal and political superstructure and to which correspond definite forms of social consciousness.... At a certain stage of development, the material productive forces of society come into conflict with the existing relations of production or – this merely expresses the same thing in legal terms – with the property relations within the framework of which they have operated hitherto.
>
> (1987 MECW 29: 263)

A result establishing the persuasiveness of Marx's insight for contract law appears as Chapter 5. In a straightforward way the analysis of the somewhat technical legal doctrine of consideration – a doctrine which has been part of Anglo American law for over 400 years – can be explained on the basis of Marx's analysis of value.

But securing the philosophical underpinnings of that analysis led to an interrogation of the foundations of social theory. For all the ink spilled explicating Marx's value analysis, its scientific basis required elaboration. Marx announced he was doing science and under the press of positivist philosophies of science, this was understood in a way that had Marxists chasing after a calibration of labor hours with a stop watch. The inevitable frustration of that enterprise – it is not the hands of a clock but ounces of gold that measure time in Marx's analysis – led one way or another to the renunciation of his analysis of value. Given physical quantities of goods and labor entered into a suitable input output matrix, it seemed possible to establish prices directly, and value therefore was redundant. Also, under the sway of logical positivism's rejection of metaphysics, the search for any notion of an unobservable causal determinant manifested only in the phenomena of price was thought vulnerable to the economist's hard-bitten use of Ockham's razor – "value," Joan Robinson said, "is just a word" (1962: 47).

Indeed. "Value" is just a word. But Marxists could be forgiven for thinking instinctively, if not with a full consciousness of what they were about, that perhaps value, the thing to which the word referred, was not. Yet efforts to recover Marx's analysis in response to positivist effacing of it more often than not explored alternatives to the project of science or, in the spirit of critical theory, understood that word in the way in which the German word "Wissenschaft" can be used, that is, in the broadly hermeneutic sense of "knowledge."

Other developments also left to the side the scientific dimension of Marx's thought. While renewed and rigorous attention to the significance of Hegel's *Science of Logic* represented an important advance and at its best acknowledged a distinction between logic and cause in no way incompatible with the perspective of science – Tony Smith proposed a "logic of material practices" largely open to naturalist investigations of the causal structures of social life (1993: 20) – other appeals to Hegel insisted on the "ontological import" of Hegel's idealist framework and emphasized conceptual logic because "capital has in part an ideal reality" (Arthur 2002: 8). Where Marx complained of the rule of *things* over persons, on this approach, "[s]elf-moving abstractions have the upper hand over human beings" (*id.*). Without determination, abstraction became the starting point of study and the critique of empiricism showed "how reality cannot conceivably be different from the inter-subjective conception of it" (Reuten and Williams 1989: 47).

Meanwhile, postmodern Marxists (Cullenberg 1999; Resnick and Wolff 2004), intent on rejecting traditional economic determinism – all notions of the determination of the superstructure by the base, for example, must reflect disreputable hours Hume and Newton spent in a pool hall studying billiard balls – drew on Althusser's concept of overdetermination to refashion a decentered notion of reciprocal and mutually reinforcing causality. But on this view even Althusser in the end did not go far enough; he clung to the dominance of economics "in the last instance." Instead every vestige of levels or layering in terms of priority or importance in natural or social analysis had to be abandoned. Everything is seen as mutually constituted and determined by everything else. Rigorously anti-essentialist (and presumably having never baked marijuana brownies), the postmodern Marxist insists that in baking a cake every ingredient is mutually constitutive of the whole (Cullenberg 1999). Nothing underlies anything else and no particular source can be deemed more or less important in its causation than any other. Thus the salutary point that what counts as a natural kind depends also on the purpose of our inquiry so that nature, in Plato's metaphor of the careful butcher, may be "carved at the joints" in very different ways to reflect our different needs and interests becomes, instead, the quite different proposition that nature may be cut anywhere, skeletal joint or no, and the choice we make is altogether one of policy. Avowedly relativist, the investigator makes policy choices that apparently meet no asymmetrical resistance underlying or determining them. Science in any ordinary sense, in other words, is made impossible, and explanation, "demystified," would be better "displaced" in favor of "story telling" (Wolff 1996).

What has been missing in all such reactions to the legacy of positivist interpretations of Marx is attention to the critique of positivism mounted over the last half century by realist philosophies of science. Hilary Kornblith (1993: 6–7) nicely summarizes contemporary themes as follows:

> Indeed it was the application of the causal theory of reference to natural kinds which allowed for the elaboration of a sophisticated scientific realism.... On the account of science which began to emerge..., it is the business of science to discover the real causal structure of the world; what this means, in a word, is the discovery of natural kinds and the causal relations among them.... natural kinds make inductive knowledge of the world possible because the clustering of properties characteristic of natural kinds makes inferences from the presence of some of these properties to the presence of others reliable.

Today it is possible to read Marx for the rich anticipation he gives of these emphases, and the work that follows is an effort to contribute to that reading. I argue that by tracking Marx's careful attention to the difference between the theoretical categories fashioned as a product of scientific investigation and the real causal structures of social life to which they refer, we find in Marx important explorations of social kinds, the natural kinds of social life, and of the causal relations among them, explorations that lay the foundation for rethinking contemporary social theory.

I've gathered these essays into two parts: "Definitions" and "Transformations." Although the chapters proceed sequentially, the argument of each following the argument of the ones before, nonetheless, the individual essays are to a degree self-standing so that I think a reader with particular interests can feel fairly comfortable attacking a chapter of interest and then filling out this reading by attention to others. Through the whole it is important not to lose the essential thread, which is quite simple and direct: capital is defined by the separation of the laborer from the conditions of production and by the separation of productive enterprises from one another. I argue that it is the intersection of these two separations that shapes our world.

Part I is concerned to develop in some detail the meanings of this definition, first, in Chapter 2, by giving an account of the commodity form, then in Chapter 3 by working out the specificity of separation that characterizes capital, and finally in Chapter 4 by drawing together these two analyses to explore Marx's development of the concept of capital or of 'capital in general' as he uses this in the *Grundrisse*. These chapters can serve as an introduction to the reading of *Capital I*, and thus, taken together with Chapter 1, serve as well to introduce fundamental features of Marx's method in social science.

Part II explores the idea of transformation in two senses of the word. On the one hand in Chapter 5 I show how the social reproduction of capital as a social kind requires particular forms of law, and I work through an example of this. In class society, I suggest, the appropriation of nature by labor tends to be reflected in the appropriation of behavior by coercion; that is, I use transformation in the sense Marx spoke of the changes in the economic foundation of society leading to transformations of the superstructure. In Chapter 6, I suggest how this analysis may be extended to our understanding of justice, morality and rights, but in doing so I underscore the essential need to understand capital as a social kind not statically but as a social form in the process of transition. This point is extended in Chapter 7 where I ask what the revolutionary transformation of capital as a social kind might mean for the transition to socialism.

Acknowledgments

As will become abundantly clear, the thread that has guided my studies for decades is an insight of Charles Bettelheim that the capitalist mode of production is characterized by a double separation. I am grateful to have known him and owe a large debt to him. I thought this idea could provide the key to understanding capital as a social kind, but without the immense good fortune of being able to work with Richard Boyd I could not have developed these ideas to the degree that I have; he has had a powerful influence on my study of the philosophy of science and it was his work on natural kinds that made it possible for me to understand Marx's anticipation of contemporary themes in scientific realism. I am enormously grateful for the attention he's given to these essays. To understand realist themes in Marx's thought I knew I needed to grapple with Marx's study of Aristotle; in this I had the privilege of studying ancient philosophy with Anthony Preus. Tony is an indefatigable hiker and our conversations about Aristotle took place largely on New York's Finger Lakes Trail; it is a pedagogy I recommend. Finally, I have to this day, more than two decades later, a strong recollection of a moment in a library basement finding in a book I do not recall a footnote to Roy Bhaskar's *The Realist Theory of Science* and thinking, "That's the book I need." I was not wrong and I am grateful to Bhaskar for the provocation and direction he provided.

I'm glad also for the debt I owe other colleagues and friends who have read and commented on portions of the text. Thanks to Howard Anawalt, Chris Arthur, Andrew Brown, Paul Bullock, Ruth Groff, Robert Hollinger, John Milios, Fred Moseley, Margherita Pascucci, John Roberts, Steve Scalet, Ernesto Screpanti, Herb Shore, Tony Smith, and Melissa Zinkin. Thanks also for help from Gwenaël Engelskirchen, Marianne Rannenberg, and Alex Utevsky. Thanks especially to Judith Soleil for her support and encouragement.

Chapter 2 previously appeared as "Why Is This Labour Value? Commodity-Producing Labour as a Social Kind," in F. Pearce and J. Frauley, eds., *Critical Realism: Heterodox Elaborations*, University of Toronto Press, 2007, and appears here by permission.

The Appendix to Chapter 2 is an excerpt from "On the Clear Comprehension of Political Economy: Social Kinds and the Significance of §2 of Marx's *Capital*," which appeared in R. Groff, ed., *Revitalizing Causality: Realism about*

Causality in Philosophy and Social Sciences, Routledge, 2008, and appears here by permission.

Chapter 5 previously appeared as "Value and Contract Formation" in J. Joseph and J. M. Roberts, eds., *Realism Discourse and Deconstruction*, Routledge, 2004, and appears here by permission.

Chapter 4 is also to be published as "The Concept of Capital in the *Grundrisse*" in R. Bellofiore, G. Starosta, and P. Thomas, eds., *In Marx's Laboratory. Critical Interpretations of the Grundrisse*, Brill (the Historical Materialism Book Series).

Part I

Definitions

What is at issue here is not a set of definitions under which things are to be subsumed. It is rather definite functions that are expressed in specific categories.

Capital II (1992: 303 [II.11])

1   Introduction

Social kinds in social theory

In the pages that follow I study capital as a social kind; I argue Marx's object in *Capital* was to study capital as a social kind. Thinking in terms of kinds refers to the way we sort the things of the world into categories – water, for example, is a natural kind – and references to natural kinds in the Western philosophical tradition reach back to the ancient world. But extension of that tradition to the study of social life has hardly begun. The real start, still today largely unexplored, was the standpoint announced in the first Preface to *Capital* where "the development of the economic formation of society is viewed as a process of natural history..." (1990: 92). In the *Grundrisse* Marx suggested that we could locate defining features of fundamental social categories, their *differentia specifica*, the way we sought distinctively characteristic features of *homo sapiens*, or, presumably, other biological species (1987 MECW 29: 227–228; 1973: 852). We can study social things the way we study natural kinds.

Realism for *homo sapiens*

Today attention to kinds is very much a product of scientific realism and it will be helpful to begin by underscoring realist emphases that make sense of this approach. We can start with an unambiguous lesson of history: it has been easy to think of ourselves as the center of the universe and not hard to throw into the bargain the idea that mind is the center of us. So idealist forms of thought have always seemed as ready to hand as the common sense realist assumptions that walk us through our daily lives. Moreover, if the ultimate reality of the world is mind then there are idealist forms of realism too. Methodologies grounded in materialism, therefore, the realisms that make good sense of science, have looked first to differentiate themselves from the notion of the world as a product of mind.

For the most part this has been done by characterizing metaphysical realism as an approach that rests on the premise that the world is "mind independent." Thus, "such physical entities as stones, trees and cats exist ('are real').... [T]hese entities do not depend for their existence or their nature on our minds, nor on our awareness, perception or cognizance of them" (Devitt and Sterelny 1987: 187). Or, "[t]he natural world is taken to exist as an object independent of human thought and action. In this sense, theorizing in the natural sciences describes and explains an independent realm" (Bishop 2007: 338). Or, again, realist methodologies hold that "[t]he world exists independent of human beings, that mature scientific theories typically refer to this world, and they do so even when the objects of science are unobservable" (Wendt 1999: 47).

Now it does indeed seem that large patches of the world, from quarks to black holes, have made their way over the last fourteen or so billion years without regard to how we think of them, so there is nothing wrong with affirming the existence of mind independent things. But it is quite another matter to suppose it follows that "mind independence" is an indispensable presupposition of science and that the study of things that are "mind dependent" must have recourse to non-naturalist methods or that our study of them cannot be scientific at all. That is to say, the pairing of "mind dependence" with "mind independence" misleads: for one thing, however it be with the world, *our* confrontation with it depends inexorably on causal practice that is mind engaged, or, what is just another way of saying the same thing, in a world of causally potent things mind is part of the causal structure we are.

When it comes to studying social things, the problem becomes acute. How can we claim that the products of our common activities are "mind independent'? Engels (1988 MECW 23: 631) urged that if socialism was a science, it had to be studied like a science[1]; but if science depends on the study of things that are 'mind independent," it looks like we are deprived from the start of an object of study.

It might make sense to back up and rethink the way "mind dependence" has been paired with "mind independence." *Homo sapiens* are part of nature and while many things do not depend on what we think of them, they do not for that reason populate "an independent realm" the existence of which is "independent of human beings'" in the scheme of things we fill a very small space, but mind is part of nature and when it functions causally it functions, like other things, as a causally potent part of nature. The real distinction we need is not between things with a mind and an independent realm of those without, but a distinction instead between the causally efficacious activity that characterizes all forms of matter in motion and that curious retreat from cause that our reference to the world, semiosis, can represent.

Semiosis is the action of signs. A sign is anything we use to refer to some other thing. Smoke is a sign of fire. The word "smoke" can be a sign of the white/grey cloud belched from a smoke stack; the sound made by saying the word can refer to clouded air. Here's a pretty obvious point that can be overlooked: reference, as such, is not causal. If I point at a full moon, I don't change it, though if someone steps on it, brings rock back to earth, that does. Surely the non-causal character of reference is an evolutionary result of profound importance. The different forms of matter are differentially efficacious in the ways they work. Those differences determine how things interact: a hydrophilic molecule bends toward a moist environment and a hydrophobic one bends away. Living things develop reflexes, and the philosopher W. V. Quine suggested how reference to color became a way to differentiate the noxious from the nutritious. (1991: 165). Alarm calls emerge to signal a predator, and a dog, Justice Holmes observed, knows how to tell the difference between being stumbled over or kicked (2009: 5). In all these instances response to causal difference facilitates the accommodation potent structures of the world make with one another in their interaction. The clear emergence of the break with causation we associate with reference marks a qualitative advance. It's like a team sport where the coach diagrams a play on the sidelines. The diagram, sketched during a time out, has no effect on the game. It can have if it is implemented. But this doesn't happen on the sidelines. It happens in the rough and tumble of regulation playing time, not with pencil or chalk, but with muscle and movement. Semiosis has its source in the world of causal phenomena we observe and informs the forms of our engagement with it. But because reference itself doesn't *do* anything, it carves, as it were, a space that is disengaged, however fleetingly – one thing refers to another, without more. And because reference can reflect well or badly, can portray accurately or distort, reflect a perspective more or less partial, the space created becomes a place of meaning, of interpretation, of imagination, of mermaids and unicorns, of possibilities abstract and real, of reason and inference and other sophisticated forms of information processing, of evaluation and judgment, of knowledge and error. And thus a short lived hiatus offers space to learn more about the world than a perceptual signal alone can provide. We can infer things and properties sensuously unobservable to us and grasp their possibilities. We figure out that smoke is caused by fire and discover DNA and the genetic code. Like the coach on the sidelines our understanding of the way things work comes to inform our plans and we mobilize our engagement with the world in terms of those understandings; our practice, mind engaged, is semio-causal. Locke's insight regarding the relation of philosophy to science is apt: causally disengaged, semiosis is an underlaborer for human practice.[2]

A fully materialist realism then can be distinguished from other approaches not by a differentiation between objects that are mind independent and those that are not – we watch those efforts obliterate the possibility of naturalism in social science. A scientific realism that is naturalist depends instead on a lively appreciation of the distinction between a world of causally potent things on the one hand and what Richard Boyd has called the *metaphysical innocence* of our concepts and categories on the other (1999b and forthcoming). Our hypotheses and theories, he argues, make no non-causal contribution to the way the world is. Notice: he has not said they make no causal contribution. The point instead is that they make no *non*-causal contribution. They are metaphysically innocent *unless* they engage ordinary causal mechanisms. The coach's diagram on the sidelines is, so to speak, game-wise innocent. It makes no contribution to the outcome of the game unless it is causally implemented. That's the idea. As long as reference is causally disengaged, it is metaphysically innocent. It is the business of science, as Roy Bhaskar (1997), Kornblith (1993), and others suggest, to understand the causal structures of the world, including the causal structure we are, and we do this by exploiting the ephemeral free space that causally *impotent* reference makes possible. But it is practice where we have our being, not disengaged reference. We understand the world to change it, and this depends on our purposeful engagement with it.

Natural kinds

We understand to transform because our survival and flourishing depend on this. If metaphysically innocent reference is to serve material activity as an underlaborer, it will do this by bringing reference into correspondence with the ways we must and can engage causal phenomena. The relationship is dialectical: reference informs action and from our engagement we learn to recognize error, a perspective that is partial, and so on. Peter Railton (1991: 767–768) has captured the idea by asking whether objectivity is possible once we know that all observation is theory laden. He writes:

> That is, although we cannot even in principle, have direct access to the objects of inquiry, there may yet exist mechanisms of belief formation that incorporate feedback from the object to the inquiring subject. This feedback would force us, if we are to realize our goals, to reexamine our theory and values in such a way that our beliefs are appropriately controlled over time by the object as well as by our subjectivity.
>
> This sort of objectivity is possible even though all perceptions of and inferences about the object are mediated by theory and norms because the object nonetheless has a direct way of affecting us: causally. To have no "conceptual niche" for a given phenomenon does not in general prevent that phenomenon from influencing our fate through all-too-familiar causal mechanisms.[3]

In other words we are enmeshed in what he calls a "causal nexus" and by "regularly and ambitiously insert[ing] ourselves into [it]" we can ensure that our representations are reliably regulated by the causal structures we engage. Even though we have no guarantee that we are carried "away from error and toward truth," still, Railton emphasizes, the process "gives objects ample opportunity to affect us causally." Asking for feedback from causally active phenomena, natural or social, is one of materialism's methodological essentials. Listening to others or to nature has always been an indispensable underlaborer for doing.

Insofar as the causal things we engage are differently efficacious they will evoke different responses from us with the result that we will sort them into different kinds of things. In this, two mistakes are possible. On the one hand we can assume we have unmediated access to the causal structures of the world joined with a capacity to give a God's eye view of the way the world is – we hold a mirror to nature and report what is reflected there. Of course the only piece missing in that account is our own being in the world. Plato's *Phaedrus* (1961[265d]) is the source of the metaphor that we carve nature at its joints; in point of fact we have no access to any such joints except by carving and our understanding of the world depends on our engagement with it. In that way we find what is amenable or impervious to our efforts. Here, then, is a second point: it is also an error to suppose that we can carve anywhere anytime and any way we want. We don't make the causal structures we engage except insofar as we work with nature's laws to exploit our own causal powers, and even the causal structures of social life can be transformed only according to imperatives specific to them – I do not change transportation patterns by riding a bike, though given an appropriate level of social organization, I may very well play a part in doing so.

Natural kinds, therefore, reflect the way we engage the world by means of our practice, including scientific experiment, and this means that natural kind terms refer to the world not in some abstraction of how it is, but instead they pick out the ways it is carved by our practice. This means we engage in different ways for different purposes and although constrained by causal structures taken as given, we do not engage always the same structures in the same way for the same purposes. For ordinary terrestrial tasks, for example, we will characterize the line light follows as straight, but we will want a different characterization for paths past massive astronomical objects across large slices of cosmos. Boyd (forthcoming) takes an example from "kitchen chemistry": "sour cream" and "baking soda" are kind terms we make use of to guide the practice of making biscuits rise, but a biochemist, sensitive to bacterial variation, will draw closer causal distinctions for her work. Or suppose someone asks why another is crying: usually she will not want the answer a physiologist might give about pressure forming on the tear ducts (Pinker 1999: 314).

A further point here is that while we name to carve nature according to our purposes, we don't carve merely by naming. Bhaskar's (1997) caution against the epistemic fallacy is relevant. His phrase challenges the philosophical tendency to turn all questions of the nature of being, ontology, into questions of what we can know about being, epistemology. In our use of kind terms we want to avoid turning all questions concerning the causal structure of the world into questions of naming and reference. We refer in order to accommodate our practice to the way the world is. We can expect disappointment if we suppose reference without more will create the referents to which it refers. Certainly social kinds can be a product of labeling. Drawing on Foucault (1990) and others, Hacking (1992) has shown the way the label "homosexual" came to refer to a kind of person characterized by much more than same sex practices. But the idea that this occurs as a result of the metaphysically innocent act of labeling rather than from a potent constellation of material social practices is an illusion.[4] To take an example from Marx, even though people in business use the term "price of labor" this term does not refer to a natural kind. The "wage form" is a term that refers, and, as Marx shows, the "price of labor" plays an essential role in its reproduction by misrepresenting the nature of the exchange of labor power for a wage, but it is "labor power" which is a natural kind term and which refers to a commodity that can take a price. As a term of reference the "price of labor", Marx suggests, is irrational with basically the same status as a "yellow logarithm" (1991: 957 [III.48.1.3]).

Because things are differently efficacious, in order to accommodate our practice to them we search for those properties that are decisive in determining causal differences. But superficial properties, the stereotypes we form on our first encounter with things – "there, that bird, the one always upside down," – typically do not reliably explain such difference and thus do not always provide a reliable guide to the causal response we need in our engagement with them. Thus, Quine (1991) suggested, that in the progress of human understanding superficial differentiations based on color give way to the theoretically sophisticated similarities we associate with molecular composition. That is, in a lesson we can still learn from Aristotle, we learn to distinguish between the constitutive properties of causal phenomena, those reliably associated with them, and those that are attributive or contingent. Mao Zedong's (Mao Tsetung 1971: 96 [*On Contradiction*]) observation is relevant: different sciences study distinct objects differentiated precisely on the basis of the contradictions fundamental and particular to them. Boyd (1999a, 1999b) refers to natural kinds as *homeostatic property cluster kinds* because the causal generalizations that support successful inductive and explanatory practice depend on a cluster of causal properties or mechanisms capable of accounting for how a thing maintains itself in a stable relationship to its environment. To offer a real definition of a natural kind, then, means to identify this cluster of features. Stathis Psillos (1999: 287–88) calls the core properties that explain how a thing behaves its *kind constitutive properties*, and he adds that ultimately these are the source of the information we have about the kind. Thus H_2O refers to a molecular configuration that ultimately regulates our understanding of what water is and how it behaves.

This is an essentialism, of course, but I think it is impossible to do science without looking explicitly or implicitly for the constitutively essential. Marx, in any event, was after the inner nucleus of connection that specifically distinguished capital from other forms of social production. He persistently sought to give expression to those decisive structures that could distinctively account for capital's sturdy ability to reproduce itself in its environment – those few features that make it what we might today call a *homeostatic social kind*: "The forms of appearance are reproduced directly and spontaneously, as current and usual modes of thought; the essential relation must be discovered by science" (1990: 682 [I.19]).

Social kinds

If the premise is that we can extend our thinking about natural kinds to the study of social life, then we will be looking to follow the path charted by the passages from Kornblith (see Preface) and Railton (see p. 6):[5] as with any science our objective will be to identify the causal structures of its domain and to discover, by means of our causal engagement with them, their features and ways of acting. I will briefly highlight a few of the key factors that make this task distinctive for the study of social life, and then briefly flag also some of the objections that have been raised to such an approach. I should say immediately that I do not address the entire constellation of things people have characterized as social or human kinds – tools, artifacts, roles, institutions, mental states, and so on. While much of what I say no doubt generalizes, my focus is on capital as a social kind and what I say can be taken as limited to kinds like it.

Social kinds depend not on conventional distinctions but on differences of causal structure and of causal efficacy. Often there is a tendency to assume that just by virtue of the fact that the patterns of social life depend on our behaviors then the distinctions we make among social categories must reflect purely conventional classifications, that is, distinctions we stipulate to as a matter of agreement. "Bachelor" is often an example offered to make the point unproblematically. We define bachelor as a marriage eligible unmarried male and assume the term's reference is determined by what we choose it to mean. But no one would really be surprised to see the term extended to any unmarried person of marriageable age the way we extend the word "actor" to any person on stage or the way "you guys" in the appropriate context will refer to a person of either sex. While we may resist such "gender neutral" renderings that become so by extending the applicability of the masculine form, nonetheless, these transformations of meaning are more persuasively explained as the product of the changing causal structures of social life rather than as a consequence of stipulation or convention. Within the small history of our personal experience we see the social kind marriage undergo a transformation and this depends on hard fought changes in material social relations and the patterns of behavior that give expression to them.

Hacking (1992: 80) argues that while "what camels, mountains and microbes do does not depend on words," human kinds often come into existence hand in hand with the invention of our categories labeling them. We can agree, but, as Foucault (1990) has so powerfully shown in the work Hacking draws on, this occurs when labels engage the ordinary causal mechanisms of social life such as legal sanctions, the organization of medical treatments, behavioral controls in schools and other institutions, as well as the other numerous manifestations of relational power that characterize our interactions with one another. Kinds accompany labels when labels accompany causal interventions that alter the objective realities persons confront in their lives.

Labor-form composites as social kinds. As a social kind capital is what I call a labor-form composite. I will argue that Marx's close study of Aristotle exerted an enormous influence on his thought and this characterization reflects that fact. Suppose we extend the insight captured by metaphysical innocence to the study of social form. In fact, an important part of Aristotle's critique of Plato was that the form of the things of the world, of a house or a horse or the family that held them, made no non-causal contribution to the way things were except insofar as such forms were instantiated in matter. The things we find in existence, Aristotle insisted, are matter-form composites. Thus while we can abstract to the idea of form without matter, unless *enmattered*, form is causally impotent; equally, Aristotle thought it impossible to think of matter except hypothetically unless *enformed* – unformed matter does not exist. And here is another point: Aristotle treated *activity* as a form of matter, and, in working out his analysis of social life, Marx took over the full significance of this. The social kinds Marx studied are composites of activity and form, and, as such, causally efficacious. But only insofar as social form is instantiated in the activity of persons does this consequence follow – social relations considered abstractly are without causal purchase.

Social kinds are reproduced by the enformed activity of persons. The philosopher Roy Bhaskar (1989; 1998) has shown that the existence of social objects is established by their causal power and that this in turn is a result of the enformed activity of persons. That is, people are, so to speak, the moving parts of social kinds, but the activity of persons always occurs in some historically specific social arrangement. Importantly, such arrangements cannot be reduced to what people do without taking into account the social forms within which they act. Marilyn Frye (1983) illustrates the point by inspecting the wires of a birdcage one by one in isolation and wondering what conceivable capacity they might have to constrain a bird. Iris Marion Young (2002: 92) compares these wires in the form of a birdcage with the same wires piled in a heap. Nothing changes in the causal power of any individual wire but the causal potential of the accumulation is very different in the two cases. Also because patterns of social behavior often attain stability, we can speak of these constellations of form as homeostatic mechanisms, taking over the word from biology. Exchange, for example, is a homeostatic social form that reproduces specialized production by independent producers; that is, exchange reproduces the social division of labor, and it has done so responsive to market environments that have changed dramatically over time.

Importantly, that we borrow concepts from biology to refer to social life and that we use concepts like "social organism" or the "life process" of a social thing need have no ghostly or teleologically compromised implications. Like objects studied by the life sciences, the causal phenomena of social life go through processes that are reliably repeated, but social structures have no purposes or consciousness or goals. I will describe capital as going through a cycle that begins with a separation of laboring producers from the material conditions of production and that includes in sequence labor market exchange, production, and forms of distribution such that the circumstance of separation that initiated the cycle is reproduced and the process begun again. But all this can be done without invoking the sort of teleology that had stones being possessed of a natural desire to find earth. Processes have a beginning and end and repeated processes tend to produce the form of their beginning as a repeated result; that is the most that is being said.

Social kinds exist in their effects, constitutive and attributive. I said people are the moving parts of social kinds but they are not the only moving parts – the forces of nature also contribute to the causal efficacy of social things. Nonetheless, it is true that such causal structures exist only in virtue of and are only reproduced by the activity of persons. There is not some sort of other substance of social life that binds a social composite. Thus, because they exist only in patterns of behavior that are reproduced, we can say that social kinds exist only in virtue of their effects (Bhaskar 1989: 81). Importantly, it does not follow that we are unable to distinguish constitutive from contingent or attributive effects. Environmental rape and wasteful consumption may be consequences of the reproduction of capital, and even inevitably so, yet these do not count as effects that are constitutive of the process (though the first may very well be destructive of it). The separation of the laboring producer from the means of labor, on the other hand, is not only a constitutive cause of the process, but a necessarily consequent effect.

Social kinds never obliterate the free agency of persons. I've said people act within specific social arrangements and, though they need not be aware of this, these shape how they think and behave. There is a necessity to this: in order for social forms to be reliably reproduced people must behave in ways that appropriately correspond to what is required for a structure's persistence. But individuals remain always fully free to think or act as they choose, regardless of the roles in which they happen to find themselves. You or I could choose to forgo market exchange. Though life is no doubt markedly easier when the choices we make conform to dominant patterns of social behavior, social arrangements never obliterate the free agency of persons. Still, while people are free and social structures cannot determine how they act, for the most part people's behaviors do in fact reproduce the social forms they inhabit. That is, their behavior mostly corresponds to what is reproductively necessary for the persistence of dominant social forms. Moreover, notice that individual behaviors necessary to established patterns of social reproduction will typically occur spontaneously; just as typically their transformation must be purposive – political action that functions to reproduce the status quo can often seem removed from politics in a way counteraction to challenge existing forms cannot. Thus, "Keep politics out of education!," in Andrew Collier's example, translates into "keep education the way it is" (1989: 153), but progressive educational change will require purposeful political organization.

Arguing for social kinds

Some of the reasons deployed by those who claim social kinds cannot be studied like natural kinds include arguments that, unlike natural kinds, social kinds are not characterized by properties that are necessary and sufficient or universal and ahistorical; that, unlike natural kinds, social kinds are not mind independent; that, unlike natural kinds, social kinds are not characterized by core structures internal to them; or that unlike natural kinds, social kinds, because mind dependent, must be studied by methods that are idealist. But these challenges are not persuasive.

The local and historically specific character of social kinds. Long standing, traditional views of what it meant to be a natural kind included the idea that if a thing were a natural kind it had to be characterized by necessary and sufficient membership conditions that were universal and ahistorical. An electron, for example, would qualify: it is presumably the same wherever and whenever in the universe it is found. On this view, species distinctions wouldn't count, or indeed any of the other mechanisms of the life sciences – these are the product of local histories that would not be the same anywhere at any time. It follows that by these criteria social things like capital are clearly excluded. But while this approach still has energetic defenders (Ellis 2001, 2002), more flexible methodologies that do not explicitly or implicitly reduce all real science to the models of physics and chemistry are now readily available (Boyd 1991, 1999b, and forthcoming).

The semio-casual dependence of social kinds. More significant resistance stems from the idea that social kinds are not mind independent. But as I've explained above, this objection also reflects ways of thinking about natural and social kinds that we can move beyond. Marx gives a telling example:[6]

> The "circumstances" which determine the value of a commodity are by no means further elucidated by being described as circumstances which influence the "MIND" of those engaging in exchange.
>
> (These same circumstances (independent of the MIND, but influencing it), which compel the producers to sell their products as *commodities* – circumstances which differentiate one form of social production from another – provide their products with an exchange value which (also in their MIND) is independent of their use value. Their "MIND," their consciousness, may be completely ignorant of, unaware of the existence of, what in fact determines the value of their commodities or their products as values. They are placed in conditions which determine their reasoning but they may not know it. Anyone can use money as money without necessarily understanding what money is. Economic categories are reflected in the mind in a very distorted fashion)."
>
> (1989 MECW 32: 348)

I think Marx is not saying here that mind is incapable of influencing the circumstances that determine the social relation of value. The point being addressed instead is that the social circumstances that account for value operate independent of mind either insofar as mind is metaphysically innocent – i.e. reflects beliefs or understanding without causal purchase – or also insofar as the things on which mind is causally engaged are not relevant to those social circumstances or are not engaged at a causal level adequate to influence them. Notice that the circumstances with which Marx is concerned are "circumstances which differentiate one form of social production from another" – what I have called a "labor-form composite." In Chapter 2 I will characterize the social form that accounts for value as "interdependent autonomy": separate producers produce products useless to them as part of the social division of labor. A shoemaker who produces thousands of shoes a year does not produce them to wear. The shoemaker is compelled by the circumstances of production to resort to market. As these circumstances work themselves out in the market they also account for the value of commodities. Further – they form the shoemaker's plans and purposes. It does not follow, however, that she understands the circumstances that drive her to market anymore than we might suppose that a shoemaker of the ancient world, who knew very well the uses of water, knew that water was H_2O.

Alexander Wendt, who has a very good introduction to social kinds realism in his book *The Social Theory of International Politics* (1999), would presumably challenge Marx's account. Taking the social category 'witch' as an example, Wendt writes:

> Social kinds seem to lack the mind/discourse independent, common internal structure that is the basis for realism about natural kinds. There is no free-standing, prediscursive essence in virtue of which a witch is a witch, and thus no objective reality exerting a regulatory influence on our theorizing about witches.
>
> (71 [footnote omitted])

But the same reasoning would apply to the circumstances that account for value – presumably there is no prediscursive essence of value since it depends through and through on mind engaged social relations of labor as well as the processes of market exchange. But it doesn't follow in the case of either witches or value that there is no causally efficacious objective reality regulating our theorizing.

By "prediscursive essence" I assume Wendt has in view a mind independent biological essence that would make a woman a witch – the kind of biological essence some have sought for without success for human racial difference. Because social things are, for humans, never prediscursive, the causal efficacy of social structures is never discourse independent. It is enough that potent structures of social life reliably regulate patterns of behavior and belief. Following Railton we can test our understanding of these by stepping "ambitiously and regularly" into the relevant causal nexus. Whether we engage natural or social things, practice will provoke feedback confirming, if we are lucky, what we have understood or, also if we are lucky, disabusing us of illusions. In the case of "witch" the relevant causal nexus is not biological, without doubt; that doesn't mean there is not a deeply embedded structure of gender relations to be understood and transformed if the social oppressions expressed by the label are to be overcome. It is that causal structure that renders the reality of "witch" objective; indeed, in a given social historical circumstance the term "witch" may capture a social kind.

This suggests a related lesson to draw from Wendt's example. Just as we do not assume witches can be studied as social kinds in isolation without considering the complicated social relations that provide the context for understanding, comparably we are unlikely to understand other social kinds as the same across all times and cultures. To study bureaucracy, for example, we may first need to characterize the mode of production within which bureaucratic forms are shaped. As with any science a foundation must be established and things that seem similar may bear only analogy to one another rather than give expression to a traceable common root. It would seem to make sense to begin the study of society with "population," Marx writes, but this is an empty abstraction unless you first establish the causal relations of which population is a complicated composition (1986 MECW 28: 37; 1973: 100).

The relationality, internal and external, of social kinds. For Wendt, the witch example can also illustrate the way natural kinds tend to reflect a self-organizing internal structure that social kinds lack. Thus, while the micro-constitution of the water molecule, for example, depends on the inter- and intra-molecular forces that bind hydrogen and oxygen, by contrast social kinds, he argues, depend on external, not internal relations. The idea here is that what makes a teacher a teacher or a slave-master a master is not something intrinsic to them as persons – not some biological essence – but instead a student or slave, respectively.

The role external relations play in defining kinds in the life sciences and also in the study of social life is a difficult question for both, and I don't propose to resolve it. I will though suggest parameters that shape my own approach. As Wendt points out, the master does not *cause* a slave; the relation is constitutive. But if it is constitutive I'd want to ask why it is considered external. We can do so only if, implicitly, we assume analysis begins with individuals. But if our objective is to understand kinds characterized as social composites of activity and form, then what counts as internal will be different. That is, the starting point will not be a witch, or a master, or teacher, or producer of commodities, but instead constitutive relational processes of social life like gender, education, slavery, and commodity-producing labor. In every case, natural or social, we must look for the causal basis by means of which a thing maintains itself as what it is. In *On Contradiction* Mao Zedong reminds us that heat will turn an egg into a chicken, but that no amount of heat will turn a stone into one. The lesson he draws is that the external condition, heat, is a condition for change, but it is the microstructure of the object, its set of inner contradictions, that is the basis for change. How a plant evolves will depend on factors such as sun, temperature, moisture, soil quality, and so on, but the same plant will grow very differently in different environments depending on features distinctive to the plant itself.

Contrary to the assumptions of methodological individualism, with social phenomena we cannot assume the unrelated individual is the basis for change. There is nothing intrinsic to an individual that makes him a capitalist, of course, nor can we reduce the composite social entities we characterize as value or capital to some indifferent aggregate of individuals. Instead, we have to take into account the distinctive material arrangements that "differentiate one form of social production from another." In each case it is the specifically distinctive form of inner connection that binds individuals to nature and to each other that is the basis not only for the persistence of the social structure as what it is, but also for its transformation. What we characterize as the relevant entity, the relevant object of study, what counts as an internal contradiction and what counts as external, all depend on this.

The materiality of social kinds. Although Wendt offers a very helpful introduction to social kinds realism, because of the differences between mind independent natural kinds and discourse dependent social kinds he feels that his approach to the latter must exploit explicitly idealist methodologies. Implicit in his appeal to the way ideas constitute powers and interests is an appreciation of the way ideas become causally potent by engaging material forces, but because he lacks a concept of metaphysical innocence, he argues that "we can only properly theorize this relationship [between material forces and ideas] if we recognize that at some level they are constituted as different kinds of independently existing stuff" (112). He understands that this separation of the world into "two kinds of phenomena" is "ultimately Cartesian," but he sees "no other way to think about the problem if we are to be scientific realists about social life" (*id.*). Thus relations of production are "thoroughly ideational phenomena" (94), and a materialist who demurs will be considered to have "cheat[ed]" unless she has "stripped the discursive conditions" (136) from any claim of what material forces can do: "in the end, there can only be two possibilities, materialist and idealist, because there are only two kinds of stuff in the world, material and ideational" (137).

No. An alternative certainly exists. For a materialist there is only material stuff that is causally active, and differentially so. Instead of postulating brute material forces on the one hand and ideational stuff on the other, it's possible to recognize that as a product of evolution some of the world's material stuff developed the sophisticated ability not only to recognize and represent causal difference, but also to withhold those representations from reflexively automatic causal response. Imagination, inference, evaluation and explanation became possible and while these, as such, are metaphysically innocent, they can be mobilized by consciousness to inform action in ways that count as evolutionary success. The relevant distinction is not between two kinds of stuff but between the stuff it is the business of science to study – the causal structures of the world, including the causal structures we are – and the metaphysically innocent capacity for representation that mind (a causally active evolutionary product of that stuff) makes use of to study them.

Naming kinds

In *Pedagogy of the Oppressed*, Paulo Freire (2005) wrote that "[t]o exist, humanly, is to *name* the world, to change it" (88 [emphasis in original]). In effect, revolt against the conditions of oppression depends on critical reflection on those conditions, and this "leads [people] to move from a purely naïve knowledge of reality to a higher level, one which enables them to perceive the *causes* of reality" (131 [emphasis in original]). That is, naming causes is the first step in transforming the world in a way that is self-determined and self-affirming: "[t]o surmount the situation of oppression people must first critically recognize causes, so that through transforming action they can create a new situation, one which makes possible the pursuit of a fuller humanity" (47). Thus, "[d]ialogue is an encounter between men, mediated by the world, in order to name the world [and] ... by naming the world, transform it...." (88).

An underlying point here is that knowledge of the nature of a thing makes it possible to accommodate our purposes and practices to its demands. This is Richard Boyd's "accommodation thesis." Realism's defining feature, according to Boyd, is that "causation is not a social construction: we do not make causal relations except in so far as we ourselves function as ordinary causal phenomena" (1999b: 54), and, he continues, "what the representation of phenomena in terms of natural kinds makes possible, is the accommodation of inferential practices to relevant causal structures..." (1999b: 56). We can transform the world – this is the very mode of our existence as well as of our evolution and survival as a species – but we do so by accommodating our efforts to causal relations we either do not make, or, that, as a product of our making, often function independent of our will. We can add another dimension. Marx begins the Introduction to the rough draft of *Capital* (1986 MECW 28: 17; 1973: 83) writing: "Individuals producing in society – hence the socially determined production of individuals is of course the point of departure." But if it is social individuals who in production transform the world, then the accommodation Boyd identifies, as he argues, is an accommodation of individuals who must coordinate their activities. Social coordination in turn requires communication and, specifically, communication about the causal structures to be used or transformed. This requires naming.

Now attention to natural kinds in the philosophy of science today has been very much the work of mainstream analytical philosophy and, for the general reader, this has not been notably hospitable terrain. Yet whatever the revolutionary implications for academic philosophy, when Putnam announced in 1975 that "'meanings' just ain't in the *head*!" (1996: 13), he was recovering a thread familiar to the Marxist tradition and also integral to it. As Mao Zedong explained to the "Yenan Forum on Literature and Art" (1971: 257) "In discussing a problem we should start from reality and not from definitions," and he argued that those who took their guiding principles and policies from definitions they looked up in books would be "following a wrong method."

But the wrong method of starting with definitions was exactly the position the philosophers Hilary Putnam and Saul Kripke challenged. According to traditional theories of meaning, intension, the meaning of a term, determined extension, the things to which a term referred. Definition was accomplished by gathering properties typically associated with the use of a term and the term then extended to any object in the world that corresponded to the concept of this conjunction. We thought of properties associated with the use of the term "gold," for example – yellow, malleable, etc. – and then looked to the world to locate samples that corresponded to the concept we'd put together. But, anticipating contemporary concerns, Marx wrote, "[i]t is not a question here of definitions, which things must be made to fit" (1992: 303 [II.11]), and shifting the emphasis from meaning to reference, as Putnam and Kripke did, reversed the traditional approach. Appealing explicitly to Marxist materialism for antecedent, Hilary Putnam called attention to the idealist nature of the project that makes reference to the world follow from meaning and suggested that "The idealist element in contemporary positivism enters precisely through the theory of meaning" (1991: 179). Instead of making things fit their definitions, Putnam's approach showed how the terms we use in science "[approach] meaning through reference" (Goosens 1977: 134). It then became clear it was the job of science to learn what it was that had been picked out. As Brian Enc summarized the essential point:

the question is answered by finding out what the facts about the original object are, and not by first establishing what cluster of beliefs the speakers hold about the objects they take to be in the extension of the term and then by associating the use of the term with the objects of which a good proportion of these beliefs is true. In other words, the extension of the term gets to determine intension, rather than conversely.

(1976: 263)

Kripke's (1972) suggestion that our use of general terms in science and everyday life functioned like personal names offers a ready illustration of the point. The idea here is that the term "water" picks out a substance we drink the way name "Tom" identifies your neighbor. You might think your neighbor a saint, another person might think him a scoundrel. In either case, by using the name "Tom" each person in the neighborhood uses the word in a first instance non-definitionally, that is, to pick out the person they are talking about rather than to mean something about him. In spite of differing perspectives, by using the name ostensively they assure that they refer to the same thing.

This is the kind of precision we are after in referring to the objects of scientific investigation. We want a term that picks out a particular thing and does so in such a way that we can know when we talk of that thing that we are in fact referring to the same thing. In addition, we want to refer in such a way that if, as we expect in the normal progress of science, we are mistaken about some of the properties we associate with it, or about some of the objects we include in a term's extension, then it will be the thing itself, not our mistaken characterization that will determine the kind to which it belongs. Moreover, in pursuit of our effort to understand, we will be driven beyond those superficial qualities that initially drew our attention. The superficial properties we associate with gold, for example, account for no alchemical transmutation. On the other hand if we know that gold's microstructure corresponds to atomic number 79, then we *can* transmute base metals into gold.[7] In each instance it is the distinct causal properties of the target of our investigation that determines classification; these properties then regulate our beliefs about the thing and guide our causal interaction with it.

Naming the sensuously unobservable

There is a second defining theme of scientific realism over the last half century: while the investigations of science are always empirically grounded, it is a mistake to suppose them narrowed to observable phenomena as these present themselves to us. The radiator that has boiled over on a lonely Nevada road does not get refilled by hurrying off to the nearest mirage. Instead the microstructures that determine membership in a kind are often characterized by features that are sensuously unobservable – the quarks that make up the particles of an atomic nucleus would be an example. Thus, the causally potent entities to which we accommodate our social practice are not exhausted by what can be seen, felt, tasted, touched, or smelt. That is, our grasp of what is real is necessarily confirmed by what we sensuously experience, but it cannot be reduced to that. For example, for a good part of the last century it was a matter of dispute in the philosophy of science whether atoms could be treated as real entities, but as I write a photo of a single molecule of the compound pentacene circulates on the internet, and the atoms that make it up are clearly delineated. Logical positivists recognized the need to appeal to theoretical constructs such as the atomic constitution of the molecule, but understood such appeals heuristically – these were conceptual models helpful in guiding research; nothing meaningful could be said about whether or not things that could not be observed could claim real existence. Indeed, faced with the pentacene photo defenders of such a view would have said, "okay, but we're entitled to treat this as real now because the microscope has allowed us to see the molecule – it has extended our senses." And yet if you "see" by means of an electron microscope, or even a simple telescope, or, as in this case, atomic force microscopy, you then rely for your conclusions on theories about things like electrons and photons that you can't observe.

But now we're faced with a problem. When we use a term to refer we want to pick a thing out, point at it and distinguish it from its surroundings. But how do we mark out entities that escape our ability to point? How do we pick out the unobservables to which both philosophical realism and ordinary scientific practice are committed? Naming may work when we can point, but how do non-ostensive terms, those which do not point, identify for us things like electrons or fields or relational entities? How do we point at capital? Do we point at the boss? Point when she is in conversation with a worker? Point at the factory? At the machines? A balance sheet? Means of production? Products? Money?

Brian Enc (1976) makes clear that the only way we pick out unobservable entities is by means of theory. We start with the phenomena to be explained and postulate a theoretical entity that we propose accounts for them. We then identify the properties associated with the postulated entity as well as the explanatory mechanisms that work to explain. The burden of reference is carried by the identified properties and the explanatory mechanisms. Notice, however, a precision not developed by Enc: we can be quite wrong in our theory and successfully target important causal relations nonetheless – Boyd suggests that:

> 18th century biologists were extremely good at distinguishing between cases in which structures in two different species are homologous and cases in which they're analogous, and thus good at using the terms "analogy" and "homology" with their standard (contemporary) referents even though their conception of homology focused on questions of design [by the deity] rather than of common evolutionary origin.
>
> (forthcoming: 28; bracket added)[8]

That is, because "natural kinds are features, not of the world outside our practice, but of the ways in which that practice engages the rest of the world" (forthcoming: 19), even if we track causal structures imperfectly, reference may succeed. – though we will want to distinguish, of course, between mere success and success that reflects, fallibly, an ability to give an accurate causal account of the mechanisms that explain.[9]

Scientific realism's attention to the sensuously unobservable challenged pervasive assumptions that the things of the world are either tangible or conceptual so that if a thing was not empirical it had to be an idea. According to such assumptions, when Marx spoke of the commodity as a thing that "transcends sensuousness" (1990: 163 [I.1.4]), the reader seemed forced to understand this as conceptual or ideal because it appealed to something beyond the empirical. For example, Louis Althusser (who remained trapped between the palpable and the conceptual) wrote of the historical significance of goings on in Louis XV's bedroom by saying, "[a]s a general rule, concepts are not hidden in beds" (Althusser and Balibar 1979: 112). Indeed. But no doubt social kinds sometimes are, and Marx would have none of it:

> Where the purely general form of capital as self-preserving and self-valorising value is being considered, it is declared to be something immaterial, and therefore, from the point of view of the political economist, a mere idea; for he knows of nothing but either tangible objects or ideas – relations do not exist for him.
>
> (1988 MECW 30: 150)

The alternative Marx had in mind here invites vindication, and there is a mistake we can trace back at least to Hume. Science studies things and their interconnections, but interconnections, relations, are accessible to us only by means of thought: you can bump into a stone; you can't bump into a relation, even one like adultery that might be hidden in bed. Thus, from the fact that patterns – such as the tendential patterns of necessity that exist between cause and effect – can be discovered only *by* thought, Hume drew the conclusion that they exist only *in* thought, and he denied the existence of relations of natural necessity. That is, he subjectivized the relation between the dispositional powers of things and their material consequences. And the same dilemma was replayed with emphasis in social science: because social relations can be discovered only by thought, it was assumed they existed only in thought. But notice: while concepts, metaphysically innocent, crumple no bed sheets, and while no one bumps into a relation, it is nonetheless true that relations, materially instantiated, are causally potent. Arrange furniture in a room one way and you can walk through it; arrange it another and you can't. To be, as Bhaskar (1989: 69) observes, is just to be able to do, but in our experience things exist and do only by taking form. That is, just as we cannot imagine the causal potency of things without matter, neither can we imagine the causal potency of things without taking into account their form, and taking account of form means grasping relation. In consequence, scientific realism's vindication of the reality of unobservables led to a vindication of the reality of that which was relational – in addition to the empirically perceptible, the furniture of the world must comfortably include relations which, though discoverable only by thought, were materially instantiated, causally potent, and thus did not exist only in thought. Indeed, feedback was inevitable: the way opened to appreciating how relational interconnection is pervasive in all science, natural and social.

Epistemic access to relational interconnection depends on the power of abstraction. Here is Marx from the first Preface to *Capital*: "in the analysis of economic forms neither microscopes nor chemical reagents are of assistance; the power of abstraction must replace both"[10] (1990: 90). Recall Enc's point just referred to: we access the sensuously unobservable by postulating an explanatory mechanism connected by a causal chain to the event to be explained. The power of abstraction plays a critical role in both picking out the mechanism and tracing the interconnection to that which we observe. But too often Marxists and others suppose that abstraction means a retreat from specific properties considered concrete to an ideational space of empty generality. To abstract, the person supposes, means to look for something common, but this is done in a way that avoids or blurs properties that characterize a thing distinctively. Abstracting from all properties of a thing but color, for example, usually tells us little about what we may expect of it. Marx's manuscripts are filled with examples of the way the concept of capital was diluted by ignoring its distinctive specificity:

> *nothing is easier than to prove that capital is a necessary condition for all human production.* We have only to abstract from the specific characteristics of capital which make it into a moment of a particularly developed *historical* stage of human production.
>
> (1986 MECW 28: 189; 1973: 258 [emphasis in original])

By defining capital as stored labor, for example, we make it possible for the extension of the term to include the hunter-gatherer's spear. Marx's use of abstraction is instead like that of the experimental scientist – a way of disregarding one specific thing to focus on another. Consider the way a natural scientist uses experimental design: she tests the force of gravity by dropping objects in a tube from which air has been removed; that is, she abstracts physically from one concrete feature of how an object falls in order to isolate another specific feature, which, though unobservable, she is able to confirm by its causal effect.[11] Marx looks for features common to instances of the social relation he studies, but these are particular properties that are concretely distinctive to it, and he scoffs at a search for common features empty of any distinctively specific content.

Two different forms of the power of abstraction can be usefully distinguished. First, by means of *selective attention* we abstract from all features of a thing except those which are the particular target of inquiry. As I've just explained, this is the kind of thing a natural scientist accomplishes by the way an experiment is designed. Marx abstracts from competition to consider the causally distinctive features that account for the resort to exchange in the first place. Second, by means of *dialectical attention* we grasp the interconnection of things – a physicist, for example, notices how the strong force binds subatomic particles to form protons or neutrons. When we say commodity producers produce use values useless to them for private exchange, we grasp the form of interconnection among producers that accounts for value. Notice, whether in the study of nature or social life, if materialism is to grasp interconnection, it must be dialectical.

To sum up the last two sections: first, words we use to refer to natural kinds must be thought of non-definitionally; in our investigations they function at first ostensively rather than semantically. As Marx understood, this is a methodological point essential to materialism: meaning follows reference rather than the other way around. Second, the things of the world include entities discoverable only by thought insofar as they are sensuously unobservable or relational – the furniture of the world is not exhausted by the palpable and the conceptual. Third, the power of abstraction is both a necessary complement to scientific experiment and is also indispensable to the social sciences where ordinary experimental methods are usually unavailable. By means of the power of abstraction we focus selective attention on the distinctive causal properties of things and dialectical attention on their interconnection.

The object of Marx's *Capital*

Let me emphasize the three points I've just summarized; they are: (1) a materialist imperative with respect to the use of language – that a precondition of a terminology adequate to the investigation of social kinds is that it approach meaning through reference; (2) an ontological imperative that among the things of the world are entities not fully accessible to the senses, including relational composites such as capital; and (3) a methodological imperative that the power of abstraction is indispensable to identifying relational social kinds and their kind constitutive properties. Appreciating the power of abstraction makes possible the identification of capital as a labor-form composite and the identification also of its simplest properties in their interconnection. Though these are discovered and expressed by definite categories of thought, they do not exist in thought. Thus equally essential is the recognition that it is not possible to reduce relational composites such as capital to either the empirical or the conceptual. Nevertheless, by recognizing that even the sensuously unobservable can be a real object, we can refer to such things by means of theory, work out their real definition by attention to the causal features that distinctively characterize them, and allow these features to regulate our beliefs about them. We persist in approaching meaning through reference.

Conversely, lack of attention to these points accounts for the inconclusive consideration given by the Marxist tradition to the scientific object pursued by Marx in *Capital*. Plainly neither empiricist nor rationalist methodologies clear adequate paths if the objects of our ontology include the non-empirically real. Althusser, who certainly appreciated the significance of relation and structure in Marx, and who sought alternatives to traditional methodologies, considered that every upheaval in the practice of theory could be correlated with a transformation in the definition of the object studied. Nonetheless, he thought that Marx did not succeed in making clear how the concept of capital formed by his analyses was different from that of classical political economy, nor was he altogether consistent in his elaboration of it. (Althusser 1979: 145; 191). From the perspective of critical theory, Backhaus, a former student of Adorno, reached much the same conclusion. He posed the following question: "whether contemporary economics or Marxian economics has developed a terminology which was adequate to its object" (1992: 85) and concluded neither had done so – indeed the relevant questions had scarcely been asked. Plainly, if capital is a thing it grounds no social science – as Backhaus explains, it would be impossible to capture capital's changes in form – but neither can it form the basis of science if it is merely something conceptual or ideal. As a consequence Backhaus concluded that the path forward lay in the "no man's land" between philosophy and science (75). It would be in some such domain, he suggested, that an objectivity transcending sensuousness yet capable of accounting for the material potency of value could be found. But while Marx had criticized Ricardo for acting as if value were merely a matter of empirical fact, Backhaus thought his achievement was incomplete:

> This critical question must now be turned against Marx himself. Where does he succeed in doing what he demands of Ricardo? The question I think points to the most serious flaw in Marx's work. He is right to call for the development of an objective concept of value. ... But the work he handed over falls short of this goal and remains but a fragment. Like Adorno, Marx himself demands the working out of a concept which "the thing has of itself," that is, "an objective concept."
>
> (88–89)

An ontology exclusive to, and exhausted by, palpable objects and concepts persists here in the riddle of how a personified thing may at the same time exist as a reified concept, and Backhaus does not pretend to solve the conundrum. But noticeably not included in the features of being thus placed on offer are real objects discoverable only by thought because not sensuously observable. Value is objective, as I will show in Chapter 2, not because it is an "objective concept," but because it is a relational composite grounded in the separation of productive entities from one another. The social kind of commodity-producing labor accounts for the value relation and is fully accessible to social science. Backhaus' perception that Marx fell short of his effort to adequately articulate the object of his science reflects the unacknowledged (and dogged) persistence of positivism's legacy: science is reserved exclusively for the empirical.

Turning from empiricist readings of *Capital*, Althusser, who in *Reading Capital* finds a "frontier impassable ... in principle" (1975: 190) between knowledge and the real, proposes to ground Marxism as a science squarely on the "mere conceptuality" (195) of capital. Marx's object in *Capital*, he argues, is the ideality of capital: "the object of his theory is an *idea*, i.e. it is defined in terms of knowledge, in the abstraction of the object" (*id.*). The "ideality of Marx's object" must be opposed to "actual historical reality" (*id.*). Thus, while he observes that Marx's "whole object [is] only the concept of the specific difference of the capitalist mode of production" (196), still, in spite of the English data Marx mobilizes, Althusser rejects the idea that his object can be found in English capitalism; he adds, "Marx, therefore, does *not even study the English example*, however classic and pure it may be, but a non-existent example" (194 [emphasis in original]).

I would like to draw as sharp a distinction as possible between the methodology of the essays that follow and this approach. If the term 'capital' refers to a social kind, then actual instances of it in England, Germany, and elsewhere will fall within its extension. England was a particularly important source of examples because its decisive features stood out most dramatically. These instances do not become conceptual or ideal because they must be grasped by means of abstraction. Althusser – and he is not alone (E. P. Thompson's energetic critique of *Reading Capital* reflects the same error[12]) – ignores the capacity of reference to selectively disregard even important features of capital in order to locate causal structures which are most decisive in accounting for its distinctive character.

Such structures are not coherently accessible to Althusser also because of his critique of essence. He finds a persistent tradition in and around Western philosophy that associates essence with a conceptual ideal or spirit given manifestation in the empirical things of the world – it is the idea of the oak at work in the oak, for example, that alone is capable of explaining the totality of the oak's manifestations. He challenges this, correctly, as in effect a category mistake; what I have called (following Boyd's usage) metaphysically innocent concepts are made to appear as if they are a causally potent part of being. The DNA of the oak is no doubt at work in the tree's process of unfolding, but not the idea of it. Yet Althusser is wrong to associate Marx's appeal to essence with this tradition (1975: 189–190). Marx wants to establish the material interconnections that establish distinctively what capital is in the way H_2O establishes distinctively what water is such that anything that is H_2O is water, and anything that isn't, isn't. He uses the word "*Kerngestalt*," a German word formed of the word for kernel or nucleus, "*Kern*," and the word for form or shape or frame, "*Gestalt*" (1991: 352 [III.15.1]; 1970 MEW 25: 254). H_2O, if you like, is water's *Kerngestalt*. So Marx is after the nuclear structure of capital as a social kind, and just as there is no category mistake in saying that the expression H_2O refers to a molecular structure that counts as water's constitutive essence, so too there is no category mistake in suggesting that the separation of productive entities that produce for private exchange captures the kind constitutive properties or essence of the labor-form composite that accounts for value. The relational separations to which I will refer in studying both value and capital are neither conceptual or, in the fullness of what they are, empirical. They are nonetheless causally potent, real, and serve to differentiate capital from other modes of production.

Althusser notices that often we are blind to what we nevertheless see – Ricardo could not grasp surplus value, though profit, rent, and interest were laid out before him. But, in truth, for lack of attention to the realist emphases in

Marx's work, blocked vision characterizes a good bit of Althusser's own reading of Marxist texts. He relies on Marx's excerpt, "The Method of Political Economy" (1986 MECW: 37; 1973: 100) but ignores the specification there of the search, by means of thinner and thinner abstractions, for the "simplest determinations" of social things, those fundamental social structures that, according to the text, can serve to ground explanation. Similarly in Althusser's reading of Mao Zedong's *On Contradiction* he picks out the concept of the principal contradictions of a process and notices how the principal contradiction can change as events unfold because of a shift in the importance of the elements that make it up (Althusser 1990). But he does not draw attention to Mao's use of the concept of a fundamental contradiction – the contradiction that will distinctively characterize a process through all its phases. In each case the omission is significant; Althusser misses the terms used to refer to materially essential explanatory mechanisms that capture the specificity of capital.

A consequence of this is a suppression of the search for essential causal determination in favor of an expansive notion of overdetermination inspired by Freud. And, indeed, in highlighting the determination of events by the totality of factors at work in them we're offered a compelling illustration of the need for social kind methodology in social theory. Attention to the way events can be overdetermined has no doubt made an important contribution to historical and other social research, but it cannot explain why kinds like capital persist as what they are in social life. In Chapter 5 I look at a legal relation that has persisted in essentially the same form for over 400 years. In any particular circumstance, application of the rule which gives it expression is without doubt overdetermined, yielding, for example, the everyday event a judicial decision represents. But the persistence of this rule and relation in the very much the same form for over 400 years cannot be explained in that way. Marx criticized Bailey for arguing that the causes of value included anything that influenced the mind of the person who entered exchange (1989 MECW 32: 348). In effect, Bailey's argument was an early form of overdetermination theory offering no stable causal structure to study because of the infinity of factors contingently at play. Marx rejected this. He wants to ground analysis by specifying those few causal circumstances that differentiate one form of social production from another.

The real definition of capital

The paleontologist Olivier Rieppel argues that the goal of scientific investigation can be expressed by "definitions that have explanatory power in that they establish a causal link to the underlying causal powers of the objects being defined" (2005: 19). The business of science, in other words, is real definition. H_2O is the real definition of water. That is, if meaning is approached by reference, then definition will not be a matter of how we use words – what we call a nominal definition – but instead an approximate, fallible and revisable product of reference, investigation and understanding. We can compare the nominal definition that Locke offered for gold – a word we use to mean a yellow, malleable, fusible metal – with what would be offered as a real definition today: "gold" refers to the element with atomic number 79. Specifying an atomic number can provide a real definition because it picks out a unique atomic structure.

Other than for Marx's own efforts, there has been little attention to the philosophy of science's use of real definition within the Marxist tradition. In his important book on the *Grundrisse*, Roman Rosdolsky did call attention to Marx's effort to define capital by working out the concept of "capital in general," but, as Michael Heinrich observes, Rosdolsky did not develop the concept with any clarity or in any detail. "Capital in general," he understood, was Marx's effort to specify features common to all instances of capital rather than features particular to individual capitals, but the definition he offered was incomplete: "What all capitals have in common is their capacity for expanding their value" (Rosdolsky 1977: 44).

While all instances that fall under the extension of the term "capital" will seek to expand value, this definition is incomplete because it does not identify a causal structure capable of explaining how all capitals expand value. For a social kind like capital a real definition must specify the distinctive form taken by the relations of laboring individuals to nature and to each other in the process of production. In *Capital II*, Marx writes:

> Whatever the social form of production, workers and means of production always remain its factors. But if they are in a state of mutual separation, they are only potentially factors of production. For any production to take place, they must be connected. The particular form and mode in which this connection is effected is what distinguishes the various epochs of the social structure.
>
> (1992: 120 [II.1.2])

We want to show how capital's capacity for expanding value is the result of its particular combination of these elements.

A core definition that will do this may be simply stated. Drawing on an insight of the French political economist Charles Bettelheim (1975: 77), I argue that the kind constitutive properties of capital can be characterized by a double separation of first, productive entities from one another, and second, a separation of the laboring producers from their means of labor. Actually I will want to gloss the second of these two separations by making explicit an important consequence: a worker's separation from all means of realizing her labor means a condition of absolute impoverishment such that by entering the labor market she is compelled, in exchange for a wage, to relinquish control during the working day of her life activity itself. She is commanded by another. But because, as we shall see, the capitalist to whom the laborer is subordinated is a mere cog, a personification, nothing but a means by which value can take on a will and consciousness of its own, the working producer in fact finds herself subordinated to the dynamic of value and value's self-increase.

Now value taken as a relation of labor expenditure accounted for by the separation of independent producers who produce for commodity exchange, is a property of labor's own product, thus the conditions of production from which the laboring producer is separated are values. That is, the specific manner in which the combination of labor and its means occurs in the productive mode of capital's existence, the labor-form composite that characterizes capital as a social kind, means not only separation, but the subordination of the working producer to her own product come to rule over her. We can therefore call the condition of separation on which capitalist production rests an alienated separation. As such, it penetrates the labor process itself, becoming embodied even in the machine. Rather than a working producer controlling her tools and using them to transmit activity to the material worked on, the machine, becomes independent, dominates, disciplines, and regulates her work; the worker becomes an "insignificant accessory" to its function. Thus, even the social powers of combined labor confront laboring producers as properties of products that rule over them. Unthinkingly we might assume the labor process is a way for working producers to appropriate nature to need. Instead, labor serves the fundamental purpose of capital – to appropriate a surplus in excess of value originally invested. In fact, while necessary labor – the labor required to produce the bare minimum of things a laborer needs to survive – would seem an indispensable precondition to the production of surplus labor, for capital the reverse is true: if surplus labor cannot augment value, labor will not be employed at all. In sum, the specific manner in which the factors of production are united in capitalist production means the appropriation of living labor by objectified labor for the sake of increasing objectified labor. Because this is a consequence of the structure of the alienated separation with which we began, and because it functions to reproduce that structure, Marx suggested that the separation of the laborer from the conditions of labor and the appropriation of living labor by objectified labor are merely the same social relation viewed from opposite poles. In the one instance we consider capital as structure; in the other as activity. In either case we give expression to the fundamental determination of capital as a social kind. I spell out these processes in Chapters 3 and 4.

Michael Heinrich rejected Rosdolsky's analysis of capital in general, arguing that a "generic concept embracing all the common characteristics of many capitals does not hold up" (1989: 66; see also 2007). But he did not pursue Marx's search for real definition as a result. Instead he concluded that Marx's effort was necessarily incoherent insofar as a gathering of all important characteristics shared by individual instances of capital could not be achieved if, as Marx insisted, only features abstracted from competition were to be considered. Thus, Heinrich argued, as Marx worked through the penultimate draft of *Capital* the effort to persist with the concept of "capital in general" "shattered" under his contradictory demands. It had to be abandoned.

Notice that Heinrich's assumption that capital in general must embrace all the characteristics common to many capitals is a demand that actually has its source in traditional theories of meaning and reference rejected by realist methodologies in the philosophy of science – reference is approached through meaning rather than the reverse. In his effort to elaborate a concept of capital in general Marx does not try to gather all the important characteristics we associate with use of the term "capital," but only "the quintessence of characteristics" which distinguish it from other forms of production. This extends even to value itself. Thus, in the differentiations he makes, Marx seeks to capture "the quintessence of characteristics which distinguish value as capital from value as simple value or money" (1986 MECW 28: 236; 1973: 310). Heinrich construes this as seeking "to embrace those characteristics which have to be added to value in order for it to become capital" (1989: 66). But the distinction Marx has in mind is not additive. While capital definitely does presuppose the value relation so that those features given expression by the real definition of commodity-producing labor are incorporated in capital and become part of its definition, capital is distinct from value not simply by addition or subtraction of properties, but in *kind*. That is, the addition of the separation of laboring individuals from their means of labor to the separation of productive entities one from the other produces a social composite as different in kind from the latter as a weekday on the floor of the New York Stock Exchange is different from a market day in the Middle Ages. Common threads persist but the world has been remade.

Heinrich's argument that Marx abandoned the concept of capital in general is also compromised because, at least in part like Althusser, he does not consider Marx's use of the phrase to have targeted an object that is real: " 'capital in general' is not to be understood as the concept of a real object, such as an individual capital: it has no direct empirical correlate..." (1989: 66). (Query: what is the "direct empirical correlate" of an individual capital?) Here Marx's anticipation of realism in the philosophy of science has been obscured by the pervasive assumptions of empiricism. But the methodologies of contemporary scientific realism have emerged and flourished very much because they make the straightforward claim that scientific practice is impossible without taking into account real objects that are not empirical. The example underscores, therefore, how attention to realism in science can open the way to a clearer understanding of Marx's project, of the questions it posed, and the way it foreshadowed contemporary concerns.

According to Heinrich, the concept of "capital in general" "shattered" because as Marx's analysis proceeded he could no longer limit it to characteristics abstracted from competition – it had to include essential features like the average rate of profit or tendencies like concentration or centralization or the falling rate of profit, all of which are important to full understanding of how capital works. As I've already explained, this challenge rests on assumptions about the function of definition that I think Marx did not share. But there is another distinction Heinrich has missed here that will be important in the essays that follow. Heinrich fails to distinguish between the constitutive and attributive features of the object of study. As the Aristotelian Alan Code writes, "A material composite is not the same as its essence" (1984a: 117). In Marx we cannot confuse, as I will show below, the causal structure constitutive of the social form of value or capital with the fully developed forms of their phenomenal manifestations – exchange value, money, price, centralization and concentration, the average rate of profit, corporate business forms, etc.

Conclusion: extracting realism's kernel

Without doubt the influence of Hegel on Marx's thought was profound. In the Postface to the second edition of *Capital* he wrote, "I openly avowed myself the pupil of that mighty thinker." Nonetheless, it remains true that Marx thought it necessary to proceed methodologically in some fashion directly contrary to Hegel's approach:

> My dialectical method is, in its foundations, not only different from the Hegelian, but exactly opposite to it.... With him it [the dialectic] is standing on its head. It must be inverted, in order to discover the rational kernel within the mystical shell.
>
> (1990: 102–103)

Engels emphasized often the basic idea by insisting that for Marx it is the real interconnections of the things of the world that are the basis for the dialectic, not the reverse, and when the things of the world change, the concepts we form of them must keep pace.[13]

I argue it was Marx's debt to Aristotle, a debt he absorbed with increasing attention to the science of his day, that offers the key the inversion required here. Marx sought to develop the "form determinations" of the object of study and no doubt there were important Hegelian influences in this. But the influence was first of all Aristotelian and, as I will suggest, the "simple determinations" of form he sought to ground social explanation reflected an appropriation of lessons from the middle books of Aristotle's *Metaphysics.* Thus, methodologically, I see Marx looking back to Aristotle on the one hand but looking forward in a way consistent with the perspectives of scientific realism on the other.

As early as his Doctoral Dissertation (1975 MECW 1) Marx appears to have drawn from the *Metaphysics* a critique of the materialists of the ancient world rooted in his concern for scientific investigation. On the one hand, in the face of an abstract self-consciousness independent of matter and thus divorced from its constraints (Epicurus), or, on the other, of matter itself considered abstractly and without potency in the world (Democritus), Marx insisted on the embeddedness of form in the materiality of things themselves. The connection of this theme to his social theory, I suggest, became quite significant. The key to a critical under-standing of political economy he found located in the social forms of labor instantiated in the material activity of production such that the basis of social life might be found in an effectively Aristotelian composite of activity and form. Marx therefore set himself the task of studying the forms of labor across history and took these as the foundation of historical and social science.

My attention to the Aristotelian roots of Marx's thought, therefore, is not for the sake of denying his debt to Hegel, but rather to insist that the rational kernel he sought to extract from Hegel's method was scientific – if oaks are to illus-trate, Marx would be after the double helix, not some animating idea, and he would be after that fallibly, revisably, open always both on the one hand to even simpler determinations and on the other to any resonance from "the rich totality of many determinations and relations" (1986 MECW 28: 37; 1973: 100) that account for the actual reproduction of the organism in its environment. His dialectic is a way of referring to the distinctive interconnected causal properties of things and a way of expressing these in definite categories.

2 Why is this labor value?

Commodity-producing labor as a social kind

First, I don't ask "Why is *this* 'labor value'?" but instead "Why is this *labor* value?" The latter question, I hope to show, is decisive for social inquiry. It opens on an understanding of the social composite of labor and form, of *enformed social labor*, that is the basis for commodity production. As a result, an answer to it can ground our understanding of those societies that depend on the production and exchange of commodities.

For Marx, the question's significance seems to me to reflect the influence Aristotle had on his thought. Moreover, what he did with it prefigures contemporary methodologies of critical scientific realism: we may characterize the form of social labor that produces commodities as a natural kind and offer a real definition of it. As a consequence, asking "Why does labor take the form of value?" shows not only the continuing relevance of Marx's work as a social theorist but also how it continues to anticipate what we may ask of social science today.

The critique of Ricardo

We can begin with Marx's relation to David Ricardo, an issue that has become something of a hot topic in the study of Marx and one that goes to the nub of how we read him today (Milios *et al.* 2002). Marx judged that Ricardo had made an enormous scientific advance by showing clearly that labor was the substance of value. But he thought also that Ricardo had ignored questions of social form (1990: 173–174 [I.1.4]). From this, over the past quarter century a powerful tradition has developed emphasizing that the understanding of capitalism must begin with the analysis of the social form of value.

According to this tradition – called value-form theory or "new" and also "systematic" dialectics – value is typically understood as a category of exchange reflected in the forms of valorization, exchange value, and money, and the idea that value may be characterized as the labor materially embodied in commodities is rejected. "Substance," conceived of as labor, and labor conceived of as a physiological expenditure of effort, a natural phenomenon, are counterposed to social form and rejected as the basis of value analysis; instead, value, often understood as empty of content except insofar as this is constituted by money in exchange, is taken as primary. By this measure, Marx is considered to have broken incompletely with classical political economy and his analysis in *Capital* is thought to be still clumsily burdened with Ricardian notions of embodied labor; as a result Marx fails to present systematically or coherently a thorough-going form analysis of the capitalist mode of production. Much reconstruction is required and we get new theories of labor, value, exploitation and so forth. (Arthur 2002, 1993; Taylor 2000; Reuten 1993; Reuten and Williams 1989; Williams 1988; Eldred and Hanlon 1981).

Once your attention is called to it, no one can read the first chapters of *Capital* without recognizing the significance of "form" to Marx's analysis: there is the commodity form, the value form, the natural form, the elementary form, the accidental form, the equivalent form, the general form, the money form, and so on. "Form determination" is essential to his investigation. But, in fact, while calling attention to the question of form, value-form theory has pretty systematically noticed only one-half of Marx's critique of Ricardo, and this has muddied everything. Christopher Arthur (1979: 68), for example, wrote, "By the value form Marx means the form of appearance of value." But Marx's critique of Ricardo was double: the failure to develop value's forms of appearance was part of it, but, even more fundamentally, Marx also noticed that Ricardo had not asked why labor takes the form of value in the first place. Here is *Capital*'s presentation of Marx's fundamental point:

> Political Economy has indeed analyzed value and its magnitude, however incompletely, and has uncovered the content concealed within these forms. But it has never once asked the question why this content has assumed that particular form,[1] that is to say, why labour is expressed in value, and why the measurement of labour by its duration is expressed in the magnitude of the value of the product.
>
> (1990: 173–174 [I.1.4])

This is an interesting question. It does not ask how it is that value appears in exchange in the form of money. It is connected to that question, but, it asks, more fundamentally, how it is that value comes to be what it is.

Marx and Aristotle

At some point, reflecting on Marx's challenge to Ricardo, I realized I'd heard the question Marx posed before, or at least something very close to it. I realized the place I'd heard it was in the decisive chapter of the pivotal book of Aristotle's *Metaphysics*, chapter 17 of Book Zeta. It was the fundamental question posed, in a way the fulcrum on which the whole structure of the *Metaphysics* turned. Scott Meikle calls Marx an "Aristotelian in metaphysics" (Meikle 1991: 296); this echo, therefore, seemed an important link to follow.

Aristotle argues that ordinarily when we explain we try to show how we predicate one thing of something else. Why do animals have joints? Why is there noise in the clouds? But we often mislead ourselves when the predication is implicit – constitutive rather than attributive – and we then ask something Aristotle thought unhelpful. "What is a man?" he thought such a question. Here we are not asking about some attribute or property that a person has, like smooth skin or dark hair. Instead we are asking what it is to be human. We are asking what it is that constitutes a human person as human. For this, Aristotle thought, we needed a question that located the generative basis of fundamental change. We want to know how this thing that is human comes to be so. We are not investigating changes that we attribute to a subject the way dark hair turns gray or skin wrinkles. Instead we're interrogating the kind of change that causes the subject to be what it is in the first place. For example, we shingle a roof and notice the house has changed, but what has changed when fire burns it to the ground? If we say the timber has changed to ash, this is true, but the timbers are not the house. They are only the material for the house. The question we need to ask is why these materials constitute a house. If we ask "what is man?" we want to know not that man is a thing of flesh and bones, but instead why these flesh and bones constitute a man. Why, in other words, recalling Marx's question, does this content assume that form? And Aristotle's answer to this question provided for him the key to the investigation of the *Metaphysics*: the basic reality of things, primary substance, primary being in the most fundamental sense, is the constitutive form of things. A thing's causally potent constitutive form is the most fundamental content it can have.

In other words, and to abbreviate necessarily, Aristotle was after the underlying structure or principle of an entity that determined and conditioned or organized its development (Lear 1988: 19). But to make this clear, he found he had to differentiate two ways in which the substratum could be understood to be underlying: "for example, an animal may be the subject to which attributes are referred, or [the substrata] are materials to be given actualization" (Aristotle 1960: 158–159 [1038b; text in brackets supplied]).[2] If we study forms of appearance we study the first of these – how a subject as substratum manifests itself in its attributes. If we study the second, we study the way the materials which make up an entity are formed so as to constitute it; in a bit of Aristotle congenial to the street, we study the "what-it-is" of a thing (1960: 134 [1029b]).

Now in the second case, for the things of nature, matter is substratum, but as such it is not the primary reality – for itself, formless, matter can't be considered more than "undetermined possibility" (Reale 1980: 212) and is impossible really to think of except hypothetically. As it actually appears, it always exists as constituted by form, *enformed*, and as enformed, it is causally potent, a power in the course of actualization. Thus, the significance of the question at the end of Book VII of the *Metaphysics* lies in this – it gets at the potent form that ultimately organizes the power and processes of development of an entity. It does this by locating that power in its fundamental causal structure or form. In the *Metaphysics*, Reale argues, ontology, the study of being, just reduces to ousiology, the study of substance. And primary substance is, in the most basic sense, an aetiology, the study of a thing's generative essence or constitutive cause (1980: 358).

As a consequence, it is important never to reduce our understanding of the Aristotelian concept of substance, *ousia*, to an ontology of things (Kosman 1994: 212). The most basic reality of the world for Aristotle must be understood as structure or power or activity (Moravcsik 1991; Kosman 1994). It is always an underlying nature in the process of actualization, an organizing principle that can account for how an entity might develop or persist as the kind of thing it is.

This distinction between the constitutive and attributive form of an entity is exactly the sort of distinction Marx thought political economy had to make. Ricardo had discovered labor as the substance of value, but he did not know how it was enformed. He argued that the value of a thing could be attributed to the amount of labor expended on it, but he didn't show how the social form of the activity of labor was constituted. By contrast, for Marx the concept of a bare, physiological expenditure of labor is best understood the way Aristotle understood matter. As the expenditure of labor in general, it can only be conceived of, like matter, as formless, no more than undetermined possibility. That is, labor only ever occurs historically within specific social forms, as *enformed*. And just as to understand a thing we must explain how it is constituted by matter and form, how it is enformed, so too if we wish to understand a mode of social labor we must locate the generative structure that organizes the developmental process of its actualization. This is its constitutive form, the historically specific underlying structure that makes it what it is. Labor's constitutive form is not a property of it the way sweat is a property of a person expending physical energy. Labor's constitutive form is not an attribute it *has*, like a physical product has density or texture, but the form it *is*, the structure of the actual process of production that makes the product a commodity in the first place.

The point can be underscored by recalling Marx's claim at the beginning of §2 of Chapter 1 of *Capital* that he "was the first to point out and to examine critically this twofold nature of the labour contained in commodities" (1990: 132 [I.1.2]). Yet Ricardo had distinguished use-value from exchange value. But for Ricardo exchange value was an attribute of the product measured by the quantity of labor expended on it and he did not investigate social labor's constitutive form. For Marx on the other hand, the products of labor, insofar as they were values, expressed a relation – a relation of persons to their labor expenditure[3] – and he then went on to make precise exactly what the relation was that could account for the necessity of comparing the labor of individuals as values. We turn now to the characterization of this social relation.

The social form of commodity-producing labor

How shall we characterize the social composite of activity and form that constitutes commodity-producing labor? In §2 of *Capital*'s first chapter Marx offers a succinct but complete definition: "Only the products of mutually independent acts of labour, performed in isolation, can confront each other as commodities." (1990: 132 [I.1.2]). I develop the argument for this characterization as it is presented in *Capital*'s first chapter in the Appendix to this chapter. Here I want to show how the argument is worked out in the *Grundrisse*, one of Marx's drafts for *Capital.*

In discussing the form determinations of capital, Marx looks back to what he calls the "simple determination" that generates exchange value. He writes,

> In the first positing of simple exchange value, labor was structured in such a way that the product was not a direct use value for the laborer, not a direct means of subsistence. This was the general condition for the creation of an exchange value and of exchange in general. Otherwise the worker would have produced only a product – a direct use value for himself – but not an exchange value.
>
> (1973: 266–267; 1986: 197)

The point is decisive: this is a structuring of labor itself. Moreover, it is a caus- ally potent structuring. The laborer produces use values for herself that are of no direct use to her. Because the laborer here is assumed to produce separately from others, fully responsible for her own production, in order to obtain the means to sustain her own existence and to produce again, she *must* resort to exchange.[4] The structure therefore is one that relates the laboring subject necessarily: (1) to nature – she produces for herself products not useful to her; and (2) to others – she produces independently. I've characterized this structure as a form of "inter- dependent autonomy" (Engelskirchen 1997).[5] It is a relation of production, the form determination we're looking for. It is the generative causal structure that forms the basis of value and the commodity form.

Notice that by abstracting in this way to the simplest determination of the commodity form itself, we lose the level of precision required to locate the actual relation of direct possession connecting the laboring producer to the means of production other than in the two respects just specified. Here's what I mean: Marx's reference to "the worker" and my use of the gendered personal pronoun can both mislead insofar as they tend to evoke the image of an isolated individual laborer who is part of a mode of petty commodity production. But to suppose that the simplest determination of the commodity implies necessarily a simple commodity mode of production would be to confuse levels of abstrac- tion. We here specify the underlying structural relation that characterizes the commodity form, not the social totality referred to by the concept of a mode of production. Thus, the commodity form may have its source in units of produc- tion as diverse as the farm of an isolated peasant, an artisan's small business, a patriarchal estate, a slave plantation, a capitalist enterprise, or a worker collect- ive during the transition to socialism. That is, in his analysis of the commodity, Marx abstracts to two bare facts only: whatever the relation of direct possession that connects the working individual to the means of production, we know actual living labor is executed under conditions of separation from other units of production and occurs in conditions where the product is not useful except to others. From the existence of a commodity we know living labor has been carried on separately and for others. To go further, to know for example how the commodity becomes the universal form of the product of labor, requires an additional, different and more concrete analysis.

Nonetheless, we do have the composite of social labor that constitutes the commodity form of the product of labor. Recall Marx's observation in the Preface to the first German edition of *Capital*: "But for bourgeois society, the commodity-form of the product of labour, or the value-form of the commodity, is the economic-cell form" (1990: 90). The structure of living labor identified in the passage from the *Grundrisse* above is the underlying causal structure that accounts for this.

From Aristotle to contemporary scientific realism

For Aristotle the things of the world were composites of matter and form and Marx applied this to the study of the historical forms of labor: he found the explanation for value and its expressions in exchange in a particular configuration of living labor. I turn now to show that this structure of labor may be considered a social kind. Preliminarily, a word on terminology: I take it that if natural kind methodology can be extended to the study of social life, then we can refer to the causal mechanisms of society as falling under natural kinds. Typically it is convenient to speak of social kinds, and I will do so here, but this is not meant to mark off a difference other than of subject matter. The naturalism I appeal to is unqualified. That is, we can speak indifferently of natural kinds in the social or natural world. As an additional point, if we do succeed in identifying and describing the causal structure of a natural kind, then we say we have offered a real definition of it.

Perhaps two emphases characterize most fundamentally work on kinds in the contemporary philosophy of science. First, there is a recognition that natural kind terms can serve the objectives of science by enabling us to pick out the fundamental causal structures studied by different sciences. In this respect natural kind theory reflects a blend of both the attention of working scientists to the dispositional properties of things (Wagner 2001) and also the attention of philosophers of language to the causal theory of reference (Kornblith 1993). Second, there is a recognition that natural kind terms function to accommodate the demands of our practice – scientific, productive, political, or other – to the causal structures of the world (Boyd 1999a; 1999b). That is, our practice, natural or social, requires that we get it right about the way the world is, and also that we be able to communicate accurately about this. To put it in terms familiar to progressive social theory, we interpret the world to change it. When we get it right, natural kind terms facilitate our ability to pick out the causal structures of the world and make our use or transformation of them possible.

According to Stathis Psillos (1999) the concept of "kind constitutive properties" best characterizes the features of an entity to which we refer in our use of natural kind terms. This concept identifies an entity's essential causal description. Thus, kind constitutive properties, like the combination of hydrogen and oxygen in a water molecule, allow us to explain how an entity behaves and how it persists as the kind of thing it is. Importantly, they also account for, and causally produce, the body of information we have about the thing (1999: 287–288). As Psillos explains, the causal origin of the information that water is a colorless, odorless liquid that becomes a solid at zero degrees centigrade is found in the chemical bonds joining atoms of hydrogen with those of oxygen.

Commonly we expect the sensible properties of a thing and the generative mechanisms that account for them to differ fundamentally – the atoms of hydrogen and oxygen that make up a water molecule aren't wet.[6] That is, while the manifest properties of a thing may trigger our initial identification of it – we notice tigers have stripes – generally such properties are inadequate to secure the reliable extension of the term to all members of a kind. A liquid, Psillos reminds, can be colorless and odorless but kill you if it is not H_2O (1999: 285). In other words, it is the fundamental causal properties of a thing that determine how it will behave. As Günter Wagner has suggested, the natural kind problem is essentially a search for the "fundamental units [that] play a causal role in a process" (2001: 6). Richard Boyd refers to the homeostatic clustering of causally important properties or mechanisms – those responsible for a thing's ability to maintain and reproduce itself as the kind of thing it is.

A comparable distinction between the underlying causal structures of social life and the manifest appearances they generate was of course an abiding theme of Marx's work. In *Notes on Wagner*, his last writing on political economy, he made fun of the abstract method of German academicians like the economist Adolph Wagner precisely because they thought they understood a thing when they had observed its manifest properties (Marx 1975: 201 [1989 MECW 24: 547]). In this they acted like "the old chemists before the science of chemistry: as cooking butter, which is simply called butter in everyday life … has a soft consistency, they called *chloride, butter of zinc, butter of antimony*, etc.… [emphasis in original]." The common name "butter" comes to be applied to all manner of substances with a soft malleable consistency. But to refer to the sensible features compounds such as zinc chloride and antimony tri-chloride share with edible butter tells nothing about their constitutive structure, nor can we use them to give a reliable account of what such compounds are or how they behave. For that we need an understanding of their molecular structure, knowledge ultimately embedded in background chemical theories. Marx drew this lesson from his study of science and found it applicable to the study of political economy. Recall his reference in the Postface to the Second Edition (German) of *Capital* to tracing out the "inner connection" of the forms of development of the material studied (1990: 102).

Making a distinction between the manifest properties of a thing and its fundamental causal structure invited a consequence of which Marx was fully aware – there is no way to identify structures which are essential except through and by means of background theories and hypotheses. Psillos writes:

> Only theories can tell us in virtue of what internal properties or mechanisms, as well as in virtue of what nomological connections, a certain substance possesses the properties and displays the behavior it does. Similarly,

only theories can tell us in virtue of what internal properties an item belongs to *this* rather than *that* kind. And only theories can tell us whether a certain collection of entities, samples or items is a candidate for a natural kind.

(1999: 288)

Always, our grasp of something, whether of water or value, depends on a background of theoretical knowledge.

Enthusiasm for social kinds

Despite the appeal of natural kind theory to many working scientists (Rieppel 2004; Wagner 2001; Keller *et al.* 2003), the extension of kind methodology to the study of social life has been halting. For natural scientists the appeal no doubt rests at least in part on their demonstrable success in identifying the physical and chemical make-up of things. In fact, for the natural sciences a sense that the constitutive causal structures they study make it possible for us to characterize what they are and how they behave has entered popular consciousness – everyone knows water is H_2O and if you explain to someone that the real definition of water is H_2O you will have no difficulty explaining that this means the chemical formula captures the nature of water such that anything that is H_2O is water and anything that isn't, isn't. But there is no comparable recognition for the achievements of social science. No doubt there are a variety of reasons for this, not the least of which must include the ideological and even apologetic character of much social theory. Here, I address briefly two important tendencies often thought to compromise the extension of kind methodology to the study of social life.

First, traditional thinking about natural kinds tends to assume models from physics and chemistry, and such models are often thought to reflect necessary and sufficient membership conditions that are exceptionless, ahistorical and unchanging. Thus, working at least in part on the basis of such assumptions, philosophers of social science have often concluded that the categories of human action do not lend themselves to treatment as kinds.[7]

A most uncompromising expression of this traditional view is found in the work of Brian Ellis (2001, 2002). The "new essentialism," he explains, holds that kinds must be unambiguously distinct from one another and characterized by properties independent of history, location or circumstance the way spin, charge and mass characterize an electron regardless of when or where it is. Further, the way we characterize a natural kind, according to Ellis, is dictated exclusively by nature; for his essentialism, kind definitions must be independent of the investigator's interest or practice.

Plainly, if these views capture what we mean by natural kinds, then necessarily there are no such things in the human sciences. Ellis (2001: 187) writes: "the economy of a country is not an object that belongs to a natural kind, and the processes of the market are not instances of natural kinds of processes." As he explained a few pages earlier (2001: 178):

Human laws, institutions, social structures, cultures, and political organizations, and so on are not members of natural kinds. But, according to scientific essentialism, all causal laws are grounded in the essential dispositional properties of natural kinds. Consequently there can be no causal laws of social behavior or development that are specific to the kinds of things that are the subject of social theory.

The argument, however, needs to proceed the other way around. Our first objective must be to identify what potent structures exist in the world, including the social world, and then establish how they are to be best characterized.[8]

Richard Boyd's "enthusiasm for natural kinds" (1991) rejects this traditional baggage both for the study of nature and social life. He argues instead that the insistence that kinds be unchanging, ahistorical, intrinsic, foundational and exceptionless with necessary and sufficient membership conditions is itself neither necessary nor sufficient to explain the way we use natural kind terminology across the diverse domains of science: "The natural kinds that have unchanging definitions in terms of intrinsic necessary and sufficient conditions that are the subjects of eternal, ahistorical, and exceptionless laws are an unrepresentative minority of natural kinds (perhaps even a minority of zero)" (1999a: 169). Like social kinds, biological kinds, for example, often reflect fuzzy boundaries, must be understood historically and in relation to locally specific environments. Moreover, Boyd argues, there is no one true way to understand living organisms or many other natural kinds, including social kinds. But none of these features gets in the way. It is a matter of being clear on what it is our reference to kinds is meant to do. For example, in explaining that there is a *"necessary* indeterminacy" in the extension of species terms, Boyd recalls that for Darwin: "speciation depends on the existence of populations which are intermediate between the parent species and the emerging one." As an important consequence,

> Any "refinement" of classification which artificially eliminated the resulting indeterminacy in classification would obscure the central fact about heritable variations in phenotype upon which biological evolution depends, and would thus undermine the accommodation of the classificatory resources of biology to relevant causal structures.
>
> (1999b: 68)

On the one hand, Boyd insists, causation is *not* a social construction: "we do not make causal relations, except in so far as we ourselves function as ordinary causal phenomena." On the other hand, the way we appropriate the world is constructed – it is always relative to our practice and how we interpret it. "Natural kinds," he writes, "are features, not of the world outside our practice, but of the ways in which that practice engages with the rest of the world" (1999b: 66). Thus they explain a kind of achievement. By contributing to our success in picking out causal structures essential to the demands of practice, kind terms help to accommodate our practice to them.

In sum, "Kinds are practice dependent but ... *the world is not*" (1999b: 55; [emphasis in original]). We carve the world at its joints, surely – it offers us no alternative – but we do not always carve at the same joints or in the same way or for the same purposes. We learn to understand its causal structures, including those we make, in order to align our practice with them – again, we interpret the world in order to change it.

A second worry compromising the extension of natural kind theory to social life follows from recognition of the mind dependence of social phenomena. This leads to conclusions which seem distinctly un- or anti-naturalist of the sort that suggest social kinds are constituted by ideas (Wendt 1999) or that they are compromised by the looping effects described by Hacking (1995). A news item from the late spring of 2006, for example, reports that 17 percent of students at Cornell and Princeton practice "self-injury" in the sense of self-mutilation, cutting, burning, and so forth: the person intends to hurt themselves but does not intend suicide.[9] The label seems new. But once classified in that way, people may relate differently to a person so labeled, see them differently, act differently toward them, and the person labeled may see themselves differently also, reinterpreting their past, looking differently on the future, and so forth. Some worry that media coverage may contribute to instances of such injury. Alexander Wendt (1999: 71) suggests that even the causal theory of reference seems to break down in such instances, insofar as it can be the very act of naming that may create the entity studied rather than a structure independently regulating one's reference to it.

As the critical realist Roy Bhaskar (1989: 84) argues:

> the social sciences are part of their own field of inquiry, in principle susceptible to explanation in terms of the concepts and laws of the explanatory theories they employ; so that they are *internal* with respect to the subject matter in a way in which natural science is not. This qualifies the sense in which the objects of social scientific investigation can be said to be intransitive, or exist and act independently of it.

Naturalism is thus qualified by an ontological limitation: "social structures, unlike natural structures do not exist independently of the agents' conceptions of what they are doing in their activity" (1989: 79).

Bhaskar's contribution to underlaboring for social theory has, it seems to me, been enormous, and it is in virtue of that contribution that I want to question the suggestion that mind dependence constitutes in any way a limit on naturalism as applied to the study of social life.

For Bhaskar, naturalism is qualified because social structures are not ontologically intransitive – a term he uses to refer to the way the things of the world act independent of our knowledge, thought or description of them. By arguing instead for an unqualified naturalism, I mean that the objects of social life can be known without recourse to ghostly or supernatural considerations, of course, and also that they can be known without recourse to *a priori* beliefs or foundational principles.

Knowledge of social kinds, like that of science generally, is of causal structures discovered *a posteriori* that exist and act independent of our theorizing.

It is important to see why this position is not paradoxical with respect to the mind dependence of social kinds. One way to do so is to step back a minute from Bhaskar's assertions. As creatures, as things of nature, as natural causal structures, we are entities with a mind. Intentionality, as Bhaskar has shown, is integral to what it means for us to act causally. It is part of the causal structure we are. So of course, insofar as social structures are constituted by the causal activity of human individuals they are not independent of mind.

But does this render social structures unlike natural structures? If we were to make an appropriate comparison we would have to ask whether natural structures are independent of the causally potent components that constitute them. H_2O is not a causal structure that exists independent of the molecular and intermolecular bonds manifested in the action of hydrogen and oxygen on one another reciprocally. That is, given that mind is part of the causal structure we are, we seem forced to read Bhaskar's proposition to make the absurd assertion that natural structures, unlike social structures, *do* exist independent of the causally potent components that make them up.

Without doubt, the human sciences are distinctive in that they include the study of mental phenomena as features of their domain. But these are not qualifications or limits on the possibility of naturalism – the constitutive causal structures in play are the object of study in all sciences. Whether we distinguish psychology from sociology or chemistry from physics, the basis for differentiation lies in how we classify just such structures.

The real point with respect to the question of mind dependence is instead addressed by the "metaphysical innocence thesis" I introduced in Chapter 1. Realists in the philosophy of science agree that mental conceptions like the adoption of particular theories may have tremendous causal effects on their target social objects. But when constructivists and others suggest that this limits the extension of naturalism to social life, expect disagreement: as Richard Boyd argues, particular theories may have a causal effect, but the theories and beliefs we adopt make no non-causal, logical or other conceptual contribution to the thing investigated. They will be causally efficacious just to the extent that, and only to the extent that, they engage ordinary causal mechanisms:

> for realists, human social practices, like the adoption of theories and classificatory schemes, are *metaphysically* innocent: they affect the causal structure of the world only *via* the operation of the intermediary causal mechanisms which supervene on the causal structures studied by the various special sciences and not also in some additional way studied only by philosophers practicing conceptual analysis.
>
> (Boyd 1991: 144)

Reasons cause action, but to do so they must supervene on ordinary causal mechanisms.

The kind constitutive properties of the commodity form

Undoubtedly, the extension of natural-kind theory to the study of social life has also been hobbled by the abstract character taken by many theoretical discussions of social kinds. Here, especially, attention to Marx's work, so rich in relevant examples, can make a helpful contribution. Let me summarize the example I presented above.

To begin, it is important to notice that the nature of value cannot be understood except as a consequence of the social form of commodity-producing labor. Value as such can be explained as a social relation of persons with respect to the expenditure of their labor. But this cannot be understood without spelling out that the social relation instantiated in this quantitative relation is a specific form of the relation of laboring persons to nature and to each other.[10] The kind constitutive properties of that specific form of social labor are two: persons labor independently and they do so as part of the social division of labor – they produce goods useless to them for private exchange. This is a real definition of the commodity form of social labor. When labor takes *that* form, then reciprocally related quantities of labor expenditure in society will tend to take the value form and value will tend to be expressed by means of commodities and money in the quantitative ratios in which goods exchange. The commodity form of social labor is a social entity, the real definition of which identifies for us the causal structure that accounts for the commodity form of the product of labor and the value form of the commodity.

Notice that we discover these essential characteristics of the commodity form through investigation *a posteriori* and we can test them empirically: if labor is characterized by the separate production of products not useful to the producer, then there will be a tendency for the product to take the form of a commodity and it will tend to be exchanged for value in the market. Moreover, this will be true under a wide variety of social circumstances.[11] Under capitalism the commodity is the general form of the product of labor, but of course historically this has not always been true. Nonetheless, even where it is not true, the causal tendencies generated by enformed commodity labor may be incompletely realized or even deformed as they are overridden by the effects of other and conflicting social structures. Still, if the constitutive properties of this living structure exist, it may be possible to mark the traces left by their causal force. Ancient Rome's forms of law, so readily adaptable to the exigencies of bourgeois life, may offer one dramatic example of such residue.

Importantly, the kind constitutive properties of the commodity form of labor identify a causal structure that exists independent of our theorizing. Thus, where production is exclusively of use values useless to the producers of them – an activity that certainly depends on the conception producers have of what they are doing – then resort to exchange is compelled. Exchange, in turn, functions homeostatically to provide each producer with the goods and services necessary for subsistence and new production. In so doing, the original causal structure of social labor is reproduced. It should be added here, in part in response to Brian

Ellis (2001), who argues that metaphysical necessity has no meaning in reference to social laws, that the particular form of natural necessity appropriate to enformed commodity labor may be styled *reproductive necessity*. That is, it will be contingent whether a particular social form is to be reproduced, but if it is, this cannot be done unless critical features of the processes essential to it are present. For example, the independence of productive entities, which is the material basis not only for value but also for the legal relation of private property, requires the prohibition of theft. This requirement doesn't mean that the social form of commodity producing labor cannot be reproduced if any theft occurs. Neither does it mean that all thieves will be caught or every theft punished – value does not generate exceptionless laws. It does mean that the commodity form is inconsistent with theft and that some qualitatively significant level of suppression must obtain if this form is to be reproduced.

It is also the case that no matter what we think or theorize, the kind constitutive properties of commodity-producing labor will tend to persist and reproduce this social form until they are themselves transformed. This task – as the persistence of commodities and monetary calculations in the former Soviet Union illustrates (Bettelheim 1975) – depends on more than wishing away the manifestations of an underlying social structure. Boyd's metaphysical innocence thesis applies. Regardless of our theories or ambitions, transforming the causal structure that accounts for the commodity form requires engaging intermediate causal mechanisms that can make theory a material force. For one, large scale social organization capable of overcoming the autonomous separation of productive units is required. And that, in turn, requires understanding what such overcoming could mean. On both these points, see Bettelheim's seminal work, *Economic Calculation and the Forms of Property* (1975).

In an essay responding to Hacking's discussion of natural kinds, Boyd (1991) identified three key features of "the central core conception of natural kinds" and argued that, properly understood, each applied fully to social kinds. The foregoing analysis illustrates his point. First, he argues that the definition of a kind must be arrived at *a posteriori* rather than by social convention. I noted above that we discover the social form of commodity-producing labor by investigation *a posteriori*. Second, the kind must be defined by properties which characterize a causal structure that exists independent of our theorizing. This, as I explained immediately above, does characterize the composite of activity and form that constitutes commodity-producing labor. Third, there must be a causal relation between the instantiation of the kind and the use of the kind term in reference. That is, as Psillos remarked, the origin of the information we have about a kind must be located in the constitutive properties of it and thus it is the kind's causally efficacious structure that in the end regulates how we deploy the term (Psillos 1999).

This last point I think is demonstrably true of Marx's use of terms associated with the commodity form of labor, including, above all, the term "value." Opposed to empty and vague metaphysical appeals to value, Joan Robinson claimed some years ago that value "is just a word" (1962: 47). By contrast Marx has given an account of the term that roots our use of it in our understanding of an underlying causal structure capable of accounting both for the social relation of persons that he characterizes as the value relation and also for the fetishistic expression of that social relation by means of products in exchange.

Marx and the continuity of scientific reference

If enformed commodity labor provides a real definition of the social kind of commodity-producing labor, this offers a context for evaluating value-form theory's charge that Marx's break with Ricardo was wavering and incomplete. The question here is one of the continuity of scientific reference. Consider two different examples from the history of science.

First, Antoine Laurent Lavoisier's contribution to the science of chemistry constituted a decisive rupture with that science's earlier understanding of combustion insofar as he rejected the category phlogiston and proposed instead the existence of a new chemical element, oxygen. The category to which Joseph Priestly clung, phlogiston, in fact did not refer to anything. According to older chemical theory phlogiston was a substance given off during the course of combustion. But there is nothing in nature that corresponds to this account – oxygen combines with other elements in combustion to form oxides. Second, by contrast, Psillos explains that nineteenth-century references to the luminiferous ether did refer to the same entity science later came to call the electromagnetic field. In that case, although the conceptions earlier physicists held were inaccurate, still the core causal description they gave of the ether did refer to an energy-filled medium of the kind required for the propagation of light waves, and these features, more fully understood, characterized the core causal properties attributed to the electro-magnetic field (1999: 290–298).

A distinction Psillos draws from Larry Laudan clarifies the difference. That two scientific theories possess a "shared explanatory agenda" is not enough for the continuity of scientific reference. Instead, there must be also a "shared explanatory ontology." For example, Aristotle's theory of natural place, Newton's theory of gravitational action at a distance and Einstein's theory of the curvature of space time refer to a shared explanatory agenda – they want to solve the same problem – but, they do not refer to some one causal structure. In other words, we cannot reduce the continuity of scientific reference to the problem being explained, but rather must insist on continuity in the causal agent accounting for the explanation. Suppose a discarded theory is incomplete and also wrong in significant particulars. Still, there may be referential continuity if the fundamental causal properties to which scientists now refer show some important overlap with the causal description earlier scientists used. This did not occur in the case of phlogiston because there is no substance in nature given off in combustion, and thus no causal properties that function in the way phlogiston theory required.

In the preface to the second volume of *Capital* Engels raised such questions about Marx's place in the history of political economy. "But what then did Marx say about surplus-value that was new?" (1992: 97) he asked, and offered an explanation that compared Marx's achievement with that of Lavoisier in the science of chemistry. Priestly had actually produced oxygen in the laboratory, but, because he could not escape the old theoretical categories, he did not know what he had found. Lavoisier, by contrast, subjected the categories of chemistry to reevaluation and concluded that Priestly had in fact stumbled upon a new element. Engels continues:

> Marx is related to his predecessors in the theory of surplus-value as Lavoisier is to Priestley and Scheele. The *existence* of the part of the value produced that we now call surplus-value was established long before Marx...
>
> [Marx] saw that what was involved here was ... rather a fact which was destined to revolutionize economics, and which provided the key to the understanding of the whole of capitalist production – for the person who knew how to use it, that is. With the aid of this fact Marx investigated all the existing categories of economics, as Lavoisier had investigated the existing categories of phlogistic chemistry with the aid of oxygen. In order to know what surplus-value was, he had to know what value was. First and foremost, Ricardo's theory of value itself had to be subjected to criticism. Marx therefore investigated labour from the point of view of its value-forming quality, and established for the first time *what* labour, why, how it formed value, and that value in general is nothing more than congealed labour of *this* kind...
>
> (1992: 98–99 [emphasis in original])

Lavoisier's revolution in chemistry required that he abandon the concept of phlogiston, which did not refer, in order to fashion a category that did. Is Marx's relation to Ricardo the same?

Not in this respect. There is no doubt Marx revolutionized the categories of economics, but he did not abandon a concept which failed to refer for one that did. Engels pointed out earlier in the preface that Ricardo had developed a theory of value that "became the starting-point of all subsequent economic science" (1990: 93). Plainly, Ricardo's theory of value could not have become the starting point for subsequent economic science if it did not refer. By contrast, Priestly had physically produced oxygen but did not produce a theoretically coherent theory of it. Theoretically, he offered nothing that could serve as a starting point for any form of chemistry.

Marx's relation to Ricardo therefore was not really like that of Lavoisier to Priestly. Marx developed, deepened and clarified the theory of value he inherited from Ricardo, but he did not abandon the scientific object to which Ricardo referred. Marx was not the first to use the term 'labor' to refer to the causal agent that produced value. Instead, Engels argues, he was the first to understand *what* labor it was that produced value, and why and how it did so. He found that value was nothing but "congealed labour of *this* kind." Notice the distinction implicit here. The substance of value is congealed labor, but the underlying nature of this, the causal structure capable of accounting for value as a social kind, must be found in the historically and socially specific constitutive properties of commodity-producing labor.

That Ricardo had no grasp of the form of labor that constituted the product of labor as value does not compromise either the continuity of scientific reference nor does acknowledging such continuity compromise the significance of Marx's theoretical revolution. On the contrary, Psillos argues, such progress is normal in the course of science:

> This is as it should be. It signifies the open-ended character of scientific concepts and of scientific inquiry itself. A fuller characterization of the putative entity can be discovered only by further scientific investigation. Nor is it reasonable to argue that before a full characterization becomes available the scientists who employ the relevant term do not refer to anything at all.
>
> (1999: 295)

Conclusion

Recall once more the critique of Ricardo with which I began: if between Ricardo and Marx there is referential continuity – if both Marx and Ricardo refer to the same causal agent – then the advance represented by Marx's work is not well characterized as a rupture. As profound as his analysis of the social form of labor was, both he and Ricardo referred to the same causal agent. The distinction between a shared explanatory agenda and a shared explanatory ontology must be underscored. Smith, Ricardo, Marx, neo-classical theory, Sraffa, value-form and others do share a common explanatory agenda. All offer explanations for the ratio in which goods exchange. The question is whether they present a shared explanatory ontology – do they refer to the same causal forces of social life? If, as I believe, Marx and Ricardo do, then the rupture on offer will likely break not just with classical political economy, but with Marx as well. In the end value-form theory proposes a different scientific object.

Here is the critical thing: beginning with the seminal 1969 article of Backhaus (1980), value-form theorists have not understood the distinction presented at the beginning of *Capital* between value and its nature. In effect, they missed the distinction Marx took over from Aristotle between substance, in the sense in which a substantial thing may be the *subject* of predication (this dog, Fido; this man, Socrates), and primary substance, *ousia*, the constituting or substantial form of that subject as a kind.[12] In the first case, we refer to the commodity as a product of private labor produced for exchange and something that exchanges in a ratio regulated by the quantity of value producing labor expended on it; in the latter case, we refer to the kind constitutive properties that characterize the causal structure of social labor giving rise to this process. In consequence, the value-form tradition tends to substitute theories of value's forms of appearance for value's constitutive form. In the event, an inversion occurs: value's forms of appearance – exchange value and money – are called upon to play the role actually accomplished by value's kind constitutive properties. At the limit because no sense can be made of the substantial content of value, value comes to be considered "pure form" (Arthur 2002: 155; Reuten and Williams 1989: 65) and as such "without content" (Arthur 2002: 155).[13] There no longer appears to be an underlying causal structure for scientific reference to pick out (Murray 1993: 51; but see Murray 1997). Alternatively, value is understood as constituted by exchange (Arthur 2002: 96), and in contradistinction to Marx ("money does not arise by convention" [1986 MECW 28: 102; 1973: 165]), we are offered explanations of money as conventional, a fiduciary store of value, and as itself without value (Reuten and Williams 1989).

Marx (1990: 152 [I.1.3]) anticipated the underlying error:

> Our analysis has shown that the form of value, that is, the expression of the value of a commodity, arises from the nature of commodity-value, as opposed to value and its magnitude arising from their mode of expression as exchange-value.

"Nature" here can be understood as value's essence, the causal structure of labor that, as the commodity's simplest determination, forms its organizing principle. Value-form theory shifts the object of social investigation instead: emphasizing the constitutive role of exchange, the theory sets labor's potent material structure aside. As a result the touted reconstructions of Marx get situated on terrain he left behind.

What we have made, we can often unmake and refashion, but to do so we need references to the world that accurately present the task confronting us. Bettelheim (1975) showed many years ago that overcoming the persistence of commodity categories during the transition to socialism requires, among other things, overcoming the separation of productive units from one another. In both ordinary language and science, we interpret the world using the terminology of natural kinds in order to get right our efforts to change it.

Appendix: Backhaus and the analysis of *Capital*'s first chapter[14]

In a seminal essay in 1969, Hans Georg Backhaus, a student of Adorno, offered a critique of the first two sections of *Capital*. The argument goes like this: Backhaus argued that there was a "defectiveness of the presentation" reflected above all in a "break" or "gap" between the first two sections and the third. According to Backhaus, the whole importance of Marx's critique of political economy was the line of demarcation drawn with Ricardo. Ricardo, unconcerned with social form, had dissolved value into labor, the substance of value. But he had offered no analysis of value's forms. By contrast, Marx's attention to the value form in §3 of *Capital*'s first chapter showed the possibility for a decisive rupture with classical political economy. Nonetheless, Backhaus thought there was a problem. Enormously sensitive to the difficulty of his opening analysis, Marx had taken such pains to popularize the first two sections that he had compromised the methodological structure of his problematic. There was a capitulation to Ricardian analysis: specifically, labor presented in §§ 1–2 as the substance of value is developed as nothing more than the bare physiological expenditure of human effort. There is no concern for an explanation that either shows or will prepare the way for a consideration of social form. The transition from §2 to §3 is therefore unmediated and "pseudo-dialectical." We are left with an incomplete break with classical political economy that has undermined not only the dialectic of Marx's presentation, but also its critical bite.

Backhaus' essay, together with renewed attention to Marx's debt to Hegel, has led among value-form theorists (e.g. Arthur 2002; 1979; Taylor 2000; Reuten 1993; Reuten and Williams 1989; Williams 1988; Eldred and Hanlon 1981) to a reconsideration of Marx's analysis of value. Christopher Arthur (2002), for example, argues that Marx's introduction of the subject of labor into the first sections of *Capital* is done "far too hastily" (2002: 87) and he offers instead an analysis of the value-form without any consideration of labor at all. Labor does enter, but only after the logic of capital has been developed and as a result of contradictions presented in that connection. In his analysis of commodity exchange, Arthur treats value as an expression of "pure form" (2002: 155), abstracted from all materiality, which, by analogy to Hegel's concept of pure Being, becomes the source of all subsequent development of the logic of *Capital*.

The question is whether value-form theory's rejections of Marx's presentation in the first sections of *Capital* can be sustained. I argue that it can't. Ironically, the reason for this is that value-form theorists have ignored precisely the social form of labor presented in §2. By claiming that Marx there reduces value to the bare physiological expenditure of labor, Backhaus and value-form theorists do, like Schumpeter and others, indeed make Marx into a Ricardian, but only because they miss the underlying causal structure he has located, the thing that allows us to characterize labor's form as a social kind. In this early stage of the analysis of the commodity, these theorists tend to consider social form only in connection with the forms of manifestation of value presented by Marx in §3 of *Capital*'s first chapter. They bypass the *constitutive* form of value presented in §2, a causal structure capable of accounting for value's forms of manifestation. This leads quite explicitly to an inversion whereby value is instead constituted by its forms of manifestation, in particular, money, and Marx's political economy gets reconstructed accordingly. By focusing on the analysis of the forms value takes in exchange, Marx's insistence on the social forms of production is lost.

A remarkable claim

To understand how Marx analyzed the social form of commodity-producing labor is to understand value as a social kind.

Marx begins §2 by reminding us that the commodity presents itself as something useful and as something that has value in exchange. He remarks immediately that §1 also established that the labor that produced commodities has a two-fold nature – labor insofar as it found expression in value and labor insofar as it was the creator of use values. He then adds quite a remarkable claim: "I was the first to point out and examine critically this twofold nature of labour contained in commodities. As this point is crucial to an understanding of political economy, it requires further elucidation." (1990: 132 [I.1.2]).

Now the group to which Marx has reference in claiming that he has moved to the front of the line includes William Petty, Ben Franklin, Adam Smith, Jean Baptiste Say, and David Ricardo, and others, not to speak of Hegel, who while not a political economist, nonetheless found an important place for the study of the political economy of value in the *Philosophy of Right*. This suggests it is time to pay attention. Marx is either puffing or something important is going on.

The fifth paragraph following this first one, that is, the sixth paragraph of the section, begins, "To sum up, then." Plausibly the detail we're invited by the first paragraph to consider has been presented in the intervening four paragraphs. We need to track the argument in them.

The first of these paragraphs is a single sentence. A commodity, Marx established in §1, is a use value offered in exchange. That is, a commodity must be a useful object, but it is not just a useful object. For one thing, if it is useful but not produced by labor, it is not a commodity. For another, if it is consumed directly by its producer it is not a commodity. Instead, in order to be a commodity a useful object must be exchanged. Moreover, it is exchanged in some or another proportion with another commodity, and, roughly, this is its exchange value. So a commodity is a useful thing that is a bearer of exchange value; that is, it stands in a variety of exchange relations with other things. The single sentence of the second paragraph of §2 offers a simple example of two commodities, 10 yards of linen and a coat, standing in a 2 to 1 relation to each other – the coat has twice the value of 10 yards of linen.

In the next paragraph, the third, Marx notices that the coat is the result of a particular kind of useful activity, tailoring. He adds that labor, considered from the perspective of the way in which it manifests itself in a useful product, is called "useful labor." This is one aspect of the twofold character of labor.

In the fourth paragraph, Marx observes that just as two use values, the linen and the coat, are qualitatively different, so is the labor which produced them. But it is just this qualitative difference that drives their producers to exchange and thus makes it possible for the results of useful labor to function as commodities. "Coats cannot be exchanged for coats," he writes. The commodity form, in other words, requires the distribution by means of exchange of the products of aggregate social labor to need.

In the fifth paragraph, Marx considers labor insofar as it is productive of value, the other aspect of the twofold character of labor. This is a point of detail not yet developed either in the preceding paragraphs of §2 or in §1. We learn here that because the useful labors expended in producing goods offered for exchange are qualitatively diverse, these labors are part of the social division of labor. But Marx immediately emphasizes that while the division of labor is necessary for the production of commodities, the converse is not true – there can be a division of labor in society without the production of commodities. Ancient societies that divided work among the members of a community without resorting to exchange offer one example. A factory offers another – labor is specialized within a factory and the object of production passes from hand to hand without the intervention of market exchange. Markets emerge when production is carried on by persons or groups of persons producing independently as part of the social division of labor. Thus, Marx concludes, "Only the products of mutually independent acts of labour, performed in isolation, can confront each other as commodities" (1990: 132 [I.1.2]).

It should not escape our attention that this is the point "crucial to an understanding of political economy."[15]

That is, if we're following the text, the next sentence begins the sixth paragraph: "To sum up, then" (1990: 132 [I.1.2]).

What Marx has presented here is a structure of social labor, a social form that generates value. We can ask whether the features identified constitute those homeostatic dispositional properties that characterize a social kind.

By returning to §1 we get a better sense of the significance of the point in the flow of the analysis. In §1 Marx explains that exchange value, the proportion in which values of one product exchange for values of another, is constantly changing. A book worth $10 today is worth $20 tomorrow and $30 in another town. The phenomena that characterize exchange value seem relative and accidental. As such, assuming nothing more, exchange value is a poor candidate for a social kind.

But since the similarity commodities share in exchange does place them in relation to one another in determined proportions, Marx concludes that exchange value must express something common to the use values exchanged. Long ago, however, Aristotle noticed that use values offered for exchange are incommensurable (1962: 127 [1133ᵇ19]). Marx therefore concludes that the act of exchange must take place in total abstraction from use value in the following sense: use value motivates the exchange, but it does not explain the ratio of exchange; in fact, any given use value can exchange for any conceivable other so long as they are presented in the right quantitative proportions. Marx adds also that if we abstract from all consideration of use, we abstract from every material element of the product that determines use. Use value must become then simply the bearer of the one causally distinctive feature that commodities still have in common – labor. Each commodity is a product of labor. Insofar as this labor has been expended on a product, transforming it to use, it is value. While this labor, because expended, is not the living labor located in the actual process of production that constitutes the value relation, still, expended labor, like living labor, can be quantitatively measured by the duration of the living labor that formed it and thus living labor can serve as a measure of the value each product of labor represents.

An early criticism of Marx's analysis here, one that has persisted, is that commodities share in common an infinite number of properties – they all exist under the stars, they all exist at some specific distance from London, they all are the object of need, and so forth. Most of these alternatives are trivial and fail because we know intuitively they do not causally regulate exchange – distance from London is an example. And the problem with need, despite the heroic efforts of mainstream economics, is this: to regulate the exchange of incommensurables, needs would have to be commensurable, but they are not.

So we're left with labor. Labor is the thing products have in common that may plausibly be understood to regulate exchange. But we're stuck still. The concrete useful labors that produce useful objects for exchange are themselves incommensurable. The tailor who goes to market demanding 30 yards of linen for a coat because 10 yards are produced in a half day and the coat took him a day and a half to produce may be as likely to wind up with a quarrel as with linen.

It is this problem that provokes us to look not just for labor as the source of value – the limitation of Ricardo's analysis – but also to consider the *form* of social labor. In fact it is the causal structure of commodity producing labor that both generates the problem of commensurability in exchange *and* the solution to it. Recall how we have characterized that structure: independent producers produce use values useless to them. We are immediately presented with the problem of finding an appropriate ratio for goods to exchange. In order to distribute aggregate social labor to need, goods must change hands.

But by generating the need for exchange, this causal structure of interdependent autonomy also generates the solution to the problem. Use values are not use values unless they are consumed. That means they must be exchanged in order to be used. Since any product whatsoever can be exchanged for any other as long as each exists in an appropriate quantity, the total amount of productive labor devoted to the production of commodities can be considered an aggregate. That is, when products exchange, as they must, they are equated practically by the act of exchange and thus the entire mass of aggregate concrete labors that produced them can be considered one mass to be distributed to social need. Each product then represents a proportion of this mass.

An analogy from the physical sciences making news while Marx was working through his analysis of the commodity may contribute to understanding. In 1857 The German physicist Rudolph Clausius for the first time explained the kinetic theory of gases in a satisfactory way.[16] A container filled with gas of any sort consists mostly of empty space. The molecules that make up the gas exist there in a condition of random motion. Collisions, which are also random, affect the speed of the molecules. Some go faster than average, some less. This means that the kinetic energy of individual molecules, which is an expression of their mass and speed, will vary. Nonetheless, the temperature of a gas, whatever its chemical composition, is proportional to the average kinetic energy of its molecules.

Now there is a point worth emphasizing here: it makes no difference what gas or gases are mixed in the container. Heavier molecules will move more slowly than lighter ones, but at the same temperature, their average kinetic energy will be the same. In this respect we can abstract from the chemical composition of the molecules.[17] We can even call this, legitimately, a "real" abstraction.

Much ink has been spilled over "real" abstraction in Marx and the concept has become something of a *deux ex machina* in a good deal of recent literature. In the case of a gas, we're entitled to call what we're left with when we abstract from chemical composition "real" because the average kinetic energy we now take as our exclusive focus remains fully present and causally effective. What do we mean by real abstraction then?

This can have no other meaning than that the features rendered irrelevant by the process we investigate have lost their causal significance for our inquiry. They are causally irrelevant to explanation and understanding. In natural kind terms, they do not serve induction or explanation by helping to accommodate our practice to the causal structures of the world.

The meaning of "real" abstraction in Marx is the same. Consideration of the material and useful properties of objects produced as commodities *are* casually relevant to exchange – as we have seen they are what drive people to exchange. But these same properties make no relevant contribution to establishing the commensurable ratios in which goods exchange.

Labor expended is different. Far from abstracting from the different concrete labors that contribute to exchange, these labor expenditures constitute value. Reference to the kinetic theory of gases may once again be helpful. For any gas, temperature is proportional to the average kinetic energy of the molecules, but this does not at all mean that the speed or actual kinetic energy of every molecule is the same. Instead, the total kinetic energy of a system depends on the different masses and random speeds of the individual molecules. When distributed over the number of molecules in the system, average kinetic energy is proportional to temperature, and thus as the average speed of individual molecules increases, temperature will increase. The speed of any particular molecule will deviate from average, but, at constant pressure and volume, average kinetic energy is a causal composition of these particular speeds taken together with their molecular mass, not an abstraction from them.

In commodity exchange we abstract from the useful effects of labor, but we do not abstract from the different concrete expenditures of labor conducted all with varying intensities deviating from any average of them. Just as at a given temperature the chemical composition of a gas does not affect the average kinetic energy of its molecules, so too for commodity exchange the useful effect of labor is irrelevant to establishing value. But just as kinetic energy depends on the actual mass and speed of the different molecules of a gas, value depends on the concrete labor expenditures of different units of production. Temperature is an expression of average kinetic energy jointly produced by the random motions of all molecules. So too, value is an expression of the average of all the different concrete labor expenditures of which a market is made. We can only conceptually abstract from these different concrete expenditures by thinking of the value of a product as a causal composition of them.

Think of it this way. The different speeds of gas molecules are the product of random collisions. Goods taken to market are reduced to expended labor that can be considered homogeneous by the collisions of exchange. Following Marx, (see p. 49), I suggested that any two products can be equated practically in the market in some specific ratio – some given proportion of the one for the other regulates the exchange of potatoes, say, for widgets.[18] But for this to happen, widgets and potatoes must be, each one respectively, homogeneous in kind. Suppose four people each produce a widget and all the widgets produced are effectively identical in their features and qualities. One does this in two hours, the other in four, the third in six, and the last in eight. As a result of competition, and because they are the same, the widgets will tend to sell for the same price. This means that competition will reduce all different expenditures of widget labor to homogeneity. The labor time contributed by the production of widgets to aggregate social labor is 20 hours. Since each widget, no matter who produced it or how efficient the process of production was, is rendered equal to every other by competition, each tends to represent five hours contributed to this total, though no one actually produced a widget in five hours. But this deviation of the actual labor expenditure from the social average for producing widgets does not mean that those specific expenditures are causally irrelevant to the constitution of value. On the contrary, value is the causal result of them. The expended labor that is the source of value is abstract because the useful effects of labor are causally irrelevant, not because the duration of labor expenditure is causally irrelevant.

There is one more lesson we can draw from the foregoing analogy. The development of the causal theory of reference has had the effect of clarifying a distinction that earlier attention to the philosophy of language sometimes confused. We call Hesperus the evening star and Phosphorus the morning star, but they refer to the same thing – the planet Venus. Since reference is the same but meaning different we're forced to recognize a distinction between the thing referred to and our meaning – meaning which may very well, as in this case, be context specific. So too we can see that temperature and average kinetic energy refer to the same thing – we reduce them both to the motion of molecules in a gas – but can recognize also that they are used in different contexts to mean quite different things.

On the analysis just given we can make a comparable distinction between Marx's use of the concepts of abstract labor and value. Like temperature and average kinetic energy, both terms refer to the same thing – a quantitative relationship of the respective expended labors socially required to produce the commodities brought to market – but these two terms do not mean the same thing.

Value connotes the relative weight such labor expenditures give the products of labor in exchange. Abstract labor, by contrast, is paired with and understood in relation to concrete labor – it connotes the way expended labor is reduced to a homogeneous and common measure by the random collisions of exchange.

Reconsidering the defectiveness of Marx's presentation

Does this specification of the social form of commodity-producing labor respond to the critique offered by Backhaus and the theorists who have followed his lead? I think it does. First, the idea that there is a defectiveness of presentation in first sections of *Capital* is the result of ignoring exactly the point Marx emphasizes, "the pivot on which a clear comprehension of political economy turns" (1967: 49) – the social form of labor. As we have seen, it is the social form of commodity-producing labor that gives rise to the problem of commensurability in exchange – producers are independent and produce use values that are useless to them. But this same social form also gives rise to the means for the problem's solution. Because any product may exchange for any other in an appropriate proportion, producers entering exchange abstract necessarily from the concrete usefulness of their labors and each product is a bearer of value to the extent of its contribution, as a result of exchange, to the aggregate total of labor distributed to need.

By ignoring the social form of labor specified in §2, value-form theorists have been led to argue that abstraction from use in exchange means abstraction from all materiality in the process. Value could thus better be understood at this early stage of the analysis as "pure form" and "without content" (Arthur 2002: 155; Reuten and Williams 1989: 65). It is clear, however, that this approach misreads §2. In the act of exchange, abstraction is made from all consideration of use and of all material properties of goods that account for their use. But there is no abstraction either from the duration of labor expenditure or from the materiality of the *social form of labor* that causes exchange! Exchange does not abstract from, but depends on, the material division of labor in society; equally exchange does not abstract from but is a causal consequence of the separation of units of production one from the other.

In sum, the labor that produces the product in the commodity form is itself form determined in two ways: it is produced independently and it is produced as part of the social division of labor. As I have argued, these causal features of labor's social form offer a real definition of the form of commodity-producing labor as a social kind.

Labor as the substance of value

No doubt Backhaus and others would respond to the criticisms I've made by noticing an omission – I've said nothing about his claim that in the first sections of *Capital* Marx reduces value to the bare physiological expenditure of labor. However it be with your analysis, these theorists might argue, this reduction has nothing to do with social form. Consider the way Marx concludes §2:

> On the one hand, all labour is an expenditure of human labour-power, in the physiological sense, and it is in this quality of being equal, or abstract, human labour that it forms the value of commodities. On the other hand, all labour is an expenditure of human labour-power in a particular form and with a definite aim, and it is in this quality of being concrete useful labour that it produces use-values.
>
> (1990: 137 [I.1.2])

On a quick reading of this passage we could conclude that the bare physiological expenditure of labor explained the source of value and the concrete form of labor explained what made labor useful. But we can read more carefully. First, there are not two different labors here, of course, and attention to labor's *useful* form does not efface the *social* form presupposed by the labor expenditures that produce commodities. That is, the labor that produces a commodity must count as one labor with distinct causal consequences, each of which realizes different causal results. When we focus on its definite aim – weaving or tailoring is meant here – we consider its useful form. When we focus on it as an expenditure of independent labor functioning as a part of a complex social division of labor, we consider its social form or value.

To consider the labor expended on commodities from the point of view of its social form, we consider its "quality of being equal, or abstract, human labour." But the abstract or equal character of human labor is not something that belongs to the bare physiological expenditure of human effort in all times and all places as such. In the Introduction to the *Grundrisse*, Marx observes that "there is no production in general" (1986 MECW 28: 23; 1973: 86) only production in specific social and historical circumstances. In the same sense there is no "labor in general." The particular social form in which the labor "in the physiological sense" takes an equal or abstract character consists in the separation of units of production that produce goods useful to others but useless to themselves. As a direct causal consequence producers exchange and the process of exchange then renders causally irrelevant the useful effects of their labor to the regulation of the exchange; instead all labor is reduced by exchange to a homogeneous commensurability in terms of labor time.

Nor in the study of labor's social forms throughout history do we disregard useful effects in all times and all places. Quite the contrary. There is no labor in general and if the physiological expenditure of labor is to be considered without regard to its useful effects, this necessarily presupposes a historically determined social form of labor in the actual activity of production. Marx presented the essential features of this in the first paragraphs of §2. Backhaus' argument that in §§ 1 and 2 Marx presents the substance of value as the mere bare physiological expenditure of human effort misreads by ignoring this. It is only in virtue of Marx's explicit specification of the social form required that labor's product can appear in the commodity form as a manifestation of equal or abstract human labor.

3 Separation and subordination

The real definition of capital as a social kind

The separations of capitalist production

In 1969, in a seminal theoretical work, *Economic Calculations and the Forms of Property*, Charles Bettelheim characterized the capitalist mode of production by referring to the *double separation* on which it depends:

> The capitalist character of the enterprise ... is due to the fact that its structure assumes the form of a *double separation: the separation of workers from their means of production* ... and the *separation of the enterprises from each other*. This double separation forms the central characteristic of the capitalist mode of production, and it serves as a support for the totality of contradictions of this mode of production.
>
> (1975: 77 [emphasis in original])

I've shown how the separation of entities of production from each other in the context of the social division of labor offers a real definition of the social form of commodity-producing labor. Here I want to consider the separation of workers from their conditions of production. Assuming the separation of productive entities from one another, Bettelheim's observation suggests a real definition of the capital relation that might be straightforwardly completed as follows: capital is the separation of laboring producers from the conditions of production. In fact, I will want to qualify this by specifying that separation is alienated and that the conditions of production are values. Alienation will add the concept of subordination or subjugation in the sense in which Marx speaks of "capital's specific social determination" as "capital ownership which possesses the capacity of command over the labour of others" (1991: 505 [III.23]). Further, specifying that the conditions of production are values will reinforce the point that the separation of productive entities is presupposed and provide dimension to our understanding of alienation – in the end, labor is subordinated to its own products and these dominate it. Thus, I will conclude that the social relation picked out by the concept of capital is the free worker's alienated separation from and subordination to the conditions of production as values, a separation that penetrates the labor process itself. This description offers a real definition of capital.

I'll proceed as follows: I'll begin by giving an introductory overview of capital as a social kind and will situate the problem of giving its real definition against what we may call the fundamental *aporia* of it. I'll then give a more fully articulated analysis by giving attention to the dynamic without which capital's definition cannot be understood; I will consider capital's separations not only as the premise of capitalist production, but also as starting point, as process and as result. In Chapter 4 I'll offer a summary drawing together the themes presented in this and the previous chapter by tracing the way Marx worked out the concept of capital in his draft for *Capital*, the *Grundrisse*.

Abstraction and simple determination

In earlier chapters I've argued that offering a real definition of a thing is a way we fashion conceptual categories we require to pick out the essential properties of its causal structure.[1] These in turn enable us to account for the way the entity behaves and persists as the kind of thing it is. Water is H_2O. This chemical formula identifies for us the causal structure which we find invariably presented in samples of the stuff we call water; it accounts for the information we have about water and, properly understood, enables us to account for how water will tend to behave in response to the different conditions in which it finds itself. As a result the category H_2O makes it possible for us to accommodate our explanations and practices to the causal reality water presents. Extended to the study of social life, we may refer to natural kinds as social kinds (Boyd 1991, 1999a and 1988). Hence, to offer a real definition of capital is to offer a definition of capital as a social kind. We look for the causal structure of capital, its most fundamental form of material organization, the essential characteristics that explain what it is, how it persists as what it is, and how we can expect it to behave over time. To offer a real definition is, in the language Marx used, to identify the *differentia specifica* of a social form – those determinations that establish how the object of study is specifically different from other things. Recall that by locating the causal structure that specifically differentiates properties constitutive of it as a kind, we distinguish between the social kind as a composite whole and its essence.

The abstraction of "capital in general"

In the *Grundrisse* Marx used the concept of "capital in general" to thread together his effort and clarify the social relation captured by this category. I will consider his explorations there more fully in Chapter 4. For now, it is enough to notice the following:

> Before we go any further, one more observation: *capital in general* as distinct from particular capitals, does indeed appear (1) *only as an abstraction*; not an arbitrary abstraction but one which grasps the *differentia specifica* which distinguishes capital from all other forms of wealth or modes in

which (social) production develops. These are determinations which are common to every capital as such, or which make any particular sum of values into capital. And the distinctions within this abstraction are likewise abstract particularities which characterize every type of capital...

(1986 MECW 28: 378; 1973: 449 [emphasis in original])

Marx's use of the concept of abstraction is important here and bears comment. First, abstraction is being used to fix reference. We make an appropriate distinction between the concept and its referent, between reality's "determinations of existence" and the categories of mind that give expression to them.[2] We deal with theoretical abstractions that refer to the real and determined phenomena of social life.

Second, all abstraction strips away from particularity, but in Marx's usage we need to understand this stripping away in the way Peirce used the word "prescind" (1992: 2–3) – it is a form of disregarding some particular features of a thing in order to attend to others. While our effort is to locate particular features that instances of capital have in common, and the abstraction we seek is general in that sense, it is misunderstood as a search for less and less specific generalities. Marxists who have used abstraction to arrive at structureless or contentless categories claimed to present an appropriate starting point for analysis at the highest level of generality reflect this error. In the last chapter I suggested how value-form theory treated value as "pure form" in the sense that it is "without content." The appeal here is to an understanding reflected in, as an example, Stace's classic presentation of Hegel's *Logic*:

Suppose we take any object in the world and proceed to abstract from all its attributes. This table, for example, is square, hard, brown, shiny. Abstract from the shininess, and we are left with the proposition, "This table is square, hard, brown." Abstract from the brownness and we are left with "This table is square, hard." Abstract lastly from the hardness, and then from the squareness, and we are left with "This table is." "*Is*" is the last possible abstraction. Being is the first category.

(1955: 87)

Now, however it be with Hegel, this is not the method of science nor Marx's approach to the study of social life. Abstraction is always a stripping away from particularity, but we have to remember the distinction between the theoretical concepts abstraction enables us to fashion and the richly specific concrete subject to which those abstractions refer. Marx writes "the most general abstractions arise on the whole only with the most profuse concrete development, when one [phenomenon] is seen to be common to many, common to all" (1986 MECW 28: 41; 1973: 103 [brackets in original]). Features of the commodity form, for example, become general as a result of capitalist production; when social production is organized by capital almost all products are produced as commodities. But that does not mean that the distinctive features of social life that characterize the social form of commodity-producing labor are any less specific or require a less precise characterization of their decisive causal properties. As used by Marx, abstraction is a tool that enables us to access features that are general in the sense that they are common to particular capitals, but these are specific causal determinations of social form, not empty generalities.

Nor is the move from particularity to common features of the richly profuse real object a stripping away to what is indifferently common. If we want to definitively identify the specific polymers of which Stace's table might be made, it will not be enough to abstract to hardness or color or Being, even if we spell with a capital "B." We attend instead to precisely those features that contribute most crucially to explanation or induction and leave aside the rest. With respect to capital in general as a social form, we abstract to those specific features of social life that "distinguish capital from all other forms of wealth." We abstract to those features that constitute capital's *differentia specifica*. In terms of contemporary scientific realism we identify those causal properties or mechanisms that characterize capital as a natural kind.

I want to develop this approach by reference to Marx's fragment on method, "The Method of Political Economy," but I need to repeat for emphasis the point just made. What distinguishes types of abstraction is not what one abstracts *from*, but what one abstracts *to*. In experimental science, for example, experiment is designed as a means of abstracting from distracting features of an environment in order to reveal without disturbance those causal features that are the target of inquiry. We disregard or screen out innumerable details irrelevant to our task in order to focus on features that render the mechanism or process studied distinctive.[3] If we do this to identify the features of a thing that distinguish it as a natural kind, we will select features that particular instances of the kind share with others of the same kind and show how in their interconnection those features account for the persistence of the kind as the kind of thing it is. It is only in this sense that we speak of capital in general – we identify those causally potent properties common to capital as a social form. Moreover, instances of capital may have many features in common, even many that are fundamental, but in picking out what will distinctively define capital as a social kind we look only to those few characteristics that account for or organize its development and their interconnection, that is, those that are constitutive of it. The centralization of capital, for example, is an inevitable manifestation of capitalism and common and fundamental to it, but it is not an essential attribute of the real definition of capital.

We also miss what is decisively distinctive about the concept of capital in general if we abstract to features that capital shares with other forms of social production. Marx writes in the *Grundrisse*:

> *Nothing is easier than to prove that capital is a necessary condition for all human production.* We have only to abstract from the specific characteristics of capital which make it into a moment of a particularly developed *historical* stage of human production. The irony is that if all capital is

objectified labour which serves as means for new production, not all the objectified labour that serves as means for new production is capital. *Capital is conceived of as a thing, not as a relationship.*

(1986 MECW 28: 189; 1973: 258; [emphasis in original])

And he makes a similar point in a last chapter of *Capital's* third book by explaining why we cannot treat all social forms for the distribution of a surplus product as the same:

> The identity of the different modes of distribution thus comes down to the fact that they are identical if we abstract from their distinctions and specific forms and cling on just to their unity in contrast to what distinguishes them.
>
> (1991: 1017–1018 [III.51])

If we abstract to features of a thing in no way specific to it, we will classify it together with other entities of the most diverse sort and be unable to give a distinctive account of its operation. Many objects other than Stace's table are shiny, brown, hard and square – a lacquer box, for example – and we can always readily find properties a thing has in common with others. We less readily find those that account for the *kind* of thing it is. Carl Hempel (1945) discovered a paradox by noticing that the statement "all ravens are black" is logically equivalent to "all non-black things are non-ravens."[4] Why doesn't a red balloon provide evidence, then, to support the proposition that "all ravens are black"? But we can search endlessly among non-black things without ever identifying a causal feature that allows us to explain the blackness of ravens. Richard Boyd clarifies what makes a generalization methodologically relevant, that is, "projectable:"[5]

> You were able to discern the true [generalization] because your inductive practices allowed you to identify a generalization appropriately related to the causal structures of the phenomena in question.... Your deployment of projectable categories and generalizations allowed you to identify a *causally sustained* generalization.
>
> (1999a: 147)

"All non-black things are non-ravens" is logically related to "all ravens are black," but logic alone does not invariably secure the connection we need for confirmation. Explanation depends on a search for distinctive causal specificity, not indifferent logical generality, and science organizes its search for evidence accordingly.

The method of political economy

An important part of the significance of Marx's fragment, "The Method of Political Economy," is precisely the pains taken to detail these points:

It would seem right to start with the real and concrete, with the actual presupposition, e.g. in political economy to start with the population, which forms the basis and subject of the whole social act of production. Closer consideration shows, however, that this is wrong. Population is an abstraction if, for instance, one disregards the classes of which it is composed. These classes in turn remain an empty phrase if one does not know the elements on which they are based, e.g. wage labour, capital, etc. These presuppose exchange, the division of labour, prices, etc. For example, capital is nothing without wage labour, without value, money, price, etc. If one were to start with population it would be a chaotic conception of the whole, and through closer definition one would arrive analytically at increasingly simple concepts, from the imagined concrete, one would move to more and more tenuous abstractions until one arrived at the simplest determinations. From there it would be necessary to make a return journey until one finally arrived once more at population, which this time would be not a chaotic conception of a whole, but a rich totality of many determinations and relations.

(1986 MECW 28: 37; 1973: 100)

This needs following step by step.

First, while it appears correct to begin with "population," taken at the outset as subject, we can form only a vague concept insofar as the abstraction is without determination. Here "abstraction" is used not as a verb, thus referring to a tool we can use to pick out more precise reference, but instead as a noun; it tells us that the category "population" with which we've begun is more or less empty of content. In this sense the word "population' is left ungrounded and it lacks meaningful reference; according to Devitt and Sterelny's (1987: 61) pertinent explanation of "empty names," it lacks an underlying causal network to which we can trace reference. Marx in fact refers to a concept without determination as, literally, an "empty word," "ein leeres Wort." To ground explanation we need to identify those determinations that account for the thing to which we refer. More. Insofar as reference is causally ungrounded our conception of the whole is "chaotic;" the abstraction we use for reference is, in the phrase Marx used in my initial quotation describing "capital in general," "arbitrary," and we risk selecting from among features empirically presented the sort of false abstraction used, for example, by economists who want to evaluate the revenue of a nation according to the needs it can satisfy. Marx responds: "it is a false abstraction to treat a nation whose mode of production is based on value, and organized capitalistically into the bargain, as a unified body simply working for the national needs." (1991: 991 [III.49]).

Instead, such a nation works for and measures its national product by the accumulation and increase of value, as we shall see. For now, we notice that a false abstraction is the result of the selection of features of a thing that do not in fact give an explanatory account of its persistence as the kind of thing it is or that do not establish a grasp of the interconnection necessary to underwrite such an account. Ideological apologetics, for example, will explain by selecting those features that appeal to the reproduction of false beliefs, and these, though they misrepresent the world, may have a functional utility in reproducing the social forms of oppression. By imagining that the wage exchanges not for labor power, but for labor, for example, a notion of exchange that is incoherent, we illicitly select features of the wage bargain that do not go together but treat them as if they did.[6]

How then do we get beyond empty, chaotic or false abstractions?

The German is important here:

> Finge ich also mit der Bevölkerung an, so wäre das eine chaotische Vorstellung des Ganzen, und durch nähere Bestimmung würde ich analytisch immer mehr auf einfachere Begriffe kommen; von dem vorgestellten Konkreten auf immer dünnere Abstrakta, bis ich bei den einfachsten Bestimmungen angelangt wäre.
>
> (1983 MEW 42: 35)

In English:

> If one were to start with population it would be a chaotic conception of the whole, and through closer definition one would arrive analytically at increasingly simple concepts, from the imagined concrete, one would move to more and more tenuous abstractions until one arrived at the simplest determinations.
>
> (1986 MECW 28: 37; 1973: 100)

We proceed by means of abstraction in order to pursue "immer dünnere Abstrakta." The translation here is "more tenuous abstractions," but connotations "tenuous" can carry of "not secure" or "slight" must be ignored – they altogether misrepresent the significance of what Marx is after. The simplest determinations that are the target of his search are those that ground analysis; they provide an anchor, a foundation. The idea to be captured is of a process of abstraction that peels away to a refinement that is more and more decisive. That is, by stripping away from particularity we arrive at fewer and fewer features of the richly articulated totality from which we began. An alternative translation of "immer dünnere Abstrakta" is "ever thinner abstractions" (1973: 100). In the first preface to *Capital I* Marx explained that abstraction was the chemical reagent of social theory (1990: 90).[7] I suggested above that in experiment we strip away from distractions and noise to focus on just those things that are the target of the investigation. This is the same process. And we do so *not* by identifying features that are more general because they are less precise. Quite the contrary. We locate the more decisively specific features of the thing to which our categories refer. Our categories are more general only because they pick out particular causal properties common and distinctive to all or many instances of the target. For example, the term "cordate" is general because it is used (by philosophers anyway) to extend to all creatures with a heart, not because it refers to an organ somehow less palpable in instances where it occurs.

The means by which we locate the more precise and causally decisive features to which our categories refer Marx specifies as "nähere Bestimmung." The phrase is crucial. This is translated as "closer definition:" we move from a chaotic conception of the whole to simpler concepts "through closer definitions." "Bestimmung" can mean "definition" but it is also translated as "determination" in the sense that real dispositions are causally efficacious – we might say, for example, that the size of the house determined the number of guests (Farrell 1969: 94). And it is something of this sense which is used here. It refers to the specific particularities that determine the operation of the social form under investigation. So we deal not with a verbal definition, but with features of a social structure's real and potent causal determinations.

"Nähere" also requires explication. It is translated as "closer" or "nearer," but is used also to mean "more specific," "more detailed," "more precise." It is used to express the idea of getting to the bottom of something. In other words, contrary to the Hegelian influenced approach summarized by Stace (see p. 57), we use abstraction as a means of locating features of a thing and their interconnections with more precision. We abstract from particularity not to embrace a more rarified conceptual ideality but instead to uncover more telling specificity. Such an approach, eminently scientific, has to be fully kept in mind in understanding Marx's analysis in social theory. The "simplest determinations" one arrives at by means of abstraction are those specific determinations that are decisive because they distinguish the *differentia specifica* of a social form. We may think of them as the kind constitutive properties of a social kind.

The simple determination of social things

I want to recall also my analysis of "simple determination" in Chapter 2 above. There I explained the social kind of commodity-producing labor as a particular composite of labor and form that allowed us to explain the commodity and value. I suggested that the approach generalized: a composite that constitutes a social entity like capital is always a compound of form and activity – activity only ever occurs as *enformed* and social form is only ever causally potent as instantiated in living activity, as *enmattered*. This methodology, I've argued, looks both forward and back. Marx took methods for the study of social life from the middle books of Aristotle's *Metaphysics* and in so doing crafted an approach to social theory that foreshadowed contemporary scientific realism's attention to natural kinds. Often, forms of social analysis separate the social activities of individuals from the forms in which these occur. This tendency, one way or another, is inescapably Platonist. We're left unable to explain, on the one hand, how the activity of persons produces social forms, or, on the other, how social form influences the activity of persons.

Partly the confusion is driven by a conflation of the distinct categories of 'constitution' and 'cause' in social analysis. But notice how we use these concepts differently: for example, we don't say that hydrogen and oxygen cause water; instead we say that water is constituted by these elements in relation. The same is true in social theory. Rather than saying this or that social role causes

persons to act in particular ways, we say that determinate social forms are constitutive of the activities in which persons participate. The slave relation does not
cause the master to be a master or the slave a slave. Instead, in historically specific circumstances the social form of slavery constitutes what it is to be a master
and what it is to be a slave; causal consequences then follow for individuals who
fill those roles. For the commodity form, the causal potency that drives producers to exchange is constituted by the social relation of separate producers who
produce goods not useful to them as part of the social division of labor. In each
such instance we look to the way relation of individuals to nature and to each
other is constituted in the course of living activity.

I will investigate capital in the same way. The composite of labor and form that
I locate in Marx's analysis and refer to as capital – a social relation of *enformed*
labor and of *enmattered* form – can be described as the free worker's alienated
separation from and subordination to the conditions of production as values.

The fundamental *aporia* of *Capital*

Every separation is the separation of a unity

In notes he prepared for his Doctoral Dissertation Marx observed that "every
separation is the separation of a unity" (1975 MECW 1: 493). And in *Capital
III*, in order to explain the way relations of production determine political and
legal forms, he described the unity on which they depend as follows:

> The specific economic form, in which unpaid surplus labour is pumped out
> of the direct producers determines the relationship of domination and servi-
> tude, as this grows directly out of production itself and reacts on it in turn as
> a determinant.
>
> (1991: 927 [III.47.2])

We're faced with a puzzle – it is only the unity of the direct producer with the
conditions of production in the course of production that can account for the
pumping out of unpaid surplus labor. How then can we expect to follow Bettelheim by offering a real definition of capital as a structure of separation? As I've
emphasized, Marx investigates forms of social labor as they've occurred historically and in each instance looks to the way in which the laborer is related to
nature and to others as this occurs in the actual process of production. That is, it
is not enough to understand the separation of labor from the means of production
as a precondition of production nor also as a result of production, we must
understand the separation of labor from the conditions of production as a determination of the process of production itself. But, it seems, if the laborer is separated from the means of production in the process of production, there can be no
social production at all.

The brief answer here is that neither the conditions of production nor labor
itself belong to the laborer in the process of production. In the most profound

sense, economically, juridically, and philosophically, capitalist labor – a form Marx refers to as wage slavery – is alienated labor. The specific form in which labor and the means of production are combined by capital depends on labor's incorporation into capital as a use value capital owns. The Lockean model of property presupposed an immediate unity between the laborer and the conditions of labor as her property. Because this corresponds to the model of simple commodity exchange it seems to serve as a reflection of the relation of the laborer to the conditions of labor under any form of commodity production, and therefore especially under capitalism, a form of production in which all products take the commodity form. Nonetheless, whatever tenuous appearance the Lockean simple exchange model may have made in history, Marx shows that it has only an illusory relevance to capitalist production. It mystifies. A system that appears to depend on the unity of labor and property depends instead dramatically on their separation. Crucially, we want to understand this separation.

There's another puzzle, foreshadowing the first. Marx first presents the unity of capital by means of its general formula, M-C-M', where "M" stands for money and "C" for commodity (1990: 247 [I.4]).[8] M' refers to the money with which one began, M, but augmented by some additional amount, ΔM; that is, M' = M + ΔM. The formula thus describes a circuit of exchange: money is exchanged for a commodity which is in turn exchanged for money again, but this time for money in a greater quantity than that with which Mr. Moneybags, Marx's characterization of the consummate capitalist, began. Usually (and according to the Lockean model) we think of a person introducing a product of her own labor into circulation and receiving money for it which she can then use to purchase things she needs. But with M-C-M' the circuit is different. It starts with money. And since it starts with money and also ends with money, the circuit can have no purpose other than to produce in exchange more money than the amount with which the circuit began; that is, not just M, but M + ΔM is the goal of the exchange.

But if we assume, as we must on the basis of commodity exchange, that products of equivalent value exchange, where does ΔM come from? If equivalents exchange, it cannot come from within circulation. But if it is the circulation of commodities which is to be explained, how can it have its source apart from circulation? Marx writes: "Capital cannot therefore arise from circulation and it is equally impossible for it to arise apart from circulation. It must have its origin both in circulation and not in circulation.... These are the conditions of the problem." (1990: 268–69 [I.5]

We have the fundamental *aporia* of *Capital.*

Capital's differentia specifica

The riddle is solved by a social relation: the laboring producer is separated from the conditions of production and subordinated to them. As I show more fully below, because the direct producer confronts the conditions of production in a circumstance of separation, she is driven to sell her labor power as a commodity. Now in order for anything to be sold as a commodity it must be a use value that has become a bearer of exchange value. To be a bearer of exchange value, labor, the source of value, must have been expended on it. How does this apply to the commodity labor power?

The worker produces the capacity to labor by consuming what she needs to survive from day to day; these are the commodities – food, clothing, shelter, etc. – that are necessary to produce labor power itself. It follows then that we can measure the value of labor power by tracking the quantity of labor spent on producing those goods the laborer consumes each day.

But if this is labor power's exchange value, what is its use value?

The capacity to labor, once set in motion, is used to produce a product and it is therefore the activity of living labor that constitutes the use value of labor power. Like any other commodity, labor power is purchased to be used. But the use of labor power produces more than a product. Since value is measured by the quantity of living labor expended, labor spent producing a product is a source of value. Thus labor creates not only a useful product, but also, where productive entities are separated from one another, a commodity that is a bearer of value. Moreover, since labor has the capacity to create more value than the value of those things purchased with the wage received, labor has the specific utility of creating more value in production than the value exchanged for it in circulation. That is, the labor expended to produce what the worker needs to survive is one thing. What labor can produce in a day is another. The former must be less than the latter for any developed form of social life. We can therefore account for the surplus ΔM. The capacity to labor is sold for its value in a transaction taking place in circulation, but the use of labor in production creates more value than was given for the exchange of labor power for a wage.[9]

Notice that while the use of labor creates value, living labor cannot itself have value. As I suggested earlier, the concept would be incoherent – the expenditure of living labor offers a yardstick to measure the value of things, but living labor can't measure itself except tautologically.[10] Instead, living labor is "spent" in production, and this is doubly meant. As expenditure it creates value in the product of labor, but as exhaustion the commodity labor power is devalued. Labor's capacity is lost and with that labor power's value. In this respect it is like any commodity; all are used up by use.

In *Capital* Marx introduces the separation of free laborers from the means of production in Chapter 6, "The Sale and Purchase of Labour-Power." Then in Chapter 7, "The Labour Process and Valorization Process," he makes explicit those determinants of the labor process that differentiate specifically capitalist production from features shared by all other modes of production throughout history. He presents these as follows: "First, the worker works under the control of the capitalist to whom his labour belongs;... Secondly, the product is the property of the capitalist and not that of the worker, its immediate producer" (1990: 291–292 [I.7.1]).

Notice the result. The separation of the worker from the means of production leads to the sale of labor power and this to capital's control over the labor process. Because capital owns the worker's labor activity, the laborer works under capital's control and in consequence capital uses its control to pump out surplus value, carefully monitoring everything the worker does to ensure that she produces according to capital's demands. In addition, capital's control over the process means that labor's product is appropriated in its entirety by capital. Capital controls the labor process and appropriates the product.

In sum: recall that in order to satisfy the general formula of capital, the aim of capitalist production, the capitalist had to find a special commodity in the market capable of accounting for ΔM:

> a commodity, whose use-value possesses the peculiar property of being a source of value, whose actual consumption is therefore an objectification [*Vergegenständlichung*] of labour, hence a creation of value. The possessor of money does find such a special commodity on the market: the capacity for labour [*Arbeitsvermögen*], in other words labour-power [*Arbeitskraft*].
>
> (1990: 270 [I.6])

Every commodity must have a use value in order to be a bearer of exchange value – this is what it means for the product of labor to be a commodity. Labor power, however, becomes a commodity not because its use value is a bearer of exchange value, although it is that, but, much more profoundly, because its use value is the activity that can make capital what it is: the activity of labor is a source of value, and not of value only but, instead, of a surplus value, of value that increases itself. Thus in §2 of Chapter 7, "The Labour Process and the Valorization Process," Marx explains that the capitalist uses labor power not only to produce commodities, products which are the "material substratum" of exchange value, but also to produce a greater sum of value than the value invested in production: "His aim is to produce not only a use-value, but a commodity; not only a use-value, but value; and not just value, but also surplus-value." (1990: 293 [I.7.2]). Some pages later he continues:

> the value of labour-power, and the value which that labour-power valorizes [*verwertet*] in the labour-process, are two entirely different magnitudes; and this difference was what the capitalist had in mind when he was purchasing the labour-power…. What was really decisive for him was the specific use-value which this commodity possesses of being a source not only of value, but of more value than it has itself. This is the specific service the capitalist expects from labour-power…
>
> (1990: 300–301[I.7.2])

And, accordingly, the fundamental *aporia* of the study of capital has been solved:

> Every condition of the problem is satisfied, while the laws governing the exchange of commodities, have not been violated in any way. Equivalent has been exchanged for equivalent…. Yet for all that he [the capitalist]

withdraws 3 shillings more from circulation than he originally threw into it. This whole course of events, the transformation of money into capital, both takes place and does not take place in the sphere of circulation. It takes place through the mediation of circulation because it is conditioned by the purchase of labour-power in the market; it does not take place in circulation because what happens there is only an introduction to the valorization process, which is entirely confined to the sphere of production...

If we now compare the process of creating value with the process of valorization, we see the latter is nothing but the continuation of the former beyond a certain point. If the process is not carried beyond the point where the value paid by the capitalist for the labour-power is replaced by an exact equivalent, it is simply a process of creating value; but if it is continued beyond that point, it becomes a process of valorization.

(1990: 301–302 [I.7.2)

Notice that the structural determinations of capital on which the creation of surplus value depends are causally potent. Briefly, as a premise of the entire social process of production, the separation of laboring producers from the conditions of production compels them to have recourse to exchange so that, through purchase and sale, they may satisfy their needs. But then there is this consequence: because capital controls the process, subordinates labor and appropriates the entire product at the conclusion of the process, each direct producer is left as she began. Her capacity to labor is exhausted, but she has received in exchange a wage just adequate for her to reproduce her capacity to return the following day. She is unable by means of the wage, however, to obtain on her own access to the means of production. Thus, the appropriation of the product by capital gives expression to a social structure that causally reproduces the separation of the worker from the means of production. Additionally, the appropriation of the use value of labor by capital expresses a causal structure of control that determines the uses of labor in the process of production and the appropriation of its product.

Toward a real definition of capital

We need a fuller account of the explanation just offered; because for any stable social form "the conditions of production are at the same time the conditions of reproduction" (1990: 711 [I.23]), a sketch of the decisive phases of capitalist production is required. I characterize these as follows: (1) Premise: labor's possibility as abstract possibility; (2) Starting Point: labor's capacity as a commodity for capital in exchange; (3) Process: labor's activity as the use value of capital; (4) Results: labor's objectivity as capital.

Notice that labor's subordination is to the conditions of production as values. As I will explain more fully, because the conditions of production are values the means and materials of labor, and also the monies that represent the wage, are embedded in the circuit of M-C-M' and participate in a process of self-valorization. They represent objectified labor driven to increase. For capitalist production the labor process merely functions as a vehicle for the valorization process, so the qualification is essential.

What I have referred to here as "premise," Marx refers to as both "point of departure" and also as "starting point." On the one hand he shows how the result of capitalist production is the constant and renewed production of the structural configuration with which it begins. On the other hand he also shows how the mediation of exchange initiates the transaction that actually leads to the incorporation of labor into production as the use value of capital – thus it is the "starting point" of a "two step transaction," first exchange, then, production. In characterizing the phases of capitalist production, I've restricted my use of "starting point" to the act that initiates production itself and I've used "premise," to pick out the material circumstance that motivates the process as a whole.

Premise: labor's possibility as abstract possibility

Labor's possibility as abstract possibility is the free worker's separation from and subordination to the conditions of production as the premise of capitalist production.

The unity of the subjective and objective conditions of labor – the combination of the activity of labor and the means and instruments necessary to any form of social production – originates for capital not in a unity but instead in a manifest separation of labor from the conditions of its realization:

> The historical process was one of the separation of hitherto combined elements; its result is therefore not the disappearance of one of these elements, but that each of them appears negatively related to the other: the (potentially) free worker on one hand, (potential) capital on the other.
>
> (1986 MEWC 28: 427; 1973: 503)

This is the precondition for capitalist production.

Thus, when Marx turns to explain the "So-Called Primitive Accumulation" of capital (*Capital I*, Part 8), his attention is not on the accumulation of funds by banks or merchants or industrialists but instead on the appearance and growth of a social relation:

> The capital-relation presupposes a complete separation between the workers and the ownership of the conditions for the realization of their labour. As soon as capitalist production stands on its own feet, it not only maintains this separation, but reproduces it on a constantly extending scale. The process, therefore, which creates the capital-relation, can be nothing other than the process which divorces the worker from the ownership of the conditions of his own labour; ... So-called primitive accumulation, therefore, is nothing else than the historical process of divorcing the producer from the means of production. It appears as 'primitive' because it forms the prehistory of capital, and of the mode of production corresponding to capital.
>
> (1990: 874–75 [I.26])

What is the condition of workers divorced from all means by which they can realize their labor? What is the condition of any creature divorced from the means of reproducing its existence? No such condition can be sustained in nature for long. If such a structure is to undergird a global mode of production that is to last centuries, then this plainly is a consequence of its social arrangements.

Marx emphasizes in the *Grundrisse* that "activity without an object is nothing" (1986 MECW 28: 197; 1973: 267). Separated from the objective conditions of production, the laboring producer represents only the abstract possibility of labor. Labor capacity without an object is activity that cannot be; it is abstract in that fundamental sense. Hydrogen held near a flame has the power to explode even though it is not exploding. This is an example of real possibility. Abstract possibility is different. Abstract possibility is a conceptual thing, the domain of fanciful counterfactuals – the domain where, since what is possible may be otherwise, the opposite of whatever is possible is also possible.[11] In his Doctoral Dissertation Marx wrote:

> Abstract *possibility*, however, is the *direct antipode of real possibility*. The latter is restricted within sharp boundaries, as is the intellect; the former is unbounded, as is the imagination. Real possibility seeks to explain the necessity and reality of its object; abstract possibility is not interested in the object which is explained, but in the subject which does the explaining. The object need only be possible, conceivable. That which is abstractly possible, which can be conceived, constitutes no obstacle to the thinking subject, no limit, no stumbling-block. Whether this possibility is also real is irrelevant, since here the interest does not extend to the object as object.
>
> (1975 MECW 1: 44)

Marx's target here is the all consuming subjectivity of the thinking subject. His target in the analysis of labor as abstract possibility in the *Grundrisse* is the all consuming impotence of the subject left with nothing but the imagined possibility of labor where real labor is irrelevant. Abstract possibility produces nothing. Where the laboring producer has no access to the means of production not only is individual survival impossible but social reproduction as well.[12] Marx refers to this as labor "conceived negatively" – labor is separated from its "entire objectivity;" it is conceived negatively in relation to an objectivity that is *not* raw material, *not* instrument, *not* product. It is living labor "existing as an abstraction from those moments of its actual reality." It is a "complete denudation," a "purely subjective existence of labor;" it is "labor as absolute poverty" (1986 MECW 28: 222; 1973: 296).[13] In "Results of the Immediate Process of Production," Marx writes:

> Man can only live by producing his own means of subsistence, and he can produce these only if he is in possession of the means of production, of the material conditions of labor. It is obvious from the very outset that the

worker who is denuded of the means of production is thereby deprived of the means of subsistence, just as, conversely, a man deprived of the means of subsistence is in no position to create the means of production.

(1990: 1003)

As he observes in *Capital*,

When we speak of the capacity for labour we do not speak of labour any more than we speak of digestion when we speak of capacity for digestion. As is well known, the latter process requires something more than a good stomach.

(1990: 277 [I.6])

By contrast, labor conceived positively as real possibility is, together with nature, the source of all wealth.

Notice that the concept of labor as mere abstract possibility differs from the concept of 'abstract labor' developed in the previous chapter of these essays. In the first chapter of *Capital* abstract labor is premised on the separation of productive entities from one another. Because each producer produces independently and as part of the division of labor in society, each must go to market in order to obtain products that will serve to renew the capacity to produce. As we've seen, once at market each confronts the problem of how to measure the ratio in which goods are meant to exchange. In practice this problem is solved by abstracting from all considerations of use. Only the amount of time expended in producing a commodity is taken into account. We can turn tins of shoe polish into castles; in the appropriate quantities they have the same value. In such cases labor is abstract not because living labor capacity has been divorced from the conditions of its realization, but instead because every kind of expended labor is equated with every other as a result of an exchange of products. We abstract from all considerations of use in order to consider the portion of aggregate labor any single product represents. Because we are able to compare commodities in exchange, the social division of labor develops product diversity and specialization; abstracting from all considerations of use facilitates exchange. But where there is only the abstract possibility of labor, then all consideration of *production* is abstracted from. The very possibility of social reproduction is blocked, nor could the social relation of separation persist except for the fact that the laborer is driven to sell the commodity labor power for a wage. The profound significance of the sale of labor power for a wage, therefore, is that, if separation be assumed, it transforms the abstract possibility of labor into a real possibility; in so doing it not only restores the possibility of social reproduction but opens the possibility for the production of surplus value.

Starting point: labor's capacity as a commodity for capital in exchange

Labor's capacity as a commodity for capital is the free worker's separation from and subordination to the conditions of production in the process of exchange.

The separation of labor from the conditions of production makes labor merely an abstract possibility for the laborer, and this in turn drives the worker to sell the only saleable property available to her – her capacity to labor. It is the exchange of the commodity labor power for a wage that is the first act of the appropriation of labor by capital. Because of the labor contract, the realization of labor as a real, not abstract, possibility occurs only as capital's possibility, and not that of labor. In simple commodity exchange the commodity owner relinquishes her autonomy by entering exchange and surrendering the product of her labor. In the exchange of labor power for a wage, the laborer relinquishes her autonomy by entering exchange and surrendering control over her life activity itself. When labor is joined to the means of production her labor capacity is no longer her own. That is, although exchange opens on the real possibility of labor, this is not labor's possibility.

It serves bourgeois sensibilities to conflate the exchange of labor power for a wage with all other contracts of commodity exchange; an account of the social forms of capitalist production, however, requires that these very different phenomena be distinguished in spite of their superficial identity: the ordinary exchange contract and the wage contract between labor and capital are different in *kind*. Here more than ever we need to heed Marx's "nothing is easier" injunction – nothing is easier than to find the employment contract just another form of contract as long as we ignore precisely those characteristics which distinguish it as a feature of capital rather than of the simple commodity form. For example, the contract of commodity exchange presupposes and reproduces a relation of formal equality – the autonomy of the commodity owner is presupposed and reproduced by any commodity exchange transaction. In the labor contract, however, the laborer alienates the right to dispose of her labor capacity. In so doing she agrees to work for another, for the purposes of another and under the command of another. That is, she enters a social relation of subordination. This can only be explained as a consequence of her separation from the conditions of production; absolute impoverishment drives her to the exchange. If she had the capacity to produce a commodity of her own, she would do so.

At this point of the analysis, however, the fact of subordination remains contingent. The impoverishment that drives the worker to the labor contract seems simply a happenstance of fact. Neither separation nor subordination that is its result appears as a necessary social relation. As Marx explains in the introductory section on "Capital" in the *Grundrisse* manuscript (1986 MECW 28: 171–82; 1973: 239–250), the factual circumstances that drive commodity owner A to exchange are irrelevant to the exchange and to the relation of exchangists; no such factors play any systematic role in such transactions. Whatever particularities characterize A as a natural person – rich or poor, strong or weak, educated or unlettered – all are irrelevant to the exchange. All that matters is that A owns value and seeks someone in possession of money or commodities of equivalent value. From this perspective, the fact that a capitalist has conditions of production and the worker has nothing is of no concern – the penny of a king or pauper is worth the same.

The most important difference between the labor contract and all other contracts of commodity exchange is that of the "double freedom" on which the sale of labor power for a wage depends. In order to sell labor power as a commodity the worker must be free in two ways:

> that as a free individual he can dispose of his labour-power as his own commodity, and that, on the other hand, he has no other commodity for sale, i.e. he is rid of them, he is free of all the objects needed for the realization [*Verwirklichung*] of his labour-power.
>
> (1990: 272–73 [I.6])

Notice here that to be free in the first sense – to be free to dispose of a commodity – is common to all sellers of commodities. But to be free in the second sense is specific to the exchange between capital and labor only – it is the privation of all means of realizing labor in production that forces the worker to sell labor power as a commodity.

In exchange the subjective and objective conditions of production, labor and the means of production, appear separately as the transaction's constituent elements. But separated they are meaningless. Labor and the means of production are meaningful and productive only when joined together. Circulation as it is used by a non-capitalist producer of a commodity is a means to obtain the food, tools and raw materials required to renew production. The producer as purchaser is rejoined to the conditions of production that replace those exhausted by her work. Both the conditions of production exhausted and those purchased belong to her; she is joined to them as her own.

By contrast, in the exchange between capital and labor, labor is kept separate from the conditions of its realization and only because of this does the worker agree to subordinate the disposition of her labor to the control of another. She obtains a wage which she can use to obtain means of subsistence. But because the value of the wage is measured by the value of subsistence, it offers no enduring access to the means of production.

Because the first act of the exchange between capital and labor – the exchange of a commodity for money – resembles an ordinary purchase and sale as it might occur in simple circulation, the features of the transaction which make it essentially different in kind get ignored. In particular, since the exchange value produced by labor includes not only the value of the wage, but also an unpaid surplus, the exchange of equivalents that characterizes ordinary market exchange does not apply to the exchange of capital for labor power. Instead, what appears to be an exchange of equivalents is in fact not an exchange at all:

> *In the exchange between capital and labour, the first act is an exchange and*
> *falls wholly within ordinary circulation; the second is a process qualita-*
> *tively different from exchange and it is only by misuse that it could have*
> been called *exchange* of any kind *at all*. It stands directly opposed to
> exchange; essentially [a] different category.
>
> (1986 MECW 28: 205; 1973: 274–75 [emphasis in original])

It stands opposed to exchange because it is the systematic appropriation of
labor's surplus without any exchange whatsoever.

As a consequence, the form of exchange between capital and labor mystifies
the social relations of capitalist production. Marx writes:

> We may therefore understand the decisive importance of the transformation of
> the value and price of labour-power into the form of wages, or into the value
> and price of labour itself. All the notions of justice held by both the worker
> and the capitalist, all the mystifications of the capitalist mode of production,
> all capitalism's illusions about freedom, all the apologetic tricks of vulgar eco-
> nomics, have as their basis the form of appearance discussed above.
>
> (1990: 680 [I.19])

To both capitalist and worker it appears that the worker is paid for the labor of
the period of time contracted for – a day, a week, a month, and so on. The activity of labor appears to exchange for a wage. But then what determines the price
of the activity? What is labor's value? These, Marx shows, are irrational questions: since the activity of labor is the measure of value, it cannot itself have any
value. The phrase, "the value of labor," is a concept that does not refer – like
phlogiston there is nothing in nature or social life corresponding to this notion.
But then by making the labor market exchange appear as the ordinary exchange
of one commodity for another in simple circulation, this confusion makes invis-
ible the actual relation of capital and labor. By mystifying the incorporation of
the use value of labor into capital, exchange plays a powerful role in reproducing
the separation of labor from the conditions of its realization.

Process: labor's activity as the use value of capital

Labor's activity as the use value of capital is the free worker's separation from
and subordination to the conditions of labor in the process of production.

Marx insists that the exchange between capital and labor that takes place in
the labor market is merely the first step in a two step transaction. The second
step is the actual use of the commodity purchased. Every purchase in the marketplace is ultimately the purchase of a commodity for its use, but it is the use value
of labor alone that is a use value for capital. We already know why. Capital
exists in order to valorize value – an invested sum is maintained and increased
but this must be accomplished by means of the exchange of equivalents. The use
value of the commodity labor power is labor itself and the activity of labor

objectified in the product of labor is the substance of value. This makes it possible for the commodity labor power to do what no other commodity can do – the use of the commodity labor power creates more value in production than the value given as a wage in exchange for the purchase of its use.

This doesn't happen automatically, though. A surplus of living labor appropriated in production over objectified labor given in exchange will occur only if the worker works beyond the portion of the working day represented by the wage. But not only this. In addition the worker must work with an intensity and care sufficient to meet the standards of competition imposed in the marketplace. If widgets are generally produced in an hour and it takes Mr. Moneybag's employees 3 hours to produce one, he will have to give up producing widgets for sale. In other words during the process of production the worker can use no more than socially necessary labor time.

This problem is complicated by the fact that the worker is indifferent to the work and its outcome. She has sold her capacity to labor in order to obtain money adequate to purchase the things she needs to survive. She has sold the right to dispose of her labor and she has given up as well any claim to the product. The process of production, therefore, is not an affair that interests her. It belongs to the capitalist and is his concern.

The consequence is that if the imperatives of capital are to be realized and if value is to maintain itself and increase, then capital must exercise control over labor in the process of production in order to ensure that the worker labors long enough and does so with sufficient quality and intensity to satisfy the demands of production. It follows that if objectified labor is to be preserved and increased, it must become possessed of a will and consciousness capable of enforcing its exigencies. Enter the capitalist:

> Except as capital personified, the capitalist has no historical value.... But, in so far as he is capital personified, his motivating force is not the acquisition and enjoyment of use values, but the acquisition and augmentation of exchange-values. He is fanatically intent on the valorization of value.... Only as a personification of capital is the capitalist respectable. As such, he shares with the miser an absolute drive towards self-enrichment. But what appears in the miser as the mania of an individual is in the capitalist the effect of a social mechanism in which he is merely a cog. Moreover, the development of capitalist production makes it necessary constantly to increase the amount of capital laid out in a given industrial undertaking, and competition subordinates every individual capitalist to the immanent laws of capitalist production, as external and coercive laws. It compels him to keep extending his capital, so as to preserve it, and he can only extend it by means of progressive accumulation.
>
> (1990: 739 [I.24.3])

These points stand out. First, the motivating force of production is not the enjoyment of use values but the augmentation of exchange value, M-C-M'. The valorization of value drives production and it is this imperative that the capitalist personifies. The social mechanism of which the capitalist is a cog is the subordination of the worker to the valorization of value. Second, through the mechanism of competition each individual capitalist experiences the dynamic of valorization as a coercive law; the capitalist succeeds in producing both the equivalent of value invested together with an added increment on pain of ceasing to be a capitalist at all. It is the preservation and increase of objectified labor that animates the course of production. Marx writes: "[i]n fact the rule of the capitalist over the worker is nothing but the rule of the independent *conditions of labour* over the *worker*, conditions that have made themselves independent of him" (1990: 989 [*Results*]; [emphasis in original]). He continues some pages later:

> The objective conditions essential to the realization of labor are *alienated* from the worker and become manifest as *fetishes* endowed with a will and a soul of their own. *Commodities*, in short, appear as the purchasers of *persons*. The buyer of labour-power is nothing but the personification of *objectified* labour which cedes a part of itself to the worker in the form of the means of subsistence in order to annex the living labour-power for the benefit of the remaining portion, so as to keep itself intact and even to grow beyond its original size by virtue of this annexation. It is not the worker who buys the means of production and subsistence, but the means of production that buy the worker to incorporate him into the means of production.
>
> (1990: 1003–04 [*Results*]; [emphasis in original])

Things in the form of commodities are purchasers of persons! And not only purchasers, but employers. Through the personification of the capitalist, things put labor to work. Marx observes that such an inversion of person and thing has invaded even the common expression of Ricardo and other economists who speak of capital as "*the means of employing labor.*" (1990: 1008 [*Results*]; [emphasis in original]). The role of the capitalist is therefore fundamentally constrained by the social dynamic to which she is subject:

> The *functions* fulfilled by the capitalist are no more than the functions of capital – viz. the valorization of value by absorbing living labour – executed *consciously* and *willingly*. The capitalist functions only as *personified* capital.... Hence the rule of the capitalist over the worker is the rule of things over man, of dead labour over the living, of the product over the producer."
>
> (1990: 989–90 [Results] [emphasis in original])

If, without discrimination and experience a person looks through a microscope at a cell, she will see a blob – all determinateness of form that distinguishes its constituent parts will be indifferently obscured. The same is the case in looking at the labor process. On the one hand there is the normal process of producing use values; on the other hand there is the valorization process, its specific social form. But to the uncritical view one sees only what one would see in any period of history – the laborer makes use of the tools and raw material of labor to produce a product. The specific social form that makes the process capitalist is obscured. But there are not two separate labor processes – a normal process and a valorization process. There is only one and, in fact, since surplus value is the driving motive of production it is the valorization process that drives the whole. If surplus value can't be realized there will be no production at all. What we instinctively think of as the normal process of production – labor joined to its raw material and instruments in order to produce use values – serves the valorization process not the reverse:

> [T]he *labour process itself* is no more than the *instrument* of the *valorization process.*... The self-valorization of capital – the creation of surplus-value – is therefore the determining, dominating and overriding purpose of the capitalist; it is the absolute motive and content of his activity.
>
> (1990: 990 [*Results*] [emphasis in original])

Taken together, control over the labor process and control of the entire product of labor express the subordination of the worker to capital in the labor process. Without the subordination of labor to the process of valorization there cannot be capitalist production. Furthermore this necessity, which begins as purely formal, in the end becomes manifest in the means of production themselves – there is an evolution from what Marx calls the formal subsumption of labor to capital to the real subsumption of labor to capital.[14] At first capital takes over the labor process as it finds it. All that changes is that the capitalist enters into a position of command and makes the production of surplus value the goal of production. At this point the subordination of labor to capital appears merely contingent. For example, the capitalist may take over the handicraft production of independent peasants without initially changing the character of the actual labor process at all. "There is no change as yet in the mode of production itself," Marx writes, and continues:

> *Technologically speaking* the *labour process* goes on as before with the proviso that it is now *subordinated* to capital. Within the production process, however, as we have already shown, two developments emerge. (1) an *economic* relationship of supremacy and subordination, since the consumption of labor-power by the capitalist is naturally supervised and directed by him; (2) the labour becomes far more continuous and intensive..."
>
> (1990: 1026 [*Results*] [emphasis in original])

A subsequent step leads through the organization of cooperation to a role for the capitalist in coordinating production; as a result labor's subordination becomes a "real condition of production:"

We also saw that, at first, the subjection of labour to capital was only a formal result of the fact that the worker, instead of working for himself, works for, and consequently under, the capitalist. Through the co-operation of numerous wage-labourers, the command of capital develops into a requirement for carrying on the labour process itself, into a real condition of production. That a capitalist should command in the field of production is now as indispensable as that a general should command on the field of battle.

(1990: 448 [I.13])

As a consequence, a divorce between the tasks of direction and execution enters the labor process – the free laborer no longer determines the goal of labor or the forms of labor discipline by which that goal will be realized.

There is a still further step. The capitalist's coordination of the labor process is at first simply a coordination of the distinct activities of different laborers. But Marx distinguishes this stage, manufacture, from the stage of large scale industry where the transformation of the mode of production extends to the instruments of production themselves. Now the coordination of production and the subordination of labor to capital are written into the material organization of capital itself:

As machinery, the instrument of labour assumes a material mode of existence which necessitates the replacement of human forces by natural forces, and the replacement of the rule of thumb by the conscious application of natural science. In manufacture the organization of the social labour process is purely subjective: it is a combination of specialized workers. Large-scale industry, on the other hand, possesses in the machine system an entirely objective organization of production, which confronts the worker as a pre-existing material condition of production. In simple co-operation, and even in the more specialized form based on the division of labour, the extrusion of the isolated worker by the associated worker still appears to be more or less accidental. Machinery, with a few exceptions to be mentioned later, operates only by means of associated labour, or labour in common. Hence the co-operative character of the labour process is in this case a technical necessity dictated by the very nature of the instrument of labour.

(1990: 508 [I.15.1)

Machinery means a 24-hour working day and an intensification of labor reflected paradigmatically in the application of social science to the task of adjusting the worker to the demands of the machine. Mental labor and physical labor are separated. Formerly the worker manipulated a tool; now workers are distributed among specialized machines: "the motion of the whole factory proceeds not from the worker but from the machinery" (1990: 546 [I.15.4]).

The real subsumption of labor to capital is the technical subordination of the worker to the machine. The conditions of work determine labor's activity.

Subordination has gone from what was at first merely a formal relationship – a necessary subordination required by the organization of cooperative labor under the control of a capitalist – to a real condition of subordination manifested in the material organization of the means of production themselves. No individual worker can take this or that piece of the assembly line home to resume production on a smaller scale. The factory can only be put into operation by associated workers. As the solution to capital's fundamental *aporia*, the constraints of value's valorization are now frozen in steel and stone and as such drive the form and pace of production.

It is important to appreciate how embedding the solution to the fundamental *aporia* of capital in the material organization of production itself establishes capital's simplest and most fundamental characterization: capital is living labor in the process of production appropriated by objectified labor for the sake of increasing objectified labor. The incorporation of labor into capital takes M-C-M', the general formula of capital, from circulation to the process of production; it is the instantiation of M-C-M' in the activity of production itself. The separation of workers from the conditions of production is not only presupposed as premise; it penetrates production itself – the machine, independent of individual workers, comes to rule over them. Work must fulfill the demands of valorization and be carried out with sufficient skill and intensity to meet those demands. In consequence, the material organization of production reproduces the subordination of the worker to capital in the course of production as a completely necessary feature of production. In the face of this, the question is whether the separation that drives the worker to this subordination remains contingent.

Results: labor's objectivity as capital

Labor's objectivity is the free worker's separation from and subordination to the conditions of production as the result of capitalist production.

In the activity of labor the subjective and objective factors of the labor process are joined in unity: labor utilizes the instruments of labor in order to transform raw materials into products corresponding to need. The products of labor therefore are the result of the activity of labor objectifying itself in the stuff of the world. But while the material trace labor leaves on any product provides important empirical data about the society in which it was fashioned, such data are typically not enough to characterize fully labor's social form. We can often guess, but really neither the texture nor taste of bread will tell us whether it was produced as a commodity by capital.

So we need to investigate social form. If the product takes the form of a commodity, then it was produced by producers who are separate and independent and who produce as part of the social division of labor. As such, the product is a bearer of value. In that event, the labor objectified in the product represents a proportionate part of the aggregate hours brought to market and leaves its trace not simply in the useful qualities of the product but also in that labor expenditure.

This means that the product will tend to exchange in the market for its equivalent, and that it is therefore embedded in the cycle C-M-C-M-C-M...

But if a commodity is embedded in the cycle C-M-C-M-C-M ... it may as readily be considered embedded in a cycle M-C-M; it all depends on where you start. As between persons who produce products as part of the spontaneously developed division of labor, the cycle C-M-C is a form by which persons give up products they don't need in order to obtain money to buy products they do need. But, as we've seen, the cycle M-C-M makes sense only if the commodity purchased with money is used to produce a product that contains not only the value M, but also an additional value ΔM. Marx therefore refers to the valorization of value as the "*differentia specifica*" of capitalist production:

> In the controversies on this question, the essential fact has generally been overlooked, namely the *differentia specifica* of capitalist production. Labour-power is not purchased under this system for the purpose of satisfying the personal needs of the buyer, either by its service or through its product. The aim of the buyer is the valorization of his capital, the production of commodities which contain more labour than he paid for, and therefore contain a portion which costs him nothing and is nevertheless realized [*realisiert*] through the sale of those commodities. The production of surplus-value, or the making of profits is the absolute law of this mode of production. Labour-power can be sold only to the extent that it preserves and maintains the means of production as capital, reproduces its own value as capital, and provides a source of additional capital in the shape of unpaid labour.
>
> (1990: 769 [I.25.1])

That is, neither the product as such, nor even the production of mere value alone can be taken for themselves as the goal of capital; capitalist production occurs only to preserve and increase value. Capitalist production produces surplus value.

We now know, however, that the production of surplus value requires a particular configuration of production. Not only must labor power be sold as a commodity, but we must show how the *differentia specifica* of capital characterize the very process of capitalist production. To do that we must show how the valorization of value is not simply the ultimate motive of production, but how it works as an imperative force structuring production itself. We locate capital's *Grundbestimmung* – its foundational determination – in production.

We have seen how this occurs – the capitalist functions as a mere personification for self-multiplying value and follows its requirements as laws coercively imposed: labor must work with sufficient intensity to preserve and maintain existing value and to create new value, and this new value must not only replace what was given as a wage, but create a surplus as well. Understood as a feature of production itself, then, capital's *differentia specifica* is the subordination of labor to the laws of capital's valorization. And this, we've seen, is possible only because of the absolute divorce of labor from its conditions of realization. Self-valorizing value, personified in the personality of the capitalist, exists as a thing apart, autonomous, obeying its own laws, and commanding obedience of the worker to them.

But if the subordination of labor to the laws of capital's valorization is to express a configuration of production that is not contingent, but instead reproductively necessary, then it must appear as a result of the process of production. We know the material result of this process is the product as a commodity. We know also that because capitalist production is the general production of commodities, every product of labor takes the form of a commodity. And we know that every commodity produced by capital is the bearer not only of value but of surplus value also. Capital purchases labor power for this very reason. While the union of the subjective and objective factors of labor must occur in any process of individual or social production, under capitalism this is driven not by the appropriation of nature to need, but instead by the appropriation of labor in order to add to value's increase.

Yet there is still another dimension to this process, the most decisive one, and one often overlooked. Not only is capitalist production the production of the product as a bearer of both value and surplus value, it produces also the social relation of capital. Recall Marx's specification of the two features that distinguish capital from other forms of social production in the labor process itself – labor works under the command of a capitalist to whom the products of labor belong:

> The labor process is a process between things the capitalist has purchased, things which belong to him. Thus the product of this process belongs to him just as much as the wine which is the product of the process of fermentation going on in his cellar.
>
> (1990: 292 [I.7.1])

But then because the wage is measured by the value of labor power only, and because labor power is measured, roughly, by the value of the products needed to reproduce the capacity to labor from day to day, capital's control over the entire product of labor means the laborer leaves the process as she began and is never able, herself, to gain access to the means of production as her own.

This means that the premise of the cycle, the presupposition with which we began, has been reproduced by the unfolding of the process itself. The result has become the point of departure. That which motivated production has been reproduced as the social form structuring it. Working in the tradition of Ricardo, Piero Sraffa in 1960 published *The Production of Commodities by Means of Commodities*, giving rise to neo-Ricardian schools of economic analysis, including among Marxists. Writing a century before, Marx more significantly showed how capital is *the production of social relations by means of social relations*. Nor would the Aristotelian implications of this characterization have been lost on him: final cause has become causally potent (social) form instantiated in the material conditions of production itself. As he explains in the concluding paragraph to his chapter on "Simple Reproduction" in *Capital I*:

> The capitalist process of production, therefore, seen as a total, connected process, i.e. a process of reproduction, produces not only commodities, not only surplus-value, but it also produces and reproduces the capital-relation itself; on the one hand the capitalist, on the other the wage labourer.
>
> (1990: 724 [I.23])

A few pages earlier he wrote:

> A division between the product of labour and labour itself, between the objective conditions of labour and subjective labour-power, was therefore the real foundation and the starting-point of the process of capitalist production.
>
> But what at first was merely a starting-point becomes, by means of nothing but the continuity of the process, by simple reproduction, the characteristic result of capitalist production, a result which is constantly renewed and perpetuated. On the one hand, the production process incessantly converts material wealth into capital, into the capitalist's means of enjoyment and his means of valorization. On the other hand, the worker always leaves the process in the same state as he entered it – a personal source of wealth, but deprived of any means of making that wealth a reality for himself. Since, before he enters the process, his own labour has already been alienated [*entfremdet*] from him, appropriated by the capitalist, and incorporated with capital, it now, in the course of the process, constantly objectifies itself so that it becomes a product alien to him [*fremder Produkt*]. Since the process of production is also the process of the consumption of labour-power by the capitalist, the worker's product is not only constantly converted into commodities, but also into capital, i.e. into value that sucks up the worker's value-creating power, means of subsistence that actually purchase human beings, and means of production that employ the people who are doing the producing. Therefore the worker himself constantly produces objective wealth, in the form of capital, an alien power that dominates and exploits him; and the capitalist just as constantly produces labour-power, in the form of a subjective source of wealth which is abstract, exists merely in the physical body of the worker, and is separated from its own means of objectification and realization; in short, the capitalist produces the worker as a wage-labourer. This incessant reproduction, this perpetuation of the worker, is the absolutely necessary condition for capitalist production.
>
> (1990: 716 [I.23; footnotes omitted])

The worker produces capital and with it the capitalist. The capitalist in turn ensures the reproduction of the worker as a wage laborer. The separation and subordination of labor to the means of production as premise, starting point, process and result of the social form of capital stand revealed as features not of natural necessity, of course – "[t]his relation has no basis in natural history...." (Marx 1990: 273 [I.6]) – but instead as what I have called reproductive necessity. It reflects an imperative necessity of social life: if capital is to be produced, then the social relation of alienated separation and subordination must characterize the phases of its reproduction. A few short sentences before the manuscript *Results of the Immediate Process of Production* breaks off, Marx writes:

> It is not just the objective conditions of the process of production that appear as its result. The same thing is true also of its *specific social* character. The social relations and therefore the social positions of the agents of production in relation to each other, i.e. the *relations of production*, are themselves produced: they are also the constantly renewed result of the process.
>
> (1990: 1065)

The real definition of capital

Behind the veil of the capitalist worker's double freedom is a structure of double separation. The worker is negatively free as impoverished and impotent and separated from all possibility of labor because separated from the conditions of labor. She is positively free as an independent possessor of a commodity; she is able to sell her labor power. Moreover, as the possessor of a commodity integrated into market exchange, she is able to act volitionally and in pursuit of her own self-interest. The separation of independent labors within the social division of labor (the separation that gives rise to the commodity form) is therefore presupposed by the worker's freedom to act as a commodity owner. But she is able to sell her capacity to labor only by sacrificing her autonomy over her very life activity; she is separated from its use and purpose and control.

With the laborer's sale of the commodity labor power, capital makes the activity of labor now possible in a process owned by it. But because the process is owned by capital, the laboring producer is subordinated to the capitalist's command; subjugation to the capitalist, however, is in fact subjugation to labor's own product. That is, because the capitalist is driven by M-C-M′, the general formula of capital, and because the capitalist functions only as a personification of objectified labor's engine of self-valorization, the process must be understood as one in which objectified labor, for the sake of its own increase, appropriates living labor in the process of production.

The essential elements of the social structure this dynamic manifests are labor *deprived of or separated from and subjugated to* its own product as value. This may be expressed structurally as the alienated separation of the free worker from and subordination to the conditions of production as values. Alternatively we may capture this as a form of activity: capital is living labor in the process of production appropriated by objectified labor for the sake of increasing objectified labor. These formulations, which Marx suggests are two sides of the same coin (1987 MECW 29: 210; 1973: 832),[15] give expression to capital's simplest determination.

Conclusion

A word on alienation to conclude. The concept of alienation is a way of expressing the appropriation of the laborer's own activity and its fruits by value and by the dynamic of value's increase. As such, alienation is the subordination of labor to its own product as a power ruling over it. As premise, alienation is the worker's separation from the means of production and subsistence as a circumstance of life. Human life, of the individual, of the community, of the species, requires the transformation of nature by labor, the kind of causal engagement with the world that makes survival possible for any living creature. In his evaluation of earlier modes of production, Marx underscored the way the conditions of labor are presupposed to the worker as belonging to her – not belonging in the sense of owning, but prior to that, a sense of belonging in the way my fingers belong to my hand. For Marx, the objective conditions of labor are labor's "inorganic body" and presupposed to the act of labor (1986 MECW 28: 409, 415; 1973: 485, 489; see also 1975 MECW 3: 275–276 ["Estranged Labour" in *The Economic and Philosophic Manuscripts of 1844*]). But under the conditions of capitalist production, the worker is separated from labor's objective conditions and as such alienated from them. Everything follows from this premise.

Labor alienated from the objective conditions necessary to its realization takes place also in the act of exchange – labor's products here confront the laborer as purchaser. In return for access to the means of reproducing her life, the worker surrenders control over her life activity and agrees to subordinate her labor to the command of another. Since that other functions as nothing more than a personification of capital itself, the laboring producer in fact agrees to subordinate her life activity to her own product attained to autonomy against her. Then in the actual process of production, living labor is subordinated to the imperatives of objectified labor's maintenance and increase. It is the dynamic of objectified labor which functions to impose a pace and discipline adequate to the task of value's self-valorization. The instrument of labor is no longer a means to transmit labor's activity to the stuff worked on; instead the machine, functioning in independence, disciplines and regulates what the worker does. And in the end, in the drama's last act, capital appropriates the product not only as an expression of the laborer's separation from the results of her labor, but also to reproduce the original conditions of her alienation.

Of course ideologies of capital saturate the social atmosphere engulfing us, functioning like pollution's grime to cover and misrepresent the real nature of capitalist production. Yet even choked as if to the point of suffocation, Marx thought working people engaged the world on a "higher plane" than those who find satisfaction in alienation:

> What we are confronted by here is the *alienation* [*Entfremdung*] of man from his own labour. To that extent the worker stands on a higher plane than the capitalist from the outset, since the latter has his roots in the process of

alienation and finds absolute satisfaction in it whereas right from the start the worker is a victim who confronts it as a rebel and experiences it as a process of enslavement.

(1990: 990 [*Results*])

That is, trapped by its mystifications, the agents of capital find the world that surrounds them sufficient though untrue. But in resistance and revolt, the oppressed, powerful in labor and its possibilities, live the searing need to throw off both ignorance and illusion and also the coercion that enslaves them:

> The recognition of the product as its own, and its awareness that its separation from the conditions of its realization is an injustice[16] – *a relationship imposed by force* – is an enormous consciousness, *itself the product* of the capitalist mode of production and just as much the KNELL TO ITS DOOM as the consciousness of the slave that he *could not be* the *property of another* reduced slavery to an artificial lingering existence, and made it impossible for it to continue to provide the basis of production.
>
> (1994 MECW 34: 246 [emphasis in original])

Alienation, then, is pregnant with force like hounds of hell, in Milton's description, kenneled in the womb of Sin.[17] The premise is labor severed from the conditions of its survival. How will you secure this? How will social reproduction take place with this separation intact and replicated? Labor gives material expression to our engagement with nature and with others; force gives material expression to our separations. In 1935, Bertold Brecht caught the significance of this in an essay called "Writing the Truth – Five Difficulties:"[18]

> The great truth of our age (to knowledge of which we have not yet been helped, but without knowledge of which no other truth of importance can be found) is that our continent is sinking into barbarism because the conditions of ownership of the means of production are maintained by force.
>
> (Brecht 1966)

"Sunk," and still short of knowledge enough to trade separation for freedom. So for "continent" read "globe."

4 The concept of capital in the *Grundrisse*

My objective in this chapter is to investigate the concept of "capital in general," a category that threads together Marx's explorations in the *Grundrisse*. I do so by summarizing and drawing together themes of the foregoing chapters and by showing how Marx's effort to work out the concept of capital corresponds to what philosophers of science today would call the "real definition" of a natural or social kind. If, as I argue, Marx has anticipated this approach, we can expect his analyses will contribute significantly to contemporary efforts to extend thinking about natural kinds from natural to social science.

Reference fixing and Marx's analysis

Start with a metaphor, one of Marx's most provocative:

> The specific economic form, in which unpaid surplus labour is pumped out of direct producers determines the relationship of domination and servitude, as it grows directly out of production itself and reacts back on it in turn as a determinant.
>
> (1991: 927 [III.47.2])

Marx returns to the same metaphor when describing the capitalist appropriation of surplus-value in 'The Trinity Formula' at the end of *Capital III*. After describing the composite structure of labor and form that will characterize any mode of production, he writes:

> we also saw that capital, in the social production process appropriate to it – and the capitalist is simply personified capital, functioning in the production process simply as the bearer of capital – pumps out a certain specific quantum of surplus labour from the direct producers or workers, surplus labour that it receives without equivalent and which by its very nature always remains forced labour, however much it might appear as the result of free contractual agreement.
>
> (1991: 957–58 [III.48.1])

It seems worthwhile to reflect for a minute on the metaphor's implications. What can it tell us? What can it tell us about the target and substance of Marx's science?

Form determination is causal determination

The idea of pumping suggests unambiguously a causal process and a causal agent. The economic form that does the pumping must be a causal structure. That is, if we're to judge by this metaphor, the "simplest determinations" described by Marx in the introductory paragraph of the *Grundrisse*'s "The Method of Political Economy" (1986 MECW 28: 37; 1973: 100), those capable of grounding social explanation, must be causal determinations. Form determination for Marx, the metaphor suggests, is above all causal determination.

It's my thought here that we've missed the significance of this emphasis in Marx's science because of the dominance of positivism in both the natural and social sciences over the last century – whether you worked with the assumptions of this approach or fought them by appealing to some variant of hermeneutics or the postmodern tradition, attention to cause was lost. But realism's reflections on the actual practice of contemporary science have opened fresh perspectives that make it possible to recover methods, emphases and insights in our reading of Marx that might otherwise have remained obscure to us.

Thus, for one, we need not assume that causal structures, if they exist, are necessarily always empirical. Under the influence of positivism Marxists have often been tempted to consider only two ontological options – either a thing was empirical or it was theoretical, merely conceptual. By contrast, over the last half century philosophers of science have learned to speak again in realist terms of causal structures that are at once potent and causally efficacious, but at the same time not observable, not empirical. Marx, never one to hide his credentials as a card carrying scientific realist, compared the search for the inner nature of capital to the effort to understand extraterrestrial motion:

> a scientific analysis of competition is possible only if we grasp the inner nature of capital, just as the apparent motions of the heavenly bodies are intelligible only to someone acquainted with their real motions, which are not perceptible to the senses.
>
> (1990: 433 [I. 12])

The simplest determinations

Notice how this comparison makes sense of the *Grundrisse* excerpt, "The Method of Political Economy:" you start with evidence perceptible to the senses but are unable to give a scientific explanation of it. You strip away apparent motions of the phenomena you explore until you arrive at their real motions – motions not perceptible to the senses. But these real motions, the "simplest determinations," allow you to intelligibly reconstruct your understanding of phenomena as they are perceptibly presented.

This, by the way, was a step that John Locke, working in the early years of the scientific revolution, could not grasp. For Locke, that which was "insensible" must ever remain a mystery to us.[1] Marx judged science had shown our capacity to grasp the inner nature of things. But for others in the traditions of mainstream thinking about science, the legacy of Locke's empiricism persisted.

The word "value," of course, refers to an imperceptible social structure, and so does "capital in general." On this reading Marx's references to the "concept of capital" or "capital in general" target that constellation of causal properties or mechanisms that constitute the simplest determination of the capitalist mode of production, an intersection of causal properties deeply embedded under capital's phenomenal manifestations. Thus Marx writes in the *Grundrisse* that searching for the defining characteristics of "capital in general" is like searching for the defining characteristics of *homo sapiens* – one looks for those features that account for what makes *homo sapiens* distinct from other animals (1973: 852; 1987 MECW 29: 227–228). Just as the biologist looks for the *differentia specifica* of a species, the search for "capital in general" is a search for what is distinctive about capital as a species of production. The *differentia specifica* of capital are those features that distinguish it "from all other forms of wealth or modes in which social production develops" (1986 MECW 28: 378; see also 1973: 449 where *differentia specifica* is translated as "specific characteristics").

Real definition and reference

To the extent that the simple determination for which we search is a causal structure, we're after what the realist philosophy of science today would call the real definition of a natural or social kind. The real definition of a thing refers to those causal properties or mechanisms that account for what it is, how it behaves, and how it persists as what it is. H_2O is the real definition of water. Notice importantly that while our effort to specify a real definition explicitly defines, what we are after is precision of reference, not the kind of thing we commonly associate with verbal definition; we are not "defining our terms" or offering a clarification of the ideas we associate with our use of the term. In this sense reference is *ostensive* rather than definitional in the ordinary sense – it points (Boyd 1979). Reference is an example of the way our use of language enables us to coordinate our causal interactions with the world; we use language to identify accurately the causal structures to which we accommodate our social practice. Even for the large theoretical elaborations any science involves, this will hold only if the things to which we refer determine the content of the terms we use, rather than that this be accomplished by the ideas and intuitions we might at any one point associate with our use of those terms.

Such an approach makes sense of what would otherwise present a puzzle. Writing in 1845, Marx and Engels wrote a tract excoriating the conceptual analysis of their day: "Let us revolt against this rule of concepts!" they announced in the preface to *The German Ideology* (1975 MECW 5: 23). Feuerbach remained stalled with the conceptual abstraction "man" and others were driven by more extravagant speculative manipulations. Thus, the social relation, family, Marx and Engels argued, must be "analyzed according to existing empirical data, not according to 'the concept of the family'" (43). In an echo of this, Hilary Kornblith (2002: 1), a contemporary philosophical naturalist, argues for the study of mind, not "the concept of mind," of law, not "the concept of law."[2] What's up then with Marx, a dozen years after *The German Ideology*, devoting some 800 pages of manuscript to working out "the concept of capital?"

Here's a solution: reference fixing, whether by pointing, or describing, or explicitly defining, is always at bottom ostensive – a matter of picking out the thing to which we refer. It is the structure of the water molecule that is the source of the information we have about water and it is by the precision with which we identify its elements that we are able to coordinate most effectively our uses of the substance. That is, theoretical concepts and their explication are essential to science. But the chemist who first said "Aha, water is H_2O" wasn't "defining his terms" – he was making a scientific discovery.

What I argue is that Marx was working with the concept of capital in the same way. He used it to pick out decisive causal structures of social life, not to stipulate the meanings he associated with his use of the term. And because he used concepts to refer, those concepts are, as are theoretical terms used in other sciences, fallible and approximate and necessarily revisable in consequence of any advance in our understanding of the thing to which they refer. This is true of all scientific work.[3]

Categories and convenience

Often people argue that the divisions we make among the things of the world are not determined by the causal mechanisms or the properties that characterize them, but instead that sorting things into kinds is a matter of convention that depends on our convenience. This is an implication of Locke's argument that nature is without chasms or gaps and that, in spite of their apparent diversity, species on the great chain of being shade imperceptibly into one another (1975: 446–47 [Book III, Chaper VI, §12]). If, by contrast, nature is, so to speak, bunched or clumped such that discrete entities reproduce themselves coherently as different kinds of things, then in our activities, linguistic, scientific, political, or other, we're obliged to accommodate our practices to the way things are. On this view we live in a world where dogs don't mate with cats regardless of how we classify them and we can give a causal account of why this is so. Again, when we offer a real definition of a natural kind we attempt to identify those causal properties that account for its distinctive stability as the kind of thing it is. By identifying water as H_2O we realize not all combinations of hydrogen and oxygen work to form a water molecule and not all combination of elements or other building blocks of nature work indifferently in any arrangement to create cohesive and stable entities.

The extension of this argument to the study of social life suggests that social things too can be more or less stable configurations that reproduce and renew themselves in relation to changes in their environment. Rather than conventionally organized categories classified according to the language user's convenience (the way many use the terms "class" or "middle class"), there are social structures also that require identification and specification if we want our social practice to respond meaningfully to them. For example, Marx differentiated modes of production according to the different social forms taken by labor's relation to nature and to others in the course of production.

Concept and referent

For its familiarity and simplicity, H_2O has become the paradigm example of the real definition of a natural kind. In fact, the idea that water is H_2O has entered popular consciousness so that we forget this is new knowledge in the history of human thought. People knew of and referred to water and its properties for millennia without knowing that its simplest determination was H_2O. While the point seems obvious, *The German Ideology*, if nothing else, underscores the importance of distinguishing between a thing and the concept we form of it. But even marxists have stumbled over this, and their missteps have led to a significant misreading of an important passage from The *Grundrisse*. In Notebook VII Marx writes that "[t]he economic concept of value does not occur in antiquity.... The concept of value is entirely peculiar to the most modern economy, since it is the most abstract expression of capital itself and of the production resting on it" (1973: 776; 1987 MECW 29: 159–160). This passage has been taken to mean that value itself, the thing to which the concept of value refers, did not exist in the ancient world. But value can exist where there is no concept of it. We might as well say, paraphrasing Marx, that "the chemical concept of H_2O does not occur among the ancients ... the concept is entirely peculiar to modern chemistry." But it would not follow that water itself did not come into being until the scientific discovery of its concept.

Anyway, identifying the essential features of "capital in general" is an effort to locate the so-to-speak H_2O of capital, its decisive underlying causal structure. We do the same thing when we define gold as atomic number 79 – we distinguish gold from all other shiny yellow metallic things by identifying the most basic causal structure both essential and specific to it. So notice, the search for "capital in general" is not an effort to gather each important property that all instances of capital share – the thing Michael Heinrich (1989; see also 2007) thought caused the concept of "capital in general" itself to "shatter." Instead it is an effort to specify those few properties of capital that are constitutive of it.

Constitutive and attributive properties

In this respect Marx's study of Aristotle is relevant. Aristotle makes a distinction between properties that are constitutive of a thing and those that may be attributed to it or are manifestations of it. All things go through a change of form, Aristotle suggests, and thus he invites us to make just this distinction in our effort to understand them – my DNA stays what it is while I wrinkle and gray.

Marx took over this insight and applied it to social life. Thus he is insistent on distinguishing between the inner nature of capital – the intersection of social relations constitutive of capital – and attributes of capital that depend on the action of many capitals on each other, that is, on competition. The thread he traces throughout the *Grundrisse* identifies features necessary to grasp capital's inner nature. Realization, for example, is part of the concept of capital, although any actual project of realization may likely confront a tangle of difficult complications arising out of the interactions of capitals on one another. But Marx abstracts from these and assumes that realization proceeds unproblematically in order to focus exclusively on the mechanisms that constitute and establish capital's essential life processes (1986 MECW 28: 376; 1973: 447). The categories of competition refer to forms by means of which capital's constitutive structure manifests itself, not to that structure itself.

I argued in the Appendix to Chapter 2 that Backhaus' seminal article on *Capital*'s first chapter ignores this distinction between constitutive and attributive form in his suggestion that there is a methodologically unsuccessful break between §2 and §3 of that chapter. He fails to notice that §2 presents value's constitutive form. The idea that in §2 we are given only the bare physiological expenditure of labor without regard to social form ignores precisely the point I appealed to earlier when I referred to the structure of labor and form that will characterize any mode of production: Marxism studies always historically specific forms of laboring individuals in their relation to nature and to others. Let me elaborate on this just a minute.

The concept of a labor-form composite

In the *Grundrisse* Marx explains the features of labor that account for the commodity form of the product of labor in terms that track the analysis briefly presented in the opening paragraphs of §2 of *Capital I*. Using the same phrase as in the "Method of Political Economy" for "simplest determination," Marx presents the social mechanism that accounts for exchange value and the commodity form as follows: "[i]n the first positing of simple exchange value, labour was structured in such a way that the product was not a direct use value for the labourer, not a direct means of subsistence" (1973: 266; 1986 MECW 28: 197).[4] Notice that this first positing of simple exchange value is explained by a structure or determination of labor. The labor that produces a commodity is form determined. This does not mean that wherever and whenever the product of labor appears as a commodity we have, say, a simple commodity mode of production. That is an entirely different thing, a whole social edifice. Here we are saying only that wherever and whenever the product of labor takes the commodity form, even if we have no idea the precise form of labor under which the product was actually produced, we do know that labor was form determined in two very material and specific ways – it involved the independent production of a use value not useful to its producer. That is, there is a labor-form composite, not necessarily involving capital, that accounts for the product of labor as a commodity.

As I've explained earlier, the idea of a labor-form composite here can be thought of as an appropriation of Aristotle's characterization of the things of the world as composites of matter and form – this is Aristotle's hylomorphism: *hylo* for matter and *morphe* for form. Also, activity, like the activity of labor, for Aristotle was something that would have fallen under the wider category of matter. For Marx, the labor-form composites studied by political economy are always ultimately causal structures formed by the activity of laboring individuals grasped in relation to nature and to others, and, moreover, grasped conceptually in the very process of production.

It is one such labor-form composite, for example, that accounts for the pumping out of surplus value in capitalist production. Thus Marx wrote in 'The Trinity Formula,' "[l]ike all its forerunners, the capitalist production process proceeds under specific material conditions, which are however also the bearers of specific social relations which the individuals enter into in the process of reproducing their life" (1991: 957 [III. 48. 3]). We can give full effect to the causal potency of just such material structures, and yet avoid reification, by drawing upon Aristotle's presentation of explanation in terms of four causal factors. First, there is a material structure of nature and laboring individuals (*material cause*), specifically shaped by definite social relations (*formal cause*), motivated by and producing a particular result (*final cause*) – and ultimately this is often a reproduction of the structure itself (that is, *formal cause* as *final cause*). To this, we add the impetus of movement: the "pumping" that drives the process is done by laboring individuals (*efficient cause*), who, by a process of inversion, confront their own activity as an alien power ruling over them. We add also the crucial point that just as the offensive power of an infantry regiment is essentially different from the power of individual soldiers aggregated (1990: 443 [I.13]), so too, the causal potency of a labor-form composite is essentially different from the causal force of a sum of laboring individuals.

The point however is to transform

One final preliminary point before I deal with the real definition of capital as such. The significance of understanding the causal structures that determine value and capital is the same as the significance of understanding the causal structures that provoke inquiry in any science. By understanding such structures we are able not only to interpret them, the limit of all traditional philosophy, but to transform. We can change base metals into gold if we know how to manipulate their atomic structure so as to change this into a structure with atomic number 79.[5] The same for capital or for value. We cannot abolish money or markets by decree, but if we understand the simple causal determinations that account for such things we can act as the causally potent creatures we ourselves are to transform them according to our ambitions. Understanding the world's causal structures, we can sometime change them, and this applies to the social world as well as the natural one. Moreover, just like any other creature, the successes of the accommodations we make to the causal structures of the world are the basis for our survival as a species, or, for lack of them, to our demise.

The real definition of capital

Capital's double separation

Over forty years ago, and with great insight, Charles Bettelheim specified the capitalist character of the enterprise in a way that offers a real definition of capital. He referred to the "double separation that forms the central characteristic of the capitalist mode of production:"

> The capitalist character of the enterprise ... is due to the fact that its struc-
> ture assumes the form of a *double separation: the separation of workers*
> *from their means of production* ... and the *separation of the enterprises*
> *from each other*. This double separation forms the central characteristic of
> the capitalist mode of production, and it serves as a support for the totality
> of contradictions of this mode of production.
>
> (1975: 77 [emphasis in original])

My argument is that the "double separation" aptly captures the *Grundrisse's* concept of "capital in general." Marx reminds that capital is not a static relation but a process so we must grasp capital's separations as an intersection of structures in process; also, we want to show how these separations penetrate production itself. But, properly understood, the category Bettelheim identifies picks out those features of capital that are constitutive of it, those features that ultimately account for what it is and how it persists as what it is.

The separation of units of production from one another characterizes the labor-form composite that accounts for value and the commodity form. As I've argued, whenever labor is structured so that it is independent and produces use values that the producer does not relate to as such but offers instead for private exchange, there you have a causal structure that tends to generate value and its forms of manifestation. To the extent a producer cannot use what she's produced, she's driven to market. Commodity production, though presupposed by capital, emerges as distinct; it forms part of capital's prehistory.

When the separation of units of production from one another is coupled to the separation of the laboring producer from her conditions of production, this generates the capital relation. Objectless labor is impoverished absolutely. Nonetheless, if the laborer not only lacks tools and materials to produce but can also dispose of her labor power as her own, then she may accommodate her circumstance to the exchange of commodities: she has produced separately a thing of value useless to her, and thus can offer that thing, her capacity to labor, for private exchange. Her labor power may then be purchased for its exchange value as the use value of capital, a commodity with the capacity to create not only value, but greater value than the wage given for it. The labor process then objectifies her activity in a product containing value adequate to replace not only the value of her wage but containing also a surplus appropriated by capital. The separation of workers from their conditions of production thus makes possible capital's fundamental determination – the appropriation of living labor by objectified labor as value for the sake of value's increase.

It is important to recognize that there is nothing spontaneous about the transition from the production of commodities to capital. In fact, as a historical matter, the simple circulation of commodities for money, C-M-C, does give rise pretty spontaneously to the circuit M-C-M, money for commodities. But this second circuit makes sense only insofar as the value originally invested is increased; in other words, the circuit actually appears as M-C-M′ (where M′ includes both the original M and an added increment). But there is nothing in the simple exchange of equivalent values that can sustain this latter circuit – the added increment appears to come only contingently from the outside – a merchant, for example, might exploit geographical differences between the prices of a thing, or a boat loaded with wheat might dock at the port of a town in famine. But there is no imperative in circulation or the relations of circulation that can account for the emergence of capitalist production, and the forms of value persisted for millennia without giving rise to it. Instead, for capitalism the bloody process of expropriation canvassed by Marx in his explanation of "The So-Called Primitive Accumulation" was necessary. Emergent capital had to break labor's natural connection to its land and tools.

The three moments of capital

In the *Grundrisse* Marx identifies three moments or stages of the life process of "capital in general" and we can trace the progress of the capital's double separation through each. The three moments are (1) the moment of the simple conception of capital as it emerges from circulation, (2) the moment of the process of production as the unity of production and valorization, and (3) the moment of capital as the unity of production and circulation (1986 MECW 28: 245; 1973: 319).

The locus of the first moment is circulation. The phenomena of circulation, we've seen, are a product of the separation of productive entities which produce use values not useful to them for private exchange.

The locus of the second moment is production. The phenomena of production under capitalism are not only a product of the separation of productive entities but also the separation of the laboring producer from the conditions of production. This is the moment of the "inner organic movement of capital" (1987 MECW 29: 70; 1973: 680), and we are here able to identify the specific characteristics that differentiate capital not only from value, but also from other forms of social production.

The locus of the third moment is the unity of production and circulation, the stage where the constitutive features of capital's inner nature are reflected in capital's full and mature development. At this stage we are able to show how the intersection of the separation of productive entities from each other and the separation of workers from their conditions of production is at once the precondition for capital, its ground and goal, and also ultimately the limit it confronts as a mode of social production.

The first moment: the simple concept of capital

Capital's point of departure arises from value as it arises out of circulation and comes to sustain itself there. Value and exchange value are presupposed. The commodity form is presupposed. This means the separation of productive entities from one another that accounts for these is presupposed. But we've seen that more is required for the circuit of self-multiplying value, M-C-M', on which the emergence of capital from circulation depends. We know that commodity production will become the general form of social production only where labor power is sold as a commodity. It is only on this basis that the commodity becomes the universal form of the product of labor and commodity production becomes generalized. As a consequence, although the circulation of commodities is explained simply by the separation of units of production, in order for the separation of units of production that produce for market to become general, the separation of laboring producers from their conditions of production is required. That is, the general formula of capital, M-C-M', and the simple concept of capital to which it gives expression, do not yet give us the basis to understand how capital sustains itself in circulation, but because capital reflects generalized commodity production we do see that it rests on both components of the double separation.

The second moment: the unity of production and valorization

We locate the source of value as self-multiplying and self-sustaining, that is, value not as pure value or money, but as capital, in the second moment of the concept of capital: the moment of the unity of production and valorization in the labor process. Here we are able to pick out constitutive features, the *differentia specifica*, of production that is capitalist, those features that form the germ out of which later developments will come (1986 MECW 28: 236; 1973: 310).

The separation that accounts for value is now presupposed. Also presupposed is the labor market exchange that introduces the incorporation of labor by capital, so the separation of labor and wealth is presupposed. Additionally, in this exchange, which introduces the labor process, the laborer surrenders control over her life activity and its fruits. Thus, the rich dimensions of Marx's analysis of the objectification of living labor as an alienation begin here as alienation in a strict juridical sense.

By surrendering control over her life activity the worker is subject to the command of the capitalist (1986 MECW 28: 234; 1973: 308), and is subjected in her work to rules, methods and goals set by another. But the capitalist is in turn only a personification of capital itself (1990: 989–991 [*Appendix: Results*]), so in the event the worker is subordinated to the imperatives of self-multiplying value. That is, because of her subordination to the process of valorization, the worker must work with an intensity dictated by the law of value and for a longer day than would be necessary to replace the value of her wage.

Also, by surrendering control over the fruits of her labor, the worker surrenders to the capitalist ownership of the product (1986 MECW 28: 234; 1973: 308); appropriated by capital, the separation of the results of labor from the worker reproduces her propertylessness. Her product becomes an alien power to which she is subordinated and on which she depends.

The defining characteristics of the separation of the worker from the conditions of production, then, are separation joined to an alienation that is its consequence. Alienation, in turn, is at once the appropriation of labor's activity and its fruits. As such it is both the subordination of labor to capital's command and subordination of labor to labor's own product as an alien power ruling over it. Taken together we are able to express this intersection of separation and subordination as follows: *the free worker's alienated separation from and subordination to the conditions of production as value is capital's simplest determination.* Marx writes:

> The worker's propertylessness, and the ownership of living labour by objectified labour, or the appropriation of alien labour by capital – both merely expressions of the same relation from opposite poles – are the fundamental conditions of the bourgeois mode of production.
>
> (1973: 832; 1987 MECW 29: 210)

Because Marx's analysis of the content of the production process of capital specifies the essential features that differentiate capital not only from "value in general" but also from other modes of production, the section from Notebook III of the *Grundrisse* on the production process as the content of capital (1986 MECW 28: 230–236; 1973: 304–310) is like the earlier section from Notebook II on the simplest determination of exchange (1986 MECW 28: 197; 1973: 266) insofar as both of these are decisively reflected in the way the argument of *Capital* presents the simplest determinations of capital and the commodity form respectively. In the Appendix to Chapter 2 above I showed how the structure of labor worked out in Notebook II was presented in §2 of *Capital*'s first chapter to establish the constitutive properties that account for the commodity form. In turn we find the constitutive properties of capital as they are worked out in Notebook III embedded in the argument developed in Chapters 6 and 7 of *Capital I.* In Chapter 6, Marx establishes the separation of the free laborer from the conditions of production as a condition of capitalist production and then in Chapter 7 he explicitly characterizes those features that distinguish capital as a form of social labor: assuming the production of value and assuming also the separation of the free laborer from all wealth, the features that differentiate the capitalist labor process are as follows:

The labour process, when it is the process by which the capitalist consumes labour-power, exhibits two characteristic phenomena.

First the worker works under the control of the capitalist to whom his labour belongs.... Secondly, the product is the property of the capitalist and not that of the worker, its immediate producer.

(1990: 291–92 [ch. 7.1])

The third moment: the unity of production and circulation

The third moment, like the first, is a point of departure. The departure, however, is not now from value, but instead from capital: value which has absorbed living labor is introduced into circulation in order to increase itself. The transformation of commodities into money and money into commodities has become part of capital's concept. The meaning here, as a matter of reference fixing, is that the moment of circulation and production considered as a whole brings into view mechanisms that account for the dynamic of capital's reproduction as a distinctive form of social labor. Abstracting to the unity of production and circulation, we look to identify those features of social life that account for capital's persistence, without for all that taking on the complications such features might encounter in a particular capital's day to day interaction with other capitals. We locate the labor-form composite that constitutes capital's inner nature and trace the dynamic essential to it as the form of capital's original presupposition, its mature development and its limit.

The machine as an incarnation of capital's double separation

For example: an important instance of how the double separation is expressed in the moment of production and circulation's unity is given by the system of machinery. Marx writes that the full development of capital takes place only where the means of labor take the form of fixed capital and fixed capital takes the form of the machine (1987 MECW 29: 85; 1973: 699). When production is organized by capital a machine belongs to a separated unit of production, of course. More profoundly, in capitalist production a machine achieves an independence that sets it over against those who labor on it. In the form of machinery, the means of labor no longer transmit the worker's activity to its material, instead, it is the machine that assigns tasks, regulates the pace of work, and dominates the worker so that living labor becomes an insignificant accessory of the machine's activity:

> In machinery, objectified labor materially confronts living labor as a ruling power and as an active subsumption of the latter under itself, not only by appropriating it, but in the real production process itself; the relation of capital as value which appropriates value-creating activity is in fixed capital existing as machinery.
>
> (1973: 693–94; 1987 MECW 29: 83)

Consider the weight of what Marx has said here: capital's fundamental determination, the appropriation of living labor by objectified labor in order to increase the latter, is incarnated in the machine. The separation of the worker from the means of production is materially embodied in the machine; the subordination of the worker to the means of production is materially embodied in the machine. Labor's experience of the machine as a force "outside itself," Marx emphasizes, "belongs to the concept of capital" (1973: 702; 1987 MECW: 88)." In fixed capital the productive forces of labor are "posited as external to labour and as existing independently of it" (1973: 701; 1987 MECW 29: 87).

The example of machinery illustrates not only how capital's separations reach full development in capital's life cycle; they illustrate also how they can be expected to account for capital's dissolution. In fact it is not only the individual labourer that becomes an insignificant accessory to production. As capitalist production unfolds, living labor itself, which, as quantity, is capital's determining element, becomes less and less important in comparison to the contribution to production made by machines and by the general applications of science and technology operative through them (1973: 700ff; 1987 MECW 29: 85ff). In part, however, the dilemma is masked by what might be thought of as capital's self-conception. In its full flowering as "fructiferous" (1973: 745; 1987 MECW 29: 129), capital generates the illusion that it can ignore labour; instead it relates to its monetary embodiment as the ground of what it has produced, "the foundation of what it has founded" (1973: 745; 1987 MECW 29: 129). M-C-M' becomes possible because its movement, instantiated in production, is no longer formal, but instead is rooted in the appropriation of living labor by objectified labor. But now surplus value relates not to living labor as its ground but instead, as if indifferently, to money capital alone. Whatever labor's contribution, the rate of profit is measured simply against total capital invested.

The double separation as a barrier to capital

Much work needs doing on all this. In effect the reproduction of capital is the reproduction of capital's double separation and this on a constantly increasing scale. But the other side of the coin called separation is indifference. In its full development capital's impulse to an unlimited development of the productive forces confronts limits in the reciprocal indifference of productive enterprises to one another and also of capital's indifference to labor. For capital, perversely, surplus labor is a precondition for necessary labor rather than the reverse. Moreover, necessary labor is restricted by the exchange value of labor power – that is, roughly, by the requirements of subsistence – rather than by an individual's rich capacity for free development through labor. As a consequence, labor's need can never provide an adequate impulse to the development of the productive forces. Nor, given reciprocally indifferent entities, can the needs of other productive units. The need others have for objects of use is ultimately subject to physical, quantitative and other measures that have nothing to do with value. The exchange value form, a consequence of the separation of reciprocally indifferent units of production, thus becomes a restriction on the production of use value.

That is, in order for production to occur, labor, machinery and raw materials must be present in the right proportions and, further, capital has a need for circulation seamlessly united to production. But not only is production determined by physical measures having nothing to do with exchange value, also each productive unit, though fully dependent on the social division of labor, confronts the indifference of alien need. Given reciprocally indifferent entities, disproportion means commodities cannot be harmoniously transformed into money or surplus labor into surplus-value. Capital's tendency to generate an unrestricted development of the productive forces is contradicted by its need to reproduce both the indifference of capital to labor and the indifference of productive entities to one another.

Conclusion: beyond capital's double separation

Marx is well known for not offering blueprints for the future. In broadest outline, however, he does suggest how the separation of productive entities from one another and the separation of workers from their conditions of production might be transformed: we look to a structuring of labor whereby associated workers take common control over their common wealth (1986 MECW 28: 95–96; 1973: 158–159). Cooperative association among units of production transforms their separation from one another, and common control by associated workers of land, raw materials and the means of labor transforms the separation of wealth and labor. These transformations in turn lay the basis for a social form of production that rests on the universal development of individuals, of the free development of their creative powers, and of the subordination of their social wealth to need through labor. Recall Marx's reference to wealth stripped of its bourgeois shell:

> what is wealth, other than the universality of individual needs, capacities, pleasures, productive forces, etc., created through universal exchange? The full development of human mastery over the forces of nature, those of so-called nature as well as of humanity's own nature? The absolute working-out of his creative potentialities with no presupposition other than the previous historic development, which makes this totality of development, i.e. the development of all human powers as such the end in itself, not as measured on a *predetermined* yardstick?
>
> (1973: 488; 1986 MECW 28: 411–412)

Ultimately, we work to develop the productive forces of labor, of which the laboring individual is the most precious, in order to develop fully all human powers. We develop the productive forces to accomplish a working out of human potentialities constrained only by the accommodation we make necessarily with nature. In its life process capital does give formidable impulse to the development of the productive forces, but this is an impulse driven to increase the value of things and it is compromised by its tendency to reproduce labor's impoverishment as well as to reproduce each capital's separation from other enterprises engaged in production. Pre-given conditions of production provide a limit to which the development of human potential must bend. By contrast, Marx imagines an unobstructed development of the forces of production, and including especially the rich capacities of the laboring individual, not limited, as is capital, by the social form of its reproduction:

> Although limited by its very nature, [capital] strives towards the universal development of the forces of production, and thus becomes the presupposition of a new mode of production ... where the free, unobstructed, progressive and universal development of the forces of production is itself the presupposition of society and hence of its reproduction; where advance beyond the point of departure is the only presupposition.
>
> (1973: 540; 1986 MECW 28: 463–464)

But "[f]or this," he adds, "[it is] necessary above all that the full development of the forces of production has become the *condition of production*; and not that specific *conditions of production* are posited as a limit to the development of the productive forces (1973: 542; 1986 MECW 28: 466).

The concept of capital's double separation refers to conditions of production capital must reproduce and by which it is constrained. While at first this double determination of labor is a form for the development of capital's productive power, it becomes at last a punishing shackle.

In the end, capital's appropriation of the social form of labor responds poorly to labor's human form. Labor, Marx observes, is purposeful activity. A content more fully adequate to this would not receive living labor as capital does, as quantity merely, but would instead give full material expression to labor's purposeful accommodation to the totality of our conditions of life – to associated labor's self-determined unfolding of human needs and abilities best suited to the accommodation we make necessarily to nature.

Appendix: a note on value as a social kind

Until now I have characterized the labor-form composite that accounted for the commodity and value forms of the product of labor as the social kind of commodity producing labor. But I will now refer to the same causal structure as a simple determination of the value relation. Is value a social kind? Because of what we've learned from the study of capital as a social kind, I think it's readily apparent that it is.

First of all, like capital, Marx speaks of value as a social relation. We speak of the value of the product of labor and in doing so have in mind the congealed labor to which the first chapter of *Capital* refers as the substance of value. By this we mean the labor expended on the product, the quantity of objectified labor the product itself can be taken to represent. But if we are to speak of value as a social kind we must speak not of dead labor but instead of a social relation of living labor in the activity of production. I've emphasized that we can only do this in a restricted sense; that the product of labor is a commodity and a value does not tell us the social circumstances which characterized the laboring producer's actual relation to nature and to others except in two ways – labor was conducted independently and devoted to producing a product useless to its producer because intended for private exchange. But those two features do characterize living labor in production, and just as when we refer to money or machinery as capital we avoid fetishism only if we understand these are not by nature capital but become so only insofar as they give expression to a specific social relation, so too we can say a product has value only because this gives expression to a particular social configuration of labor.

The parallel here can be pushed further. In Chapter 3 I showed how the general formula for capital, a formula deriving from circulation, M-C-M′, was instantiated in the activity of production insofar as objectified labor appropriated living labor to generate a surplus. Recognition of this clarified two ways in which the essential features of capital could be understood: they could be grasped structurally as a relation of separation; additionally they could be grasped as the activity of this structure – the appropriation of living labor for the sake of an increase of objectified labor.

The social relation of value as a social kind can also be understood both as a causal structure and as an activity of that structure. If we speak of the general formula of simple value, we refer to M-C or C-M, the exchange of equivalents. Insofar as production for private exchange is presupposed this relation of equivalence is instantiated in the activity of production as the conversion of living labor to expended or objectified labor rendered commensurate. This is accomplished by a process of production that presupposes the market's ability to realize the exchange of any product for any other so long as they are in appropriate proportions. That is, production for private exchange is a process that abstracts from labor's concrete useful qualities in order to render every product the bearer of a specific quantity of labor homogeneous in quality. Thus, value as a social kind can be grasped not only structurally as the separation of independent producers who produce for private exchange, but it can be grasped also as the form of labor activity that reduces living labor to expended labor that is qualitatively homogeneous.

Spelling out the parallels between simple value and capital in this way clarifies our understanding of capital as the ultimate development of the value relationship (1973: 704; 1987 MECW 29: 90):

> The exchange of living labour for objectified labour – i.e. the positing of social labour in the form of the contradiction of capital and wage labour – is the ultimate development of the *value relation* and of production resting on value. Its presupposition is – and remains – the mass of direct labour time.

Structurally the separation of independent producers who produce for private exchange is completed by the separation of the laboring producer from and subordination to the conditions of production. Because of this structure, objectified labor, reduced by exchange to a direct mass of qualitatively homogeneous labor time, can appropriate living labor activity for the sake of the increase of objectified labor.

To make clear that as material social relations value and capital are both social kinds will also draw into sharper focus the tension between the two that surfaces whenever questions concerning the legal or ideological superstructure emerge. Thus, in analyzing the legal doctrine of consideration in Part II, I will show how juridical relations of autonomy correspond to the material relations of separation that characterize value as a social kind. But we already know from studying capital that the worker who contracts for employment exercises autonomy in order to enter a relation of subjugation where she executes the commands of another in order to fulfill the purposes of another; she exercises autonomy to sell herself into a relation Marx characterizes as wage slavery. That is, because social kinds as fundamental to production as value and capital will tend to generate normative and ideological relations that correspond to them, in the case of capital these reflect the contradictions intrinsic to the double separation that characterizes capitalist production. Capital in its operation presupposes and includes simple value and in the intersection of capital and value as social kinds normative and ideological forms deriving from the separation of the means of production from laboring producers tend to contradict those deriving from the separation of independent entities of production and exchange. The abiding tension between capital's pretensions to equality and the glaring actuality of pervasive structures of hierarchy and domination is a preeminent example of this.

In sum, when I refer to value as a social kind I refer to the same causal structure of labor and form that I have referred to as commodity-producing labor as a social kind, and I will use both forms of expression. While the latter tends to emphasize the kind captured structurally as a relation of separation, the former emphasizes the activity of converting living labor into objectified labor rendered abstract and commensurate; importantly, it is the living activity of the same causal structure of social life that is referred to in either case.

Part II

Transformations

[E]very separation is the separation of a unity.

Notebooks on Epicurean Philosophy

[I]ndividuals obtain their freedom in and through their association.... For it is the association of individuals ... which puts the conditions of the free development and movement of individuals under their control – conditions which were previously left to chance and had acquired an independent existence over against the separate individuals precisely because of their separation as individuals.

The German Ideology

5   Value and contract formation

This chapter explores the relationship between value and contract formation – in effect it is an extended reflection on the first paragraph of "The Process of Exchange" in Book I of *Capital* (Marx 1990: 178–179 [I.2]).[1] The investigation shows that the explanation of a textbook rule of contract formation in Anglo-American law may be derived from Marx's analysis of value.

If the result is significant, this is for two reasons. First, the nature of what is explained is important. Remarkably, within the Marxist tradition there are few examples analyzing specific rules of law. Those examples that do exist rarely go beyond considerations of policy or interest, the immediate or surface forms in which competing classes struggle over legislation and judicial opinions. But there has been little effort to show the way the inner structure of a mode of production shapes decisive forms of legal life. Grasp of Marx's proposal that the economic base is the key to understanding the legal superstructure has suffered accordingly.

Second, the method used to generate explanation may claim attention. On the one hand I draw on the work of Volosinov (1986) to show that communications forming contractual bargains, and the forms of consciousness presupposed by them, are generated by identifiable conditions of social life: these communicative performances derive from the imperatives of the social reproduction of the product in the commodity form. Also, I show that the long standing puzzle of enforceable promise depends for its resolution not only on understanding the cycle of commodity reproduction, but also on understanding how the behavior required functions semiotically – consideration, the technical requirement for an enforceable promise, is a sign.

In addition, I read Marx as a realist doing social science. As I argued in Part I, for too long too many Marxisms have assumed that if Marx was doing science it must be positivist and employ a Humean concept of cause. Instead, advances in the philosophy of science have restored attention to the realist tradition to which Marx belonged. Rather than understanding cause as a conjunction of atomistic events whereby an antecedent event is regularly associated with its consequent, Marx understood cause as generative and drew an ontological distinction between structures of nature or society with causal powers and the patterns of events they generated.[2] Against this background, the value relation may be studied as a causally efficacious social structure capable of generating significant phenomena of social life.

Thus, it is from a perspective of what may be called depth realism that I read Marx's notes on method in the Introduction to the first draft of *Capital*, the well-known "Method of Political Economy." In Chapter 3 I quoted a fragment from this text in which Marx proposes a move from observed reality as a point of departure to the same phenomenal reality as a result – we travel a roundtrip ticket ending back where we started. But there is a difference. Like many a journey, we are transformed and do not see things as before on our return. On our return the concrete is concrete not only in the sense that we can see or hear or taste or touch or smell; it is concrete also because we understand, fallibly, how it works and how it behaves. Reality is now not only subject to observation, but also to explanation. And because the world is now a world we understand, it is also one that we can consciously change.

"Consideration" – a point of departure

The world of phenomena with which I start is the world of law – judicial decisions, behaviors shaped by law, rules, legal regulations and so on.

In this particular instance I take the rules by which contracts are formed in Anglo-American law. Although the core of contract formation, a legal doctrine called "consideration," has existed in pretty much the same form for about 400 years – a late sixteenth century London lawyer transported to a first year contracts classroom in New York today would recognize the rule – the doctrine has never received satisfactory theoretical explanation (Engelskirchen 1997).[3] A century ago the legal historian Sir Frederick Pollock called the problem posed by consideration "a secret paradox of the common law" (Pollock 1914: 129). Within more recent years an American legal scholar said the problem remains "an unsolved mystery" (Gordon 1990: 1002).

The consequences for contemporary legal scholarship have been interesting. For the most part academic lawyers would like to see the problem go away. Because they can't explain the puzzle, much energy has been devoted to showing the doctrine is senseless and unnecessary and ought to be abandoned (Ashley 1913; Pound 1945; Gordon 1991). The difficulty is, judges continue to apply it (Wessman 1993).

The rule and its mystery may be pretty simply stated. People enter contracts by promising one another. Enforcing contracts then means enforcing promises. The fundamental question for contract formation is to know what promises the law will enforce. In Anglo-American law a promise becomes enforceable when consideration is given for it. Traditionally consideration has been understood as something given in exchange for a promise (Williston 1894: 33). Recall Adam Smith's explanation of bargain: "Give me that which I want, and you shall have that which you want" (Smith 1976: v. 1, 18 [Bk. I, Ch. 2]). In order to enforce my promise to give you that which you want, you have to show that you gave or promised to give me that which I want. The act or promise committing you to give what I'm after is consideration.

Now this seems simple enough, but there is a problem. By the end of the sixteenth century it was acknowledged that courts would enforce an exchange of promises (Barton 1969: 889). Actually this step represents a not so well known world historic advance in human culture. Roman law would enforce particular categories of promises, say, sale, or it would enforce promises using particular verbal formulas, but Roman jurisprudence never developed a general theory for the enforcement of promises (Watson 1991: 53–68). That is, in Rome it was never the case that promises could be enforced simply because they had been exchanged. But this happened in England in the sixteenth century. Regardless of form or subject matter (assuming the subject of the contract was not illegal) if two persons exchanged promises, this justified enforcement. The reason English common lawyers were able to accomplish what Roman jurisprudes never could depends on the analysis on which we are embarked. If in fact rules of contract formation depend on the value relation, then the flowering of commodity production in the early modern period provides the answer.

For now, the point I want to fix is that from an early period lawyers and judges understood that one promise could be consideration for another. This was fine as a practical matter, but a theoretical problem was posed: giving consideration is a way we decide which promises are enforceable. Courts will enforce a promise you made to me if I gave consideration for it. If I sought to enforce a promise you made, a court would ask whether I gave or promised to give the thing you wanted of me. Well, I might say, I delivered to her the chairs she promised to pay me for, but she hasn't paid. Giving the chairs would constitute consideration and the promise of payment would be enforced.

But what if I said, I *promised* to give her the chairs and she promised to pay me for them, but she won't pay as agreed. What have I actually given now? If one were tempted to say that I've in effect given the chairs because I've promised to give them and my promise can be enforced, we have just reasoned in a circle. We are trying to decide whether the promise of another is enforceable. In order to establish this we've assumed my promise is enforceable. But why do we make that assumption? My promise must be enforceable because the other has given consideration for it. But the other has given a promise as well. So we would have to assume that the other's promise is enforceable if it is to count as consideration in order to establish that my promise was enforceable. And there we are. Where promises are exchanged we assume the enforceability of one promise to establish the enforceability of another. Hence, the secret paradox of the common law. The explanation of no less fundamental a problem than the theory of contract formation turns on question begging. In fact Corbin, the foremost English-speaking scholar of contracts in twentieth century, gave up trying to explain. He concluded:

Is it shocking to put a definition or rule of law in such a naked form as to show that it completely begs the question? It should not be so; for what often seems to be our favorite method of legal argument is to beg the question in complicated and repetitious terms. It should console us for our frailty that a conclusion is not necessarily wrong because it was arrived at by merely assuming or asserting it – by begging the question.

(Corbin 1963: 492)

Consoling, perhaps, but not a recipe for science.

The simple determination of value

I am going to show that the social relation of value, considered as a category of simple determination, can resolve this puzzle.

Why start with value? Briefly, we can ask, retroductively, what is presupposed by the existence of the doctrine of consideration. Plainly the state of affairs presupposed includes promises because consideration is a way of distinguishing between enforceable and unenforceable promises. But as we have seen, promises have not always played the same role in social life. Rome never developed a general theory of promises; in fact the kind of practical and philosophical reflection on promising that so readily engages us today effectively begins with Hobbes and Hume. Legal rules for the general enforcement of promises develop at roughly the same period. That is, the phenomenon of a general obligation to enforce promises emerged only in conjunction with a market economy developed to the point where the general circulation of goods and services in the commodity form was becoming the basis for production. No doubt promising has existed throughout history, but the promises presupposed by the doctrine of consideration are of a historically specific character. The world of promises to which they correspond is one that presupposes private production for market exchange. Understanding consideration, therefore, may plausibly start with the analysis of value.

Marx's text on "The Method of Political Economy," to which I've appealed, proposes to discover simpler and simpler determinations of social phenomena by means of progressively "thinner" abstractions. Importantly, the word "abstraction" is not meant here in the sense that the concept of "steel" is concrete because you can touch the thing it refers to but the concept of "hard" is abstract because taken alone the word brings nothing specific to mind. Instead, abstraction is used as a means to identify different generative mechanisms of social life taken in isolation from others. A natural scientist can often do this by effective experimental design. Comparably, in social life we use abstraction to ignore distracting elements and in order to focus on features that play an ever more significant role in accounting for social phenomena. Ultimately, in the hurly burly of everyday life the phenomena to which basic causal structures like value or capital give rise intersect in a complicated jumble of events. By means of thinner and thinner abstractions we reduce this jumble to fewer and fewer structures of determination. Consider the following from a draft of *Capital*: "... in its totality (wholeness) (or considered completely) (or in *its completeness*) the movement of capital is a unity of the process of production and the process of circulation" (1991 MECW 33: 69). But as we saw in Chapter 4, we are not able to grasp the essential features of capital if we look for them in the undigested and chaotic way the unity of production and circulation first presents itself to us. Instead, we abstract from their unity to consider the thinner abstraction the form of labor takes in the activity of production considered alone. By a multitude of intermediate steps we abstract to capital's simplest determination – the separation of the worker from the means of production. Plainly, as we abstract to a more and more slender complex of social mechanisms we must select more decisive, rather than more frivolous, determinations. If we do, as we move to simpler levels, fewer and fewer forces determining events operate and fewer features of the world present themselves for analysis. We have a better chance of understanding how the structure of powers we study tends to behave. Some of the things abstracted from, of course, are pure distractions. But we abstract also from structures of determination important in their own right, but whose study we reserve for a later stage of analysis. Notice however that there is a limit implicit in the process, one Marx makes explicit in the first pages of the *Grundrisse* "Introduction." We cannot abstract from the historically specific form under which social relations appear to "production in general." "There is no production in general," Marx insists (1986 MECW 28: 23; 1973: 86). Production always appears in a historically specific form. We can abstract to features common to all forms of production – production, for example, is always a relation of the laboring individual to nature and to others – but we can study these features only in their historical specificity.

Nonetheless, the abstraction "production in general" is not to be ignored. Because it identifies features shared by all modes of production it is a way in which we can identify the specificity of the object of study. Thus, production is always the appropriation of nature by labor, and any particular form of social production, any economic category, will always be a form of this. The value relation, for example, is one such form. This fixes its scientific content. But if we know only that the value relation is a form for the appropriation of nature by labor, we know nothing of how the value relation actually appears.

We can generalize these conclusions. Just as we could not understand the simple category of value without specifying its content, we can assume we will require similar precision with other such categories. In other words, we need to specify what any simple category we study is a simple category of. The value relation is a category of production. Consideration is a category of law. There is a difference. Plainly science would be impossible unless we were able to make such distinctions. For example, to the extent we are unable to identify the content of gravity as a scientific category, to that extent our ability to give an account of it is compromised.

So this is the first point: the categories of simple determination on which social explanation turns have a specificity that must be identified. I have specified that content with respect to categories of production – it is the appropriation of nature by labor. I have not done this yet with respect to law.

A second point. In earlier chapters I've emphasized that if we want to give an account of a social kind, it must be a causal account – the structures of social relations that are the object of inquiry are causal ensembles capable of generating the phenomenal forms of social life. In this, it is important to recognize that tracing causal connections between the inner structure of a social thing and the modes of appearance that give expression to it is distinct from studying its historical evolution. Some have suggested that the development of categories in *Capital* must be studied either as a matter of conceptual necessity or else as a question of quasi-causal historical necessity (Arthur 1998). But this is a false dichotomy. The circulation of blood is related causally to the processes of respiration in a multitude of ways. To show these causal relationships is quite different from showing the historical evolution of the heart or lungs in mammals. To show the causal tendencies that drive a mode of production is one thing, to show its historical evolution is quite a different causal inquiry. I do not mean to sever these distinct investigations, of course; I mean only to insist they can be separately studied in order to enrich our understanding of their common articulation.

I've also emphasized that for any stable social kind the causal structures that account for it function homeostatically to account also for its persistence. As Marx wrote to his friend Kugelmann (1988 MECW 43: 67 [July 11, 1868]), every child knows that a nation that stopped working would perish; production must continue or society cannot. Implicit here is a dynamic I have called reproductive necessity – it will be contingent whether a particular form of social life will appear at all, but if it does, then there are particular elements of it which must exist and be reproduced. On the one hand these are the kind constitutive properties that are the target of investigation. But what commands our attention just now is that it is the reproduction of these features that generates the need for corresponding forms of consciousness and forms of law.

In Chapter 2 I presented an analysis of the kind constitutive properties that underlie the value form.[4] For convenience, let me recall basic points of that analysis and begin by using Marx's defense of his approach in *Notes on Wagner* (1989 MECW 24) to do so. Marx summarized the steps in his analysis as follows: (1) He starts with a concrete fact of social life, what he characterizes as the simplest economic fact given by the economy of a commodity-producing society, the product in the commodity form; (2) He analyzes this form and finds it to be at once a use value and an exchange value; (3) Pushing the analysis further, he notices that exchange value is only the phenomenal form of value, that is, it is only a form under which value appears; (4) Thus he is driven to the analysis of value and finds value as such to have its source in a specific social relation of production.

Actually, as I've argued, where and whenever the production of value is found, the value relation can never itself give us a full picture of the form of production within which it is embedded. Because it exists in slave, feudal, capitalist or socialist societies – all characterized by very different modes of joining the direct producer to the means of production – it stands to reason that the value relationship itself will not fully explain these different social forms.

The value relation does, however, tell us two things about the mode of production to which it attaches. First, it tells us that the processes of production joined by the value relation take place in isolation from one another. Each process is autonomous. Second, it tells us that the production process has produced use values that are, at least in part, useful only to others. That is, producers who produce commodities are autonomous from one another but, at the same time, dependent. They are reciprocally bound by the social division of labor.

Summarizing: the causal structure underlying the value relation may be characterized as follows:

a   Every unit of production produces use values independently;
b   Every unit of production produces goods for others rather than for itself.

These two features offer a real definition of value as a social kind.

Given this distribution of the agents of production to nature and to each other, exchange emerges necessarily. Each is driven to market to meet her needs – because she produces goods she does not need, what she needs she must obtain not by production but by exchange. If she doesn't, her capacity to produce ceases. Thus, exchange resolves the contradiction that generates the commodity form of the product of labor, but it resolves it by reproducing it: by providing commodity owners with the things they need to reproduce the conditions of their existence, exchange reproduces the original social relation of autonomy and interdependence that determines the category of value.[5]

Generating law

Now I want to show how legal relations are generated by this causal ensemble. Suppose I make arrangements in London to deliver coal to you in Newcastle for so and so many pounds sterling. I can get paid in London or I can get paid in Newcastle, but in the nature of the case someone has to rely on a promise. Promises are a commitment to act in such and such a way in the future. The problem is that your self-interest tomorrow may not be what it is today. So I deliver the coal and you decide you'd prefer to do without it. You have other coal available to you. Because our relationship is ultimately one of mutual indifference, the trajectories of our self-interest may be different. Yesterday they were coincident, today they're not. So you decide not to keep your promise. But now I am left with my coal and cannot reproduce the conditions of my own existence. Social reproduction under these conditions is not possible.

But if social reproduction is not possible without a solution to this problem, then as a strictly economic relation value is unstable and could only actually exist in a very cramped and narrow form. It follows that in order to support the exchange of performance for a promise or of a promise for a promise, there must be a means of enforcing promises.

The value relation does not, of its own, generate a solution here. Institutions of force used with enough regularity to become official, and to become law, are the result of the division of society into classes. For itself, the commodity relation is unstable because commodity owners relate to one another on terms of mutual indifference. But for the location of commodity owners in a structure of class division we have to look behind the commodity relation to the social form by means of which the direct producer is joined to the means of production. Once labor power is sold as a commodity, as it must if commodity production is to be the universal form of social production, then a division of society into classes is presupposed, but this is a result of *capital*, not the commodity relation as such. In general, in any social formation whether force will be used to develop commodity production depends on the degree to which the interests of the dominant class depend on its extension. But the significant thing for our purposes is narrower than this, namely, that as a particular historical form for the distribution of labor, the value relation, wherever it appears, generates a material need for relations of coercion, that is, law. How legal relations corresponding to it come about historically is a separate theoretical question, but it is worth noting that the emergence of the rules of contract formation in England occurred during the sixteenth century, a time when, as Ellen Meskins Wood (1998) has observed, England was more effectively centralized politically than other European regimes.

Generating consciousness

Relations of consciousness are directly generated by the value form. I do not pretend to be exhaustive here, but at least in part this occurs in the following way. We have seen that under the commodity form exchange is an integral part of the appropriation of nature to use. Now, if I produce independently and self-sufficiently, I can labor without communicating with anyone. But I cannot engage in private exchange without communication. I need to cooperate with others. Social reproduction and the appropriation of nature in this form involve the other as co-participant.

It is Volosinov, in *Marxism and the Philosophy of Language*, who insisted on understanding language, and, more broadly, relations of consciousness, as resulting from generative processes rooted in actual conditions of material existence:

> This is the order that the actual generative process of language follows: *social intercourse is generated* (stemming from the basis); *in it verbal communication and interaction are generated, and in the latter, forms of speech, performance are generated; finally, this generative process is reflected in the change of language forms.*
>
> (1986: 96 [emphasis in original])

Understanding this process must begin with understanding how actual existence determines communication and how consciousness generated by the process reflects actual existence.

Exchange provides a sharply drawn example. If the commodity form is to be reproduced, the autonomy of commodity possessors must be reproduced.

A person cannot obtain what she needs by just taking it – plunder is inconsistent with the reproduction of relations of autonomy. Reproduction of value, therefore, generates relations of consciousness corresponding to the underlying material reality that characterizes the value relation. Non-interference with another person's activities and products forms in that other a consciousness that these belong to her. Further, commodity owners confront the economic fact that the goods they produce are useless to them. This forms a consciousness of the desire to obtain things they need from others. Taken together, the desire to obtain from others and the injunction on interfering with others generate consciousness of the need to appeal to the reasons of others, that is, to induce them and to cooperate with them. Each commodity owner seeks the other as a co-participant.

With regard to the above, perhaps the following point should be spelled out. Of course, history teaches that a world stable enough to exclude plunder requires institutions of common defense, law, etc. Should our analysis then start with those institutions rather than with forms of production? There are two answers to this. First, in this or that circumstance plunder or some other factor may work so that the autonomy of independent producers is not a feature of social life. Fine. Then we study some other category of social determination, not the value relation. Again, we are not for the present concerned with how value came to be. Instead, given that it does exist we want to trace how it works. As for starting with institutions of force, there is a problem. Suppose, borrowing an example suggested by Marx in *Notes on Wagner* (1989 MECW 24: 537), we are on a ship at sea. The ship's stores are available to us. The distribution of these may be changed by force so that in this sense force can be an economic factor. But no matter how we rearrange deck chairs, force itself doesn't produce anything. This takes the actual appropriation of nature by labor. It is for this reason that we start with production as the foundation of social analysis.

Volosinov argued two things: first, we must recognize how actual existence is the basis of the generative processes of communication and consciousness; second, we must recognize how forms of communication and consciousness reflect and refract actual existence. Both of these are apparent in exchange. On the one hand we see how the actual conditions of material existence create a consciousness of belonging ('this thing belongs to me'), a consciousness of the autonomy of the other, and a consciousness of a need to cooperate with the other. At the same time we see how these forms of consciousness not only reflect but also are essential to the reproduction of the conditions of existence that account for them. Without a consciousness of the need to induce cooperation in another, the social reproduction of value could not occur.

A qualification is important. Value is obviously not the only social relation shaping consciousness. Instead, consciousness is like a playing field where many determinations interact. We may say that the dollar of a pauper is worth the same as the dollar of a king, but a king can use force to imprison the pauper. Inevitably a consciousness of equality is at war with a consciousness of subjugation.

In brief compass we have seen how the legal and ideological superstructures are determined (in part) by the value relation. But if these are to be scientific objects in their own right, their content must be specified. We can take a cue from the example of production. Production is the appropriation of nature by labor. Nature is transformed and labor is the agent of transformation. Law often facilitates the transformation of nature by labor, but it is not immediately about this. Instead, law concerns the transformation or appropriation of behavior and the agent of transformation is force. Thus, we may characterize law as the appropriation of behavior by force. This is a rational abstraction of "law in general" comparable to the abstraction we form of "production in general.' But just as in the case of production, law only ever occurs in determined historical forms. So the study of law is the study of specific historically determined forms of legal relations regarding the appropriation of behavior by force.

Marx refers also to legal relations as relations of will (1990: 178 [see note 1]; see also 1985 MECW 20: 27–28 ["Marx to J. B. Schweitzer," January 24, 1865]), and in this sense law necessarily includes the ideological superstructure as a component part of what it is.

The specificity of the ideological superstructure, Volosinov shows, is representation or semiosis, the action of signs. By means of signs, we represent the world for ourselves and thus, he argues, consciousness is formed through our use of signs. On this analysis, ideology concerns the transformation of consciousness and the agent of transformation is semiosis. This is the specificity of the ideological superstructure. But as with the examples of law and production we would err to suppose to study ideology in general. We study the appropriation of consciousness by representation only through the study of specific historically determined social forms of it.

The significance of the study of consciousness for law is as follows: powers may exist unexercised (Bhaskar 1997: 229–238). That is, in consequence of the action of signs, force does not need to be exercised to be causally efficacious. Given a threat, the victim interprets the threat as a sign of what is threatened. The consequence is that persons will act under duress without actual force ever being used. Thus, behavior can be appropriated either by relations of force or by relations of ideological representation. Suppose you want persons on the other side of a boundary. You can physically carry them, place them over the boundary and wall them out, or they can interpret the communicative signs you make and move over the boundary themselves. In either case there is an appropriation of behavior.

The upshot is this. Although a threat can be efficacious without the powers on which it rests being exercised, except in the case of misunderstanding, those powers must exist if the sign is to be effective. That is, without fire there is no smoke and for that reason smoke is a sign of fire. Without the actual ability to exercise force, there is no threat. Therefore, assuming the appropriation of behavior is not going to rest on simple persuasion, then in the last analysis there must be an ability to exercise force. In this sense, law rests upon the exercise of force and it is the exercise of force that makes law law. Legal relations are coercive forms for the appropriation of behavior. That is, their specificity as objects of social science. But behavior can be appropriated either by force being exercised directly or by representation. In either event we can speak of the appropriation of will. Whether I threaten or carry someone across a boundary, in either case I have appropriated his or her will.

In "The Method of Political Economy" Marx says that Hegel is right to begin the philosophy of law with "possession" because this is the subject's simplest legal relation (1986 MECW 28: 39; 1973: 102). Marx begins his own philosophy of law in the introductory paragraph to the chapter on "The Process of Exchange" by saying that the guardians of commodities relate to one another as persons whose will resides in their objects: "[i]n order that these objects may enter into relation with each other as commodities, their guardians must place themselves in relation to one another as persons whose will resides in those objects…" (1990: 178 [I.2]). This is the commodity possessor's simplest legal relation – her relation to an object as one of belonging, as a thing embodying her will. But this simplest legal relation is a contradictory one. The will is a label we attach to the moment of consciousness that mediates between activity and purpose. Will disciplines activity to purpose. But the commodity owner has embodied her activity in a thing that for her has no purpose. As such the guardian of a commodity finds her will impotent to serve her own interests; instead, she needs the cooperation of another to obtain what she needs. This need is expressed in the proposal of a bargain. The other, reciprocally dependent, communicates responsively in return and by accepting the proposal seals their shared commitment. By mutual consent they agree to an exchange. But in the end each looks to exchange only as a means to satisfy her own ends (1986 MECW 28: 175; 1973: 243–244). Thus, although they enter a relation of reciprocal inducement, in the last analysis they are also reciprocally indifferent to one another (1986 MECW 28: 94; 1973: 156).

The contradiction between cooperation and indifference expressed in this relation of wills is in fact the driving force of contract as a form of law; it is resolved by obligating the one to the other. By means of an enforceable exercise of state power each by entering a contract appropriates another's will. By law each has a right to the activity of the other, and this right is given reciprocal legal expression in the other's obligation. Each enters contract voluntarily and in the exercise of autonomy, but finds as a consequence she is bound regardless of her will; clothed with autonomy, each exchangist enters the puzzling world of "voluntary obligation."

From value to bargain

First, an important terminological clarification. By "exchange" I mean the actual transfer of goods or services from one person to another that constitutes the economic content of a contract. By contrast, I want to limit the meaning of "bargain" to the reciprocal communicative performances, usually verbal, that establish the cooperative understanding required for exchange. Where commodities are produced, exchange is essential to complete the appropriation of nature to use and to reproduce the conditions for production in this social form. Bargain is the reciprocal communication that introduces and makes possible exchange.

The essential thing to grasp is that bargain will "reflect and refract," to use the words of Voloshinov (1986: 9), the social relation of value that generates it. As an expression of the value relationship, bargain must reflect the autonomy of commodity owners and their integration within the social division of labor. To explain bargain is to show how it refers to these characteristics of the relationship from which it derives.

First, bargain takes a volitional act by both parties to an exchange. This feature reflects the material autonomy of commodity possessors. Each process of production is isolated from others. To take herself to market, each must engage in an act of communication. But this act not only reflects the autonomy of each producer, it reflects also her willingness to relinquish that autonomy. Because it reflects an intention to embrace exchange, bargain shows her integration in the social division of labor.

Additionally, each party to a bargain forms an intent to obtain what she needs from the other. Recall Adam Smith: give me that which I want and you shall have that which you want. But the obtaining is grounded in a recognition of the autonomy of the other. Neither can obtain what she wants simply by taking it. As a consequence each party to a bargain induces the other by appealing to the other's reasons for action. Because bargain is a relationship of reciprocal inducement, therefore, each party to the bargain constitutes the autonomy of the other. As parties to a bargain act to relinquish autonomy in order to enter exchange, at the same time each meets a counterpart who constitutes her autonomy through the recognition accorded. Just as a king is not a king unless there is a subject who recognizes majesty in his person, neither is a commodity owner autonomous without the recognition accorded by the other.

An essential difference underscores the distinction between the value relation and the bargain it generates. As a category of simple determination, the value relation expresses material relationships with respect to the appropriation of nature. From an economic perspective, autonomy is a material condition characterizing separate productive processes. Dependence on the social division of labor is the same. As a matter of economic fact each process of production is dependent on exchange for the reproduction of its own conditions of existence and reproduction.

By contrast, bargain reflects the value relation as a relationship of consciousness. Free volition, a state of mind, expresses autonomy; the intent to obtain, also a state of mind, expresses dependence on exchange and the social division of labor. An awareness of belonging and of the need to appeal to another's reasons for action are equally forms of consciousness that express the contradictory relations of autonomy and interdependence given material expression in the value relation. In other words the actual processes of existence have turned a material relationship with respect to the appropriation of nature into a corresponding relation of consciousness.

From bargain to legal obligation

Bargain may be characterized as a form of mediation between the economic relation of value and legal obligation. The reciprocal communication established by bargain is a semiotic interaction that lays the foundation for an exercise of coercion. But because invoking the official machinery of coercion is a significant event, not just any communication will do. Legal rules emerge that specify exactly the communicative performance needed to lay the basis for the use of force. A promise will be enforced when the legal rules attaching to bargain are met. A communication between commodity owners becomes enforceable if it meets the rules for an enforceable bargain. If those rules are met, whether a person intends it or not, contractual obligation is triggered.

Consideration in Anglo-American law

The doctrine that expresses the rules required for enforceable bargains in Anglo-American law is called consideration. The doctrine gives expression to a set of somewhat formal and technical rules that correspond to the requirements of bargain explained above. When these rules are met, the bargain is enforceable.

A characteristic statement of the rule of consideration is given in Section 71 of the American *Restatement (Second) of Contracts* (American Law Institute 1981):

1   To constitute consideration, a performance or a return promise must be bargained for.
2   A performance or return promise is bargained for if it is sought by the promisor in exchange for his promise and is given by the promisee in exchange for that promise.

These rules define the behaviors that must occur to establish the foundation of an enforceable promise.

To begin, consideration requires an act of commitment from the promisee. Before legal obligation will be triggered, there must be a manifestation by both participants to an exchange that each has surrendered her autonomy and embraced exchange; otherwise, neither incurs contractual obligation. Unless there is a consensual embrace of exchange, obligation does not attach.

An act of commitment is the form in which the willingness to surrender autonomy and embrace exchange is manifested. It is important to see that any act involves at once both the expression of autonomy and its surrender. This goes to the nature of action. For a person to have acted means, in its most rudimentary sense, that she acted materially in some way to transform nature. This is an exercise of autonomy. At the same time something different could have been done than was in fact done. This shows a surrender of autonomy. That is, if a person lacks the ability to choose among alternatives, then whatever occurs is something that happens to her, not something that person did. Just as motion can be characterized as being and not being in the same place at the same time, action can be characterized as the simultaneous exercise and surrender of autonomy.

Importantly, this analysis extends to acts of commitment. Even though a commitment may never be fulfilled, the making of it is nonetheless an act. It involves sign formation – a material process – and choice among alternatives. One need not have manifested a commitment at all.

Because of the nature of action, then, an act of commitment can serve to establish the autonomy of the actor and her willingness to relinquish autonomy. But if an act of commitment is to trigger contractual obligation its content must reflect the value relation as well: its content must reflect autonomy and the social division of labor. The commitment must show a willingness to surrender autonomy, to embrace exchange, and not only to recognize, but also to constitute and reproduce the autonomy of the other.

In the language of the *Restatement*, this occurs when a commitment is bargained for. Recognizing the autonomy of the other, the promisor makes a commitment to exchange by making an offer: if you do this thing X (repair my garage), then I will do that thing Y (pay $3500). The content of the reciprocal commitment given by the promisee must be responsive to that which the promisor seeks – the promisee promises to do X (promises to repair the garage). Further, the commitment of the promisee must be given for the purpose of obtaining that which the promisor offers – the promisee promises to do X because she wants Y (the $3500). That is, a commitment is bargained for when:

1   the promisor seeks a performance or return promise in exchange for his promise, and;
2   the performance or return promise is given by the promisee in exchange for that promise.

The commitment given by the promisee is on the one hand responsive to what the promisor seeks from exchange and on the other hand given in order that the promisee may obtain by means of exchange. In sum: both promisor and promisee commit to surrender that which each has in order to obtain that which the other offers (Farnsworth 1999: 52–54). In this way, the content of each promise reflects both autonomy and the social division of labor. Together the promisor and promisee enter a relation of reciprocal inducement (Holmes 2009: 265).

Numerous technical rules spell out these requirements in detail. Taken as a whole they reflect the surrender of autonomy, the intent to obtain and the reproduction of autonomy. Here are some examples.

1   *Each party must commit to surrender autonomy.* The promisor does this by making the proposal sought to be enforced; the other does this by agreeing to give that which is sought by the promisor. In either case, the commitment given must be real and not illusory. A promise is illusory if it does not actually commit to anything because it leaves the one promising a way out: "I'll

mow the lawn Saturday if I feel like it," is an example. "I won't ask for my money until I want it," is another. Where an illusory promise is given, the bargain is not enforceable (*Restatement [Second] of Contracts*, section 77; Farnsworth 1999: 75). For the same reason – the lack of a commitment to surrender autonomy – a bargain cannot be enforced if a party promises something conditioned on an event that cannot occur (*Restatement*, section 76).

2   *Each party must manifest an intent to obtain.* If the promisor does not seek to obtain anything by means of her promise, then the promise she gave is not enforceable. For example, where a grandfather promised his granddaughter a large sum of money – a sum large enough to enable her to quit her job – and she did quit her job, this was not consideration because he did not seek this action from her as a condition of his promise. Under traditional rules his promise was not enforceable; he had no intent to obtain anything by means of exchange.[6]

Promises of gift fail for this reason – the promisor seeks nothing in return (compare Farnsworth 1999: 50–52). This is true even where the promisor says something like "I'll give you this painting if you agree to accept," and the other says, "I accept." The person who says "I accept" has manifested commitment, but the promisor does not seek to obtain anything in exchange (Williston 1936: v. 1, 380). If she did – for example, she wanted the other to take the painting in order to keep an heirloom in the family – then the acceptance would be consideration and would bind the promise.

Much ink has been spilled as to why the rules of consideration should distinguish between gifts and bargains. Promises of gifts, for example, often involve large monetary sums and seem of greater apparent personal and social consequence than everyday bargains readily enforced (Wessman 1996: 826). Yet, under traditional principles gift promises are not enforced. Confusion here, however, is not difficult to resolve: bargains are essential to reproduce the value form of the product of labor; gifts are not. Arguments offered to show the gift-bargain distinction analytically incoherent never consider the matter in light of the social reproduction of value.

Because there can be no intent to obtain, neither does so-called "past consideration" bind a promise. Suppose I save your life by pushing you out of the path of a car and in return you promise me a stipend for the rest of my life. On traditional contract principles your promise is unenforceable because what I did was not something you sought to obtain by means of your promise (Farnsworth 1999: 54). (I should emphasize that in this and other cases where promises cannot be enforced because they do not satisfy the rules of consideration, they may be enforced on other grounds. But this does not defeat the underlying argument any more than an airplane's flight disproves the law of gravity. These other instances must be separately explained.)

As a last example, and again according to traditional contract principles, if you find a dog or capture a criminal without knowledge of the reward previously offered for the discovery or capture, you cannot enforce the promise made for the purpose of producing such results. You did not act in order to obtain something by means of exchange (Farnsworth 1999: 67).

3   *Each party must induce the other.* Each party to a bargain must reproduce the autonomy of the other by appealing to his or her reasons for action. For example, on traditional contract principles if someone makes an offer to another by mail and the other at the same time makes an identical offer but these cross in the mail, then there is no enforceable bargain because neither has been induced by the proposal of the other (Farnsworth 1999: 67). Their conduct does not manifest reciprocal inducement.

Consideration and social reproduction

The key to the puzzle consideration has posed for over a century is to be found in the role bargain plays in social reproduction. Because commodity owners need each other in order to reproduce the conditions of their existence, they are driven to exchange. Because they are driven to exchange, they embrace commitment. But because in the last analysis they are indifferent to one another, force is necessary to bind their relationship. In consequence, bargain mediates between contractual obligation and the underlying economic relation in which commodity owners find themselves. The formal rules of bargain lay the predicate for the exercise of force necessary to sustain relationships of reciprocal commitment.

Traditional explanations of contract attempt to explain the use of force either as a means to honor the decision of the promisor in committing herself (Raz 1977) – a strange honoring now that she has changed her mind – or as a means to protect a promisee who has relied (MacCormick 1972) – though unless promises are known to be enforceable, a promisee has no expectations that justify reliance. In other words, the justification for coercively enforcing simple contractual obligation has never been well explained by looking to either one party or the other. It can be explained only in terms quite independent of either person – as a necessary means to secure the distribution of the product of social labor in the value form. Without a relationship of force to secure the commitments of bargain, the reproduction of the product of labor in the commodity form could not be sustained.

Once we view the problem from the perspective of social reproduction, the so-called "secret paradox of the common law" dissolves. Promises are enforced when there has been a reciprocal commitment to relinquish autonomy and embrace exchange. Instead of hiding a logical circle, bargains reveal a cycle of social reproduction. Promises give evidence of reciprocal commitment. This was all that was needed – a sign of commitment that by its content reflected and signaled the reproduction of the social relation of value.

Why the paradox then? We need to explore the ways in which commodity fetishism generates confusion. Marx argues that in a society where the product of labor takes the commodity form, laboring producers attribute to labor's products powers that in fact are a consequence of their own social relations with one another. Specifically, social relations distributing aggregate social labor to need appear in the "fantastic form" of the natural attributes of things, and these properties then seem to determine the quantities in which things are exchanged. (1990: 165 [I.1.4]).

Briefly, this occurs in the following way. Commodity production is social production, but it is private in form. Compare the self-sufficient production of isolated producers. Where producers are self-sufficient, the question of distributing social labor does not arise. But because each commodity producer produces for others as part of the social division of labor, there must be a form for the distribution of labor to need. This form is value, and social labor takes the form of the value of the product of labor. Yet because production is private in form, producers of commodities are not conscious of the social character of their production until they enter exchange. Exchange appears to them as their original social relation (and all contractarian social theories follow in tow). They don't see that their social relation as producers, their reciprocal dependence on one another as producers, appears under the form of the proportion in which one product will exchange for another. As a result the social character of their labor is transformed for them into a natural quality of their products. This is the sense in which social relations are between things. According to the unreflected explanations of the vulgar economist, if a bushel of wheat will exchange for two bushels of corn, it is not because wheat has absorbed a greater amount of aggregate social labor. Since the labor devoted to producing the wheat is private in form it does not appear as social labor at all. Instead this argument assumes there must be something in the natural properties of the wheat that make it twice as valuable.

Now one enters exchange in order to exchange the products of labor as values. But here is the problem: if value is reduced to a natural property of things, promises, since they are not things, are without value. How can valueless bare commitment count as something given in exchange? And if it does not, how can it lay the predicate for legal obligation?

Yet if, as I have argued, consideration is a legal relation established by reciprocal commitment reflecting a surrender of autonomy and an embrace of exchange, then traditional doctrine treating consideration as a thing given in exchange was in effect treating "a definite social relation between men ... [in] the fantastic form of a relation between things" (1990: 165 [I.1.4]). Instead of puzzling over how a promise could be a thing given in exchange, the real puzzle was how a performance given in exchange, say the delivery of a book, could constitute a commitment to exchange when it was the very thing sought.

Here we need Volosinov. A sign is a material thing that reflects or refers to some other thing (1986: 10) (the thing referred to need *not* be material). Smoke is a sign of fire. Like a promise that is given material expression in words, actual performance given in exchange can also reflect a commitment to relinquish autonomy and to embrace exchange. Performance can be a sign of commitment just as effectively as written or spoken words of promise. For example, any delivery of a thing includes at least the commitment that it is what it purports to be.

If performance can serve as a sign of commitment as readily as promise itself, then the puzzle of consideration disappears. There is no paradox or confusion in saying a commitment of an identifiable kind engages legal obligation. This is manifestly so where the commitment identified is indispensable to social reproduction. Instead it becomes clear that the puzzle stems from a failure to consider the way contract formation functions in the reproduction of value.

Final remarks

A first point: consideration shows connections of necessity between the legal relation of force to which the doctrine refers and the social reproduction of value. As I explained above, the cooperation established by exchange is inherently unstable. While it reflects a coincidence of interests, it does not reflect a shared common interest. And because the perception of self interest by different persons in different circumstances necessarily changes, a coincidence of interest achieved today may no longer hold tomorrow. Thus, if social intercourse is to be based on the autonomy of private producers; if these producers are to produce for private exchange as part of the social division of labor; and if the distribution of the products of social labor in this form is to be reliably reproduced; then coercive mechanisms for ensuring the performance of obligation are inevitable. Requirements of the doctrine of consideration mandate specific forms of communicative performance required to trigger the use of these mechanisms. Such performances are generated by the underlying structure of the value relation; reciprocally, they function causally to secure the reproduction of social intercourse in the commodity form.

A second point is necessary to avoid confusion. Just as we use the word "law" in science to refer both to the causal mechanism that generates effects in the world and to the way scientists formulate the behavior of that mechanism in words (Bhaskar 1978: 251), so, too, in law we use "rule" ambiguously to refer both to the underlying ensemble of legal relations that is causally efficacious and the verbal rules that give expression to those relations. Speaking precisely, however, the rules of consideration are verbal forms referring to a particular structure of underlying relations of force.

Judicial or executive orders directing the exercise of force, or other individual behaviors shaped by law, cannot be reduced to verbal forms. These behaviors distribute goods and determine conduct. As such, they are the forms of appearance under which legal relations such as those expressed by the doctrine of consideration appear. And just as a product may sell in the market at a price that diverges from its value, so too, a judicial order may only approximately correspond to the underlying legal relation applicable to a given circumstance – confronted always with a confusing welter of social forces, a judge may fail to grasp what is decisive in a particular case and ideology may cause her to misperceive. For the same reasons, official statements of rules, or scholarly expressions of them, may express such underlying relations well or badly. Thus, knowing the rule of consideration in any jurisdiction does not enable anyone to predict the outcome of any actual instance litigating application of the rule. Too many other factors are in play, including, famously, what the judge had for breakfast. Nonetheless, results which correspond to social reproduction have a staying power those that do not lack, and understanding a rule like consideration does make it possible to explain why the category has persisted and been expressed in pretty much the same form for 400 years.

A third point: the necessary relation established between the value relation, bargain and consideration, corresponds to the hierarchy of base and superstructure in this sense: the social relations within which nature is appropriated by labor generate corresponding relations of consciousness and force. Nonetheless, production never appears in a commodity-producing society except as production defined by law and determined by consciousness. If we look to the events of the day we see only a one dimensional mixture of law, economics and ideology. It is only by abstracting to the processes of the appropriation of nature by labor, the appropriation of behavior by force, and the appropriation of consciousness by representation that we can discern simpler determinations in the generative processes of social life. But if we want to present any such relation as it actually exists historically, then it must be shown to be embedded in a complex of determinations. It is for this reason that we can say at once that the base determines the superstructure and at the same time that the base cannot exist without presupposing the superstructure.

A final point: if the argument just given explains a legal category not previously given coherent theoretical explanation, this in itself constitutes independent evidence for the scientific correctness of Marx's analysis of value.

6 What ought to be done

Marxism and normativity

In the last chapter, I argued that a fundamental relation of Anglo-American law was generated by, and reciprocally worked to reproduce, value as a social kind. In this chapter, I suggest how the implications of this approach might be generalized. My thought is that Marx's analysis of capital as a social kind can offer fertile ground for understanding the normative structures of morality as well as law and can also ground normative standards to guide the transition to socialism. The idea that there can be a normative Marxism at all is sharply contested, as I will show. I hope to suggest that social kind analysis offers a way to respond to some of the objections that have been raised to the place of normative considerations in Marxism.

In his notes on Hegel's *Logic* Lenin proposed an aphorism: Marxists didn't understand Marx, none of them, because they hadn't "thoroughly studied and understood the *whole*" of Hegel's book (1963 LCW 38: 180 [emphasis in original]). I don't think it's necessary to read Aristotle to build on foundations Marx left for social science, but I do think it's worth reading Marx closely enough to grasp Aristotelian themes developed in his thought. The Marxism-morality debate offers an example. The familiar understanding that basic forms of justice and morality correspond to relations of production undoubtedly captures Marx's view and provides also a basis for clarifying important dimensions of social life. But context is necessary here. For Aristotle there was not only the actuality of things as they existed but also a kind of incomplete actuality – incomplete in the sense that things in a process of fulfillment express potential carried by them. Thus, a house is one kind of actuality, but the building of the house is the actuality of the process of building (1984: 343 [Physics Bk III 201^b]): "the actuality of the buildable as buildable is the process of building." Because Marx approaches social life in this way, when we approach social kinds, we have to consider them in a double perspective – on the one hand the social theorist will want to explain the causal mechanisms that account for how social kinds like capital persist; on the other hand she will also want to grasp the potential such things carry for transformation. This means grasping not only the present actuality of a social kind but grasping also the actuality of which it is an incomplete example. For Aristotle when there is a completed house, the buildable is no longer there, but for Marx social life is like a house that is never finished – there is a never ending process of remaking and remodeling going on as *homo sapiens* work out the social conditions of their flourishing in nature.

In *Capital*, Marx argued that capitalism had prepared the way for a society where the free and full development of each individual is a ruling principle (1990: 739 [I.24.3]). A plain meaning here is that capital is a social kind in transition. Thus, to say that justice corresponds to the relations of production of a mode of production like capital can never be taken statically; it must always be understood both from the perspective of the kind as it exists and also from the perspective of a trajectory of real possibility opened up by the dynamic of transformation in play. While we will notice that the norms of justice and morality provide reasons for individuals to conduct themselves in ways that reproduce existing social arrangements, at the same time we will want to grasp how others might view these critically and pursue reasons that instead look to a revolutionary transformation of what exists.

A parable of normativity: the challenge of moral naturalism

Before pursuing these themes further, let me introduce a parable I find unusually instructive. In *Balance*, a remarkable academy award winning short film,[1] a half dozen figures, identical in every way except for identifying numbers, are located on a horizontal slab suspended in empty space. How they position themselves and how they move matter – a false step and the slab tips: if one moves forward, another must move back; if one moves to the right, another must move to the left, and so on. Incongruously, they throw fish lines into the emptiness they inhabit and one pulls up what turns out to be a quite large – and heavy – music box. This catches their attention; it offers relief from an apparent boredom as empty as the space engulfing them. By turns, each holds an ear to the box to hear. Then they soundlessly quarrel over who gets to hear. One by one we see a figure pushed off the slab into nothingness until finally there is left only one last person. Now this figure has exclusive possession of the music box. But it is perched at the edge of the slab on the side opposite and the tall single remaining silhouette can't move to approach it or move to draw the box closer without tipping the slab catastrophically such that emptiness would make its implacable final claim.

I take it the parable here runs to something more than the parental injunction to, say, "Share your toys."

What we observe are two things: (1) the conditions of life that figures on the slab confront, and (2) the individual actions each takes with and among others. The nature of the slab and the so to speak natural laws it obeys establish conditions of life for those located there. These aren't negotiable. Any social arrangements individuals on the slab form will be constrained by the way the slab behaves. Think mountains or deserts or earthquakes or global warming; think physical, chemical or other natural laws. On the other hand individuals in their actions are free; each individual acts purposefully for reasons he or she chooses.

From individual actions, patterns of social practice emerge as an accommodation these individuals together make to the conditions of life in which they find themselves. Each learns that when another takes a step someone, or all, must compensate by adjusting position. That is, social practices come to mediate between the two things we initially observe – actions individuals choose for themselves and the conditions given by the slab.

In stark metaphor, then, with only these simple elements, the film offers a way to understand how normative structures of social life emerge to guide our thinking about what we ought to do. This happens as follows: while inhabitants of the slab act freely in their own interest, yet, in the interests of common survival, they must come to understand that the social practices in which they engage – when one moves to the left another must move to the right – are not simply repeated patterns. They come to realize that the patterns of behavior which they engage with others are what *ought* to happen. The social practices we observe are not merely factual patterns of behavior, but are also practices that carry normative force: if you want to survive on the slab then you ought to move to the left when someone else moves to the right. Indeed any stable pattern of social reproduction will tend to generate normative standards corresponding to what must be done if persons are to persist in the same way. Just as historically specific social arrangements mediate between the actions of individuals and nature to assure the stable reproduction of the conditions of existence those individuals engage, so too normative structures emerge to mediate between the actions of individuals and the social practices required by the distinctive character of their accommodation with nature. People act for reasons. Normative standards function to give reasons for action and also to provide reasons for criticizing the conduct of others. On the one hand we praise or approve conduct that corresponds to what ought to be done; on the other hand we disapprove or blame where conduct threatens the balance required for social life. By guiding conduct according to established norms, individuals in society act to reproduce those social practices required by the social accommodation they have made with nature. We've already seen an example of how this works in law: where a person's conduct does not correspond to what the reproduction of the commodity form of production requires – say you breach a promise – then legal enforcement ensures compliance. The normative structures of law, I suggested, were relations of force that functioned to appropriate behavior. Normative structures of morality function similarly by means of praise or blame.

There is no need to claim this as an exhaustive account. Social life involves more than the appropriation of nature, of course. But we can start there; it is the foundation of our survival as a species. Just as the social relations engaged in the appropriation of nature play a decisive role in any community's life, so too normative relations that correspond to these play a major role in shaping how individuals behave. Moral and legal reasons emerge to mediate between individual behaviors and the normative structures individuals in community require. In sum, the social practices individuals in community make in their accommodation with nature provide in very substantial part normativity's material ground.

Two points bear emphasis. First, if emergent norms correspond to and reproduce existing patterns of social practice, then, as those patterns change, the normative structures corresponding to them will have to change as well. Patterns of
social practice, in turn, will tend to change whenever the conditions of life to
which they correspond, natural or social, alter in a decisive way. To keep pace,
then, we would expect our attention to law and morality to be unceasingly *critical*. Second, if we are naturalists, then such criticism can only come from a place
that is materially grounded. The philosopher Bernard Williams (1996: 218)
thought he saw room in some such space for what he called an "unanswerable
objection" to traditional historical materialism: "that if we have doubts about the
'latest stage', then it cannot be that stage, but rather our doubts, that constitute the
latest stage." In other words, despite pretense to the contrary, materialists also
must appeal to the kind of non-naturalist rational argument traditionally dear to
philosophers because if our doubts about the latest stage of development cannot
be grounded in that stage, then they cannot find any other material ground at all.

I'll leave Williams' unanswerables unanswered for a minute for we can make
use of another parable, this one in the form of an anecdote from the *Nicomachean
Ethics*. Aristotle was impressed enough with reports of Milo the wrestler's
strength to have immortalized him in his book on ethics, and there is much to
learn from his account. In order to show the kind of excellence in activity we
identify with virtue, Aristotle explained that virtue is a mean between excess and
deficiency. Here, again, I don't think he had in mind the kind of admonition you
would get from a parent enjoining "everything in moderation;" instead Aristotle
thought to invoke the accuracy with which an archer hits the target – she neither
undershoots or overshoots but aims in a way that is exactly right. He offers Milo
as an example to clarify the point. If we know ten pounds of food is too much
for Milo and two pounds is too little, it does not follow that we can locate the
mean by arithmetic reasoning. Instead, we must find "a median relative to us"
(Aristotle 1962: 42 [Book II at 1106^{b}7.)

A whole series of reflections is possible here. First, the quantity of food Milo
needs will not depend on what he thinks or even on what his trainer thinks, but
instead on Milo's physiology independent of what anyone thinks. It will depend
also on the task or circumstance at hand. A runner might undertake one kind of
training at an altitude of 2000 or 3000 meters and another at sea level. Suppose
Milo overweight or suppose he wants to train for a different sport. Then we adjust
to compensate. In each case we appeal to Milo's nature and the adaptations he
must make to build the body to which, as a matter of real possibility, he aspires.
That is, we have, for Milo, a standard by which our judgments can be objectively
correct or incorrect. Notice also that our judgments, though objective, are not at all
judgments we apply to every athlete or every wrestler at all times and in all places.
There can be no suggestion here that an objective account must be a universal one.
A beginning wrestler, Aristotle suggests, would likely get less food.

Thus, if Milo is instructive to us it is because we found in his physiology, his
physical nature, objective standards by which to measure what he must do. Can
the same insight apply to social life? Philosophy has looked always for eternal

principles of morality and justice, and with these Marx, for one, had no patience. If we can use the analogy, then what is morally correct for members of a community will depend objectively on the nature of that community. To discover this we will want to track those specific patterns of social life its practices most characteristically reproduce. To the extent we are persuaded that different cultures are essentially different in nature, then morality will be relative to each. But remember that Milo could be overweight and what he then needs may differ from what, given his nature in that condition, he would choose. Presumably the same would be true of social life. Thus the slave culture that Aristotle awkwardly justified, for example, will reflect an accommodation to that society's conditions of life; its morality would reflect its nature as a slave society. But just as Milo, overweight, confronts a different demand than his then nature drives him to desire, we can make a comparable critique of slave society. We could say, yes, slavery could be justified: relative to its nature, the normative standards it established worked to reproduce the social arrangements of slavery. But we would go on to notice that it is the nature of a slave society itself that is in question. Early in his career Milo might have established a regime he would now reject as wrong, or even hurtful. That is, just as the standards we apply to Milo depend on what it is really possible for him to become as a person, an athlete and a wrestler, so too societies in their nature destructive of human flourishing can be held to standards materially grounded in our experience of what is really possible in social life and the insight experience has made possible. The practice of female genital mutilation, for example, may be essential to the stable reproduction of social life in a particular community, but then it is the nature of that community that we challenge. Or we can take the example of global poverty as it exists today. Either the horrific magnitude of global poverty – each day something like ten times the number of children die of starvation or hunger-related disease as people were killed in the criminal attack of September 11, 2001 – contradicts the very nature of world society as it now exists, and is immoral for that reason, or, given that another world is demonstrably possible, world society in its nature is immoral.

So here is the take-home lesson. Prying objectivity loose from the universal claims of abstract principle depends on figuring out how we may discover a society's nature: we must locate its fundamental social forms, the forms of a society's regularly reproduced social relations and practices. We must find the social relations to which its forms of normativity correspond. That is, there are no sources of normativity to be discovered without specifying the nature of the patterns of social life under investigation. That is the task of contemporary social kind analysis.

Back to Bernard Williams' unanswerable objection, then. I have said that if a society is to keep pace with its conditions of life and with those social changes necessary to respond to them, then our approach to normativity must be unceasingly *critical*. But if we are to be naturalists, such criticism will not come from doubt grounded in transcendent truths or rational argument or intuitions; criticism can only come from a place that is materially grounded in the adaptations we make or have made or can make to our conditions of life. The normative is derivative. Even as important as doubt is in pushing forward inquiry, for a materialist it can only be grounded in inferences we draw from or surprises we find in experience. Doubts do not fall from the sky, but emerge instead from our attention to contradiction in an actual present or from real possibilities foreshadowed by that present. As such, doubt and criticism will find material ground, and the unanswerable disappears. That is, we may offer a critique (1) of past social forms from our experience of the present (say, capitalism's critique of slavery), or (2) of the present from the past (say, social forms reflecting the respect many indigenous peoples shared for the environment as a critique of more contemporary market driven forms), or (3) of one cultural form in the present from another also now present (say, forms of women's oppression from perspectives of gender equality), or (4) of practices characteristic of one class by another in any society divided by hostile class antagonisms (say, sentiments of solidarity that arise out of the habit of working together to accomplish a common task as against motivations driven by competitive self-seeking), or (5) of the present from a really possible future (say, of democratic forms of industrial production as a critique of established hierarchical forms).

Notice that the social knowing implied by this kind of normative inquiry is the sort of thing that much philosophy, intent on distinguishing itself from science, has always avoided. Ethical inquiry has often been a search for moral principles that are transcendent, ahistorical and universal in their application. This was straightforwardly the case when the sources of normativity could be found in the commands of a Supreme Being located outside history. But it remains the case in the search for ethical principles that command universal human agreement because they appeal to every rational being. Even moral realist tendencies seem often to carve out some such terrain in so far as the social analysis required to undergird normative analysis is ignored. There is the assertion that moral facts are part of the stuff of the universe there to be discovered by moral science. But it is less clear where we are to locate these facts and the tools we are to use to uncover them. Often, recourse is made to our biology or our psychology, and indisputably features of these are decisive to our understanding of the kind of creatures we are. But even normative standards that have a biological or psychological source normally get mediated by historically specific social relations.[2] Marx's observation about the chemistry of exchange value is instructive: exchange value is a *social relation* and as a result "So far no chemist has ever discovered exchange-value either in a pearl or in a diamond" (1990: 177 [I.1.4]). So too, no biologist has yet found a gene for fairness, or promise keeping, though probably not for lack of grant proposals. No doubt there are moral facts but if we are to ground them, these must be tracked to the normative structures of social life that correspond to and function to reproduce the social patterns within which the production of human life occurs. Thus, without a fully scientific analysis of social life, the moral naturalist who appeals, for example, to the immorality of slavery as a transhistorical moral fact of universal human import, simply expresses the conviction that right and wrong are *really* right and *really* wrong and she is sure of it the way she is sure the earth goes around the sun. But this approaches a secular religion: we can no longer find moral qualities in a Divine Being, so we locate them in our nature and do so with a kind of faith that appeals to the progress of science – one day science will offer us a clearer picture. But what seems on its face an appropriate and judicious humility before the progress of investigation can turn out, on closer inspection, to be a way in which attention to those social relations undergirding the normative structures that shape our lives may be avoided.

To summarize: like any creature, we survive by maintaining a homeostatic relationship to our environment. The environment confronts us with conditions, some of which can be changed, some of which can't. Though we confront our environment as individuals, this is as social individuals so that our engagement with nature is always part of a social metabolism; that is, it is always mediated by historically specific social arrangements – as Marx wrote, "[a]ll production is the appropriation of nature by the individual within and by means of a definite form of society" (1986 MECW: 25; 1973: 87). What we observe, Marx suggests, are individuals appropriating nature with and among others, but the activity in which they engage is always mediated by definite social arrangements. Moreover, because those arrangements are reproduced, normative structures emerge from which reasons to motivate action are derived; people become aware of what they ought to do. In consequence, the individual behaviors required for the persistence of social life in the same form take place. We look to social kind analysis to specify the patterns of social life to which the normative corresponds and which constitute its material ground.

Normative Marxism and social kind analysis

All this is readily compatible with Marxism, of course; as we saw in the last chapter, a rule of Anglo-American law may be shown to emerge from and correspond to commodity-producing labor or value as a social kind. Surprisingly, though, that there should be a fit between the normative standards of any society and the forces and relations of production that correspond to it has been used as a basis to argue that no society can be considered unjust except on its own terms; that is, it would make no sense to impose any perspective on it not intrinsic to it. From this it is supposed to follow that Marx did not consider capitalism unjust. Allen Wood, for example, understands Marx to say that capital's appropriation of the entire surplus product without equivalent is in no way immoral because this, the appropriation of surplus value, just is what capitalism most essentially is. As a consequence, he argues that Marx saw "no fundamental moral defects in capitalism" (1981b: 123; see also 1981a) and, whatever social justice activists might think, "unqualifiedly reject[ed] moral standards as acceptable vehicles of social criticism" (1981b: 128; see also 1991).

Others have raised similar objections.[3] Steven Lukes pointed to a paradox: on the one hand Marx and Engels often scorned appeals to morality as unhelpful, if not reactionary, yet they themselves did not hesitate to excoriate those they thought deserving of moral condemnation. "Utter baseness," for example, characterized Malthus (Marx 1987 MECW 31: 347].[4] In something of the same vein, Andrew Collier (1981) developed the view that there are no specifically socialist values and that when Marxists disagree it is not about values, but about explanatory hypotheses. More: incorporating socialist values threatened to dangerously derail the socialist project; therefore scientific socialism must seek to eliminate evaluative support. Steven Lukes asks not only whether the resources of traditional Marxism offer any basis for an adequate theory of morality, but, in particular, "can a Marxist believe in human rights?" (1985: 66)

Now, as we've seen, morality provides reasons for action, and in addressing these issues it is important to hold in view what is fundamentally at stake: properly presented the issue is not whether Marxists can do without values, or whether Marx as a humanist used values to underwrite his analysis (Wilde 1998), but whether we locate the source of values to which appeal might be made in the normative structures of social life, structures which themselves correspond to the social kinds that most decisively characterize a given society. Marx's objection to morality was not that people would act according to normative demands, but instead that the morality to which philosophers loved to appeal claimed to provide an independent basis to qualify materialist analysis. Lukes wants to cling to some such terrain. But recall Bernard Williams' argument that the phenomena of doubt offered unanswerable objections to historical materialism. Marx rejected the idea that ethical values were to be found in some heavenly stockpile of rational moral principles for the same reason he would have rejected Williams' claim. The issue is not whether we should doubt and neither is it whether we should be guided by normative principles in the conduct of our lives; instead the issue is whether those doubts and values can claim material ground. Implicitly, Marx's argument is that they do whether we're conscious of it or not, and, if we are not, then pretty surely the source of those that influence us will be found in the ideologies that pervasively surround us. Further, if we're to locate a material source to ground analysis we must shift attention from norms and principles considered for themselves, say equality or fairness, to the normative structures that correspond to the social kinds we investigate. On that basis we can grasp in a common sense way the lesson of Marx's 1857 Preface to the *Contribution to the Critique of Political Economy:* social structures of law, morality and ideology form loci of struggle where people learn to advance or resist the revolutionary transformation of social arrangements that exist (1987 MECW 29: 263).

Perhaps, another parable would help.[5] Suppose a bunch of us are on a height overlooking a plain. We notice a soldier running and one of us is amazed: "Look at that soldier run! I don't think I've ever seen anyone run faster than that! My goodness! And look at the grace with which he carries his pack!" Then another might respond, "But do you notice; he's running away from the battle." Our appraisal of the soldier's virtues would not stop with his athleticism.

Consider it this way. I've presented capital as a social kind. We can add a dimension. Like any mode of production, capital is an ecological kind. If before it seemed nature could be taken for granted so that we could consider a form of production without concern for the social metabolism established with nature, this is surely no longer true. Fred Magdoff and John Bellamy Foster (2010) quote Fidel Castro: "Until very recently, the discussion [on the future of world society] revolved around the kind of society we would have. Today the discussion centers on whether human society will survive." In *Knowledge and Its Place In Nature*, Hilary Kornblith (2002: 65) makes the case that for many creatures, including humans, knowledge is an ecological kind insofar as it was selected for because of the contribution it makes to constructing a fit between an organism and its environment. The concept of a fit is an important one and can be applied to those social arrangements that define a mode of production. But in borrowing the concept, I want to insist, I make no appeal to natural selection. Nature does not notice that one mode of production rather than another confers greater reproductive success and then select it because of this differential.[6] I make the more limited point that the Darwinian revolution does call our attention to the importance of an organism's relation to its environment and remind also that where the fit is poor the organism's survival is at risk.[7] Given the enormous plasticity of human nature and the rich variety of the earth's environments, the social accommodations that have been made between human groups and their conditions of life have been many. Nonetheless, within this spectrum of possibilities we can refer, as Marx did, to higher and lower forms, picking out by such comparison the degree to which different social forms facilitate well or less well the flourishing of human individuals. Thus in *Capital I* Marx refers to the capitalist as:

> fanatically intent on the valorization of value; consequently he ruthlessly forces the human race to produce for production's sake. In this way he spurs on the development of society's productive forces, and the creation of those material conditions of production which alone can form the real basis of a higher form of society, a society in which the full and free development of every individual forms the ruling principle.
>
> (1990: 739 [I.24.3])

In this perspective the basis for cross cultural or cross system comparisons does not depend on ideal principles, but is materially grounded in a comparative evaluation of the extent to which particular social forms provide a real basis for full and free human development. In effect, if justice is the first virtue of social institutions (Rawls 1971: 3) this can no longer be evaluated without taking into account how competing social arrangements determine the metabolic exchange between society and nature and in so doing contribute to individual flourishing. *Within* any mode of production actions are just to the extent they correspond to the essential features of that mode of production. Marx wrote (1991: 460 [III.21], "[t]he justice of transactions between agents of production consists in the fact that these transactions arise from the relations of production as their natural consequence."[8] But a *mode of production* will be just to the extent that its social arrangements actualize the potential for a goodness of fit between human individuals and nature.

So how does capital do on this score?

It is not hard to conclude it is running from the battle. Capitalism, though fanatically good at what it does – the valorization of value – ranks poorly as an ecological kind. While we can take advantage of the spur capital has given to the development of the productive forces, what was once a spur is now a grotesque barrier threatening our survival. Not only has the majority of humanity been ruthlessly impoverished in body and spirit, but this has been for production's sake, for the sake of an increase in the quantity of labor amassed in things. Capital's ability to foul the environment, once so readily overlooked, destroys now the preconditions for life. The unimaginable barbarity of war without end to which it is systemically addicted leaves flesh burned to bone and radioactive dust carelessly spread to deform – indeed, capital has produced war as an assault of things against people controlled on a video screen far from the turmoil of battle, but with consequences that are actually, not virtually, horrific. "Man is the highest being for man," Marx writes, and insists on what is surely a moral imperative: that we "overthrow all relations in which man is a debased, enslaved, forsaken, despicable being" (1975 MECW 3: 182 ["Contribution to the Critique of Hegel's Philosophy of Law"]). In his preparatory drafts for the projected fourth volume of *Capital* he adds that for the ideologies generated by capitalism, "workers themselves appear as that which they are in capitalist production – mere means of production, not an end in themselves and not an aim of production" (1989 MECW 32: 175). Any organism fashions a goodness of fit between itself and its environment, but this is something capital neglects, not through omission, but because it realizes a different dynamic. Because it is driven to augment without limit the value of things, capital's social arrangements fail to realize the sustainable flourishing of human individuals in nature. That is, it is unjust in precisely what it most essentially is.

There is also this. What capitalism most essentially is, the structure on which the drive to augment value without limit rests, is the separation of the laboring individual from the conditions of labor. This relationship, imposed by force, is, Marx argues, an injustice (1994 MECW 34: 246, quoted above in the Conclusion to Chapter 3). "[W]hat is life, but activity,' he asks (1975 MECW 3: 275 [*Economic and Philosophic Manuscripts* of 1844]). But if it is activity where we have our being, then a social structure that takes as its default option the separation of the living person from the conditions of activity is unjust in what it most essentially is. To be unemployed contradicts what it is to be human.

Other themes have been developed in the Marxism and morality debate that deserve brief attention. It is important to appreciate that capital as a social kind is a composite of contradictions and these cannot be ignored in evaluative appraisals of it. On its own terms, justice and injustice contend. To appreciate this it is important to shift attention, as I've suggested, from talk about moral principles to an inquiry into material structures of normativity. We have seen how legal relations must be characterized as relations of force; this is their substance. They are not simply some shadow double of the relations of production;

they are differently constituted. The exercise of coercion makes them what they are. Where relations of production appropriate nature by labor, legal relations appropriate behavior by force.

Morality is a social kind like law but grounded in relations of approval and disapproval rather than force. In his more recent book, *Moral Relativism*, Lukes (2008: 56) offers a good catalogue of the kind of things that materially ground social relations of morality: "norm violations typically elicit punitive emotions like disgust, anger, and outrage and the behavior that expresses them, such as criticism, condemnation, avoidance, and exclusion, even the infliction of physical harm, and, not least, ostracism and gossip." There is no precedent in history, Marxist or other, where the upheaval of revolution has unrolled without judgments of admiration or condemnation and actions corresponding to these. To say that such passions must be informed by science is one thing; to say that there is no place for them in the struggle is quite another.[9]

Thus, any society that rests on hostile class antagonisms will hold in uneasy suspension competing normative standards. On the one hand there will be those that function to reproduce the means by which one class subjugates another, and dominant institutions of justice and morality will sanction these. But where there is oppression, there is resistance. While slavery in the ancient world could be considered just on its own terms, nonetheless, there was resistance to it and admiration for this.[10] With regard to capitalism Marx wrote the following passage that I originally quoted in the conclusion to Chapter 3 (1990: 990 [*Results*]):

> What we are confronted by here is the *alienation [Entfremdung]* of man from his own labour. To that extent the worker stands on a higher plane than the capitalist from the outset, since the latter has his roots in the process of alienation and finds absolute satisfaction in it whereas right from the start the worker is a victim who confronts it as a rebel and experiences it as a process of enslavement.

Of course, spontaneous resistance to injustice may go no further than a theme and variation on machine smashing and our moral admiration may only signal the need for revolutionary change while actually doing little to transform the relations of force and legitimacy that make oppression possible. Still, Marx also suggested that moral understanding could make a difference: in the conclusion to Chapter 3 I also quoted his judgment that labor's consciousness of the injustice of its coerced separation from the means of labor was for capitalism a "Knell to its Doom;" in this it was like "the consciousness of the slave that he cannot be *the property of another*," an awareness that reduced slavery "to an artificial lingering existence" (1994 MECW 34: 246).[11]

There's another set of contradictions within the framework of capitalist institutions that suffered Marx's critique. From *The Poverty of Philosophy* in 1847 (1976 MECW 6) to "Notes on Wagner" (1989 MECW 24), written the year he died, Marx made clear that petty bourgeois notions of fairness or justice or equality had their source in the social relations of capital and that only bourgeois idealists would rely on normative structures belonging to capital for the transformation of capital. Yet the normative contradictions specific to capitalism are too significant to be ignored. As I've shown earlier, capital absorbs into itself value as a social kind and contradictions emerge between ideologies generated, on the one hand, by the separation of productive units from one another and those generated, on the other, by the separation of laboring producers from their conditions of production. Thus the material circumstances which give rise to separate producers who produce independently for commodity exchange give rise at the same time to exchangists who confront one another freely on a footing of mutual recognition and equality. Thus, the social relation of separation that characterizes the commodity form accounts not only for private property, but also for our ideas of liberty and equality.[12]

But these ideas are contradicted by normative standards that have their source in the capital relation – the employment relation is one where mutual recognition leads to subjugation; where, in exchange for a wage, capital appropriates the right to another's labor, including a surplus appropriated without equivalent. As a means to reform capitalism, principles of morality derivative of the commodity form are problematic because they become pervasive only where the product of labor everywhere takes the commodity form and that only occurs where commodities are produced by capital. Still, considered for itself, commodity exchange does not presuppose subjugation and patterns of behavior that derive from it, though compromised by the self-regarding separations that constrain them, may nonetheless carry seeds of roughly straightforward horizontal relations among individuals. As a result commodity exchange relations infect capitalism, and on its own terms, with a contradiction between justice and injustice that is not trivial. Global market integration extends exchange transactions to every inch of the globe and those transactions generate the sense of equality and autonomy associated with the commodity form. But capital also extends staggering disparities of poverty and wealth that contradict these sentiments to every corner of the globe. Philosophers suggest torturing babies qualifies as a moral universal because it fills all persons with revulsion, but I have already pointed out that about 25,000 children die of starvation and hunger related causes every day. It is hard to see how this is not a form of torture to which one can remain insensitive only because it is on a scale too difficult to comprehend and is otherwise variously kept at sufficient distance.[13] Calling attention to global inequalities, arguing for the injustice of the division between the global north and the global south, calling for climate reparations – these need not be idealist appeals to the reform of capitalism on its own terms; they can be the means to signal social dysfunction and to witness, in anguish, that too many people anywhere, and almost half of humanity everywhere, live lives debased, degraded, enslaved, and forsaken by a social system intoxicated with barbarism.

There's still another contradiction that bears on the injustice of capitalism. The present contains within it not only normative ideals generated by capitalism itself, but normative principles grounded in the real possibility of an alternative future. In the *German Ideology* Marx and Engels wrote:

> Communism is for us not a *state of affairs* which is to be established, an *ideal* to which reality [will] have to adjust itself. We call communism the *real* movement which abolishes the present state of things. The conditions of this movement result from the now existing premise.
>
> (1975 MECW 5: 49)

The appeal here is to conditions of actual possibility, not abstract or speculative illusion. The justice of capitalism can be critiqued in terms of post-capitalist normative standards that may be built from already existing conditions of movement in the present. Wood thought any appeal to post-capitalist standards of justice would fail on two counts: first, it would essentially amount to an appeal to some ideal or speculative state of affairs of the sort Marx and Engels here criticize; second, even if somehow it were not that, it would still appeal to standards foreign to capitalism such that it would make no sense to measure capitalism by them. But the first objection fails insofar as normative critique can be materially grounded in conditions of real possibility disclosed by the conditions of actual movement present in what exists. And the second objection also fails because, as we've seen, no mode of production stands alone apart from the trajectory of human social development, and, most especially not capitalism, which, like a wayward soldier outrageously betrays its vocation as an ecological kind.

There is a broader aspect to the challenge to any effort to use post-capitalist standards to judge capitalism that might be thought to compromise all normative Marxism. To critique capitalist economic structures as unjust, no matter how we might locate the source of injustice, would be an instance of the so-called "naturalist fallacy" – the idea that a normative conclusion, an "ought," can't be derived from an actual or really possible state of affairs, an "is." But I think this is a mistake. We can be less squeamish about "what ought to be done" if we reclaim a materialist philosophy of labor to ground such concerns – as Marx's analysis of the labor process shows, any conscious plan to transform the world through labor must provide standards to discipline activity: if you want to fasten a screw, you ought to turn the screwdriver clockwise.[14] While it has become dogma of much modern social philosophy that the so-called naturalist fallacy has driven a wedge between the "is" and the "ought," in fact the error targeted might more appropriately be called *the transcendental fallacy*. Hume (1888: 469 [Book III, Part 1, §1]) argued that if an evaluative conclusion was to be drawn from any given state of affairs, it had to be observed and explained. That, he insisted, he'd never seen done. Instead, though an "ought,"might readily be connected with an "is," no derivation was ever provided. And thus, over the years, for supposed lack of any possible connection to be observed, the dictum has hardened into an article of faith. But Alasdair MacIntyre (2007) has shown that Hume's conclusion is only justified if you completely abandon the idea that there can be things with powers, as Hume, of course did – but as Marx most certainly did not. If a thing has power, then evaluative conclusions will follow from how well the actualization of a thing's potential fulfills its function: if someone is a sea captain, we have normative expectations without which we could not properly refer to the person as a sea captain at all.

The argument applies as well to social kinds. Social forms such as capital are entities in process reproduced by the behaviors of individuals. Recall, once again, the short film *Balance*: individuals in community become aware that the patterns of behavior that make the reproduction of social life in the same form possible are what "ought" to occur. Now with this much Marx would agree – there is nothing in any "is" statement that will entail any ahistorical or eternal principles. That's what I mean by "transcendental fallacy;" moral principles good for all times and all places may have their source in God or eternal truth or universal reason, but they have no source in any historically actual state of affairs. Even Hume could look around and insist that, from the perspective of empiricism, there was nothing in the world of events to entail eternal values. In other words, what I've called the transcendental fallacy is perfectly serviceable weapon for the defense of material-ism. But it is no use against any proper naturalism, though where the appeal to nat-uralism is incongruously coupled, as it still can be, with a search for universally valid moral principles, the transcendental fallacy remains relevant. We can recall Boyd's argument that "natural kinds that have unchanging definitions in terms of intrinsic necessary and sufficient conditions that are the subjects of eternal, ahis-torical, and exceptionless laws are an unrepresentative minority of natural kinds (perhaps even a minority of zero)" (1999a: 169). There is no reason to think social kinds such as the normative structures of justice or morality would be different from the natural kinds of the physical world in this respect, and there is no natural-ist fallacy in appreciating the way patterns of behavior that secure social reproduc-tion do entail in a material way what ought to be done if social life is to continue.

From separation to association: the example of liberty of expression

But ought a Marxist believe in human rights? Traditionally, Marxists have held as a matter of real possibility that with the dissolution of hostile class antago-nisms law and the state will wither away. Insofar as rights depend on law, then, the withering away of the state means, in the words of Marx's *Critique of the Gotha Programme* (1989 MECW 24: 87), crossing the narrow horizon of bour-geois right to a more expansive actualization of human freedom unconstrained by institutions of coercion. E. P. Thompson is a thousand times right to insist that we have seen enough of tyranny's barbarism to value the distinction between the rule of law and the arbitrary exercise of extra legal power (1975: 265) – we've seen enough too of democracy's export of barbarism and extra-legal terror.[15] But I think Thompson is not right to call the rule of law an "unqualified human good" (1975: 266). The separation of the state from civil society is a theme I have not discussed, but it is one powerfully developed by Marx as a political complement to the double separation of capital as a social kind. Transforming the separations that characterize capital cannot occur without overcoming the distinctive separations that characterize forms of state and law. Emancipation of the sort sketched by Marx is not some amalgam of the freedom of social individuals mixed together with mechanisms of coercion separated from them to ensure their freedom does not go too far. That's a bourgeois notion responsive to bourgeois fears. No human good characterized as "unqualified" will find its material ground in institutions of coercion. We can aspire to more.

But there is also this: any such aspiration must know overcoming capital's separations cannot be other than a very long historical process during which basic democratic liberties need defending and extending, nor will law's withering be accomplished by decree (a contradiction in terms if there ever was one!). That is, because the narrow horizons that characterize bourgeois rights have their source in the material separations of capitalism, they will not disappear until the separations to which they give expression actually, not merely formally, disappear. What this means can be captured by an address Marx gave to the International Workingmens Association in 1865 – he sought to clarify the problem economists called "primitive accumulation" – how the resources that gave capitalism its original impetus had been gathered:

> We should find this so-called *Original Accumulation* means nothing but a series of historical processes, resulting in the *Decomposition of the Original Union* existing between the Labouring Man and his Instruments of Labour.... The *Separation* between the Man of Labour and the Instruments of Labour once established, such a state of things will maintain itself and reproduce itself upon a constantly increasing scale, until a new and fundamental revolution in the mode of production should again overturn it, and restore the original union in a new historical form.
>
> (1985 MECW 20: 129 ["Value, Price and Profit"])

In very broad outline, this maps the task for the transition to socialism: as the *Communist Manifesto* (1976 MECW 6: 504) urged, the struggle for socialism is prepared by winning the battle of democracy. In turn, winning the battle of democracy means overcoming capital's separations.

We can miss the world historic nature of the task presented. In concluding Chapter 3, I recalled the conclusion Marx drew from his analysis of pre-capitalist economic formations – that the conditions of production were presupposed to the worker as belonging to him the way my fingers belong to my hand; nature was the laborer's inorganic body. Restoring the original bond means restoring that, but now as a belonging grasped in association with others for which democratic forms must be found. That is, restoring the laboring producer to the conditions of production is not a matter of returning the weaver to her loom or the shoemaker to his last. Capitalism has transformed the means of production so that they are social and as a result forms of association must be found whereby working people learn to manage and carry out the sustainable appropriation of nature to need democratically. It would be silly to think the bourgeoisie has prepared such forms of labor for us, or prepared us for them, or that they will fall from the sky. Nor is the democratic task presented exhausted by entering a ballot box every several years or other representative forms. These are a start; they are levers with which to begin. But the new historic form put on the agenda is an active and self-determined collaboration of persons who work without existing divisions between mental and manual labor. Through common struggle all who work will learn to manage and operate production with each other and learn also to provide together for the distribution of their common product as their common wealth.

It is against this vision of democratic association that we can situate the significance of Marx's characterization of bourgeois right as a "narrow horizon." From the beginning, Marx objected to what might be called the "metes and bounds" liberties that characterized bourgeois society. In "On the Jewish Question" he was concerned with the way the source and content of the liberties of "egoistic man" were defined as if by two fields set off by boundary posts:

> Liberty, therefore, is the right to do everything that harms no one else. The limits within which anyone can act *without harming* someone else are defined by law, just as the boundary between two fields is determined by a boundary post. It is a question of the liberty of an individual as an isolated monad.
>
> (1975 MECW 3: 162)

He framed this critique against the suggestion of a more expansive view:

> But the right of man to liberty is based *not on the association of man with man*, but on the separation of man from man. It is the right of this separation, the right of the restricted individual withdrawn into himself.
>
> (1975 MECW 3: 162–163 [emphasis added])

We can move beyond the narrow horizon of bourgeois right insofar as we move beyond rights born of separation to social relations grounded in association.

The lesson is decisive. Both in his book on Marx and in his more recent discussion of moral relativism, Lukes argues that because individuals have different conceptions of the good, rights are indispensable. Follow out the implication – we must have institutions of coercion because individuals have different conceptions of the good. Does that make sense?[16] For Marxist social theory this misses the issue – of course we have different conceptions of the good; we would not be individuals at all if we were not different individuals; instead we interrogate the material social relations that ground those differences. We cannot evaluate the consequences that follow from individuals pursuing different conceptions of the good without considering the material context from which those conceptions emerge. If they refer ultimately to the institutions of private property, then, yes, we need boundary posts to mark division. If we own and produce in common, then we must find democratic forms to resolve our differences. The fundamental issue is not whether we have different conceptions of the good life but whether those conceptions are materially grounded in social structures of separation or of association.

The right to liberty of expression offers a telling example. If working people are to find democratic forms that make association for production possible and effective, then this will be the result of communicating readily, fully, and transparently with one another over the fullest range of considerations that concern the sustainable appropriation of nature to need. Limits to communication which stem from private property, on the one hand, and alienation in the workplace on the other, stand as manifestations of separation, imperfections to be remade in construction of fully socialist relations of production. If capital's separations are to be overcome by winning the battle of democracy, the way we organize relations of expression and communication will be key.

Consider the historical trajectory. Where social reproduction is based on the separation of independent producers who produce for private exchange, then each in isolation is fully responsible for the production and reproduction of their own existence. Each is self-responsible. It follows that each individual must be free to collect all opinion, consider all errors and be able to judge for herself of all that concerns her own need, including also how she may, as part of the social division of labor, produce to meet the needs of others. She must have full access to the acquisitions of science and technology and be able to determine for herself what to believe or not to believe. Also, because mutual assent seems here the volitional foundation of social life, each person is entitled to know all that might be relevant to the affairs of the community and how the community's actions might affect her. In consequence, each must have full access to all information essential for decision making, both public and private, and the full right to express herself concerning these. Thus, the right of the autonomous individual to know, to form opinions and to speak her mind is the most persistent theme of bourgeois speech theory

From Milton's *Areopagetica* to today, the story told by these achievements represents an inspiring and hard fought advance over the suppression of expression that characterized capital's prehistory. Still, these liberties are also constrained. The separations that undergird the commodity form presuppose an autonomous individual who is not only self-responsible, but also and necessarily self-regarding. Thus, while production for market provokes a tremendous stimulus to the development of communicative freedoms, competition forces each to take advantage where she can, and expressive activity is no exception. Misrepresentation, false advertising, defamation and the like are legal wrongs, and trade secrets, patents and copyright get legal protection. With the emergence of intellectual property ideas get commodified and restrictions on the digital spread of information resemble nothing so much as, once again, a new enclosure movement fencing off ideas from ready public access and use.

There are also constraints that bourgeois theories of communication freedom rarely, if ever, consider. Because production is mediated by exchange value, ultimately each producer finds she is unable to communicate directly with others regarding the distribution of social labor to need – that is, where production is governed by the law of value, social labor cannot be directly compared. A producer has no way to communicate the quantity and character of social labor embodied in her products except by means of things. One commodity can give expression to the value of another, and by means of the money commodity, each takes a price. But it is as if each producer were a mute Geppetto who could communicate only through a block of wood his craft made eloquent. Free and direct communication about how labor should be allocated to satisfy social need remains out of reach.

Mute also with respect to all that concerns production stand the vast majority who have sold their labor power for a wage. Marcuse (1941) noticed how a worker comes alive only withdrawn from the productive life of the community in what is all too often meaningless recreation. What goes on in the factory where she is employed is not her affair; ownership belongs to another. In fact, those like Lukes concerned with the specter of rights disappeared need not speculate about a future without the bourgeoisie; they can look over a factory wall. The disappearance of rights for working humanity starts right now right here: in every place of employment ownership trumps expression. A worker may have a privilege to speak, but in all that concerns the material production of life, she has an asymmetrical and legally enforceable duty to listen. She must carry out the commands of the one to whom her labor belongs.

Discourse about rights often proceeds as if there were no alternative to the metes and bounds liberties we exercise. But surely we know from experience that it is possible to think of the other not as a boundary to our enjoyment but as a rich increase of what, as an isolated atom, any could be. "[A]ctivity in direct association with others ... has become an organ for *expressing* my own *life*," Marx wrote of the transition to communism, "a mode of appropriating *human* life." Rather than the separated individual's withdrawn satisfaction at having things, Marx emphasized the expansive social activity of doing, that is, doing so that the expression of my individuality is realized in and through my engagement with others. I become rich in listening to music, developing an eye for beauty, designing, building, experimenting, and I become rich in doing these with others; I become rich in dialogue with them, in working with them to produce and reproduce a human space in nature. "The dealer in minerals," Marx wrote, "sees only the commercial value but not the beauty and the specific character of the mineral; he has no mineralogical sense" (1975 MECW 3: 302 [*Economic and Philosophic Manuscripts of 1844*]). We can extrapolate. The captain of industry sees only a quantity of labor expended – he has no *human* sense of effort or craft.

Without doubt, the concept of individual self-fulfillment rooted in commodity private property represents an enormous advance over relations of personal dependence which characterized most pre-capitalist social forms. But the task is now to create "free individuality, based on the universal development of individuals and on their subordination of their communal, social productivity as their social wealth" (1973: 158; 1986 MECW 28: 95). In taking on this task we can hardly ignore the first glimpse of lessons hammered out in the socialist revolutions and liberation struggles of the twentieth century. Lenin, for example, emphasized that if production is not to depend on an externally imposed discipline, then there must inevitably be an upsurge of communication among producers. Only in this way can they work out for themselves the unity of will and action required for cooperation in large scale social production. Thus, he insisted, although the "mania for meetings" is ridiculed by bourgeois detractors of the revolution:

Without the discussions at public meetings, the mass of the oppressed could never have changed from discipline forced upon them by the exploiters to conscious, voluntary discipline. The airing of questions at public meetings is the genuine democracy of the working people, their way of unbending their backs, their awakening to new life.

(1965 LCW 27: 270 ["On the Immediate Tasks of the Soviet Government"])

What we find here is not only a vast extension of the right to communicate, but the seed of something even more important – communication is more than a soap box right; it is a social need. Calling the public meeting democracy of people the equivalent of "liturgical acts," Fanon (1968: 195) captured how special this must be:

The masses should be able to meet together, discuss, propose, and receive directions. The citizens should be able to speak, to express themselves, and to put forward new ideas. The branch meeting and the committee meeting are liturgical acts. They are privileged occasions given to a human being to listen and speak. At each meeting, the brain increases its means of participation and the eye discovers a landscape more and more in keeping with human dignity.

"Without comparatively complete knowledge, it is impossible to do revolutionary work well," Mao Zedong wrote (1971: 216 ["Rectify the Party's Style of Work"]), but each of us starts from a place of limits defined by our interests as individuals, by the interests of our group, by our region, and so on; any individual's view is partial and incomplete. Communication is a social need both because we cannot gain relatively complete knowledge without the special contribution the perspective of each can make and also because we need everyone mobilized around common tasks. No individual can rely solely on her own experience or on what seems to concern her exclusively. That's a metes and bounds idea. The task to which our knowing must correspond is the full and free development of each as a condition for the full and free development of all. Also, individual confusion or error can blunt enthusiasm for action; just as we need the special insight of all, we need the gathered effort of all. In other words, it is not even enough to extend the right to speak – people must be mobilized to speak. "Take the ideas of the masses," Mao explained,

(scattered and unsystematic ideas) and concentrate them through study (turn them into concentrated and systematic ideas), then go to the masses and propagate and explain these ideas until the masses embrace them as their own, hold fast to them and translate them into action, and test the correctness of these ideas in such action.

(1971: 290 ["Concerning Methods of Leadership"])

The leadership anyone can provide depends first on listening, then on synthesizing or summing up, then on explaining so all are ready aggressively to test their plans and understanding in action. This does not come without engaging views that differ and conflict. Thus there must be a struggle for unity, the kind of thing summed up in the democratic method of "starting from a desire for unity, distinguishing between right and wrong through criticism or struggle, and arriving at a new unity on a new basis" (1971: 439 ["On the Correct Handling of Contradictions Among the People"]).

Several points can be drawn out here. First, the struggle engaged is for unity among persons with whom you disagree – "as to those who see eye to eye with you, you are already united with them" (1977: 318 [SW5: "Strengthen Party Unity and Carry Forward Party Traditions"]). Second, it is the confrontation of ideas in the perspective of action to be taken that brings clarity and it is this that lays the basis for a new and stronger unity. Thus, no one should fear the correction of error – truth is not some personal property I possess and mark off for my own with boundary posts. Error encumbers advance, and "conditions must be created to help those who erred;" it is "passive just to observe" as if you were separated off from another's mistakes (1977: 302 [SW5: "On the Ten Major Relationships"]). Nor, equally, can you suppose others disinterested in your own:

> [i]f we have shortcomings, we are not afraid to have them pointed out and criticized, because we serve the people. Anyone, no matter who, may point out our shortcomings. If he is right, we will correct them. If what he proposes will benefit the people, we will act upon it.
>
> (1971: 310 ["Serve the People"])

We may decide another is wrong, but in fact ourselves err. Still, the contradiction here is not fundamentally different from what any of us does with conflict in our own chest – we're pretty sure or less sure, and we deliberate to the fullest extent we can. But when push comes to shove we act. Our knowledge is always approximate and fallible. What we can be certain of is that when we're wrong, we need to revise, and we will be glad for the criticisms that helped expose error.

The tension raised by the perception of error in another raises an additional point: in the end, respect for the personal autonomy of an individual will trump concern for error or conviction of mistake. This doesn't mean the other gets a veto where action is required, but it does mean that what must be done cannot be at the expense of our common respect for the ground of another's very capacity to act. In truth, respect has never been a bourgeois virtue. It gets lip service, but it has never been grounded in our common humanity.[17] As with other classes who have ruled in history, respect in bourgeois society has always depended on power and status. That is, respect is a terrain of struggle also. Are there socialist virtues? Start with this. Start with the democratization of respect. Start with our engaged attention to one another. We're after the full and free development of each as a condition to the full and free development of all, and the way marked out to get there is from each according to ability and to each according to need.

The so-to-speak moving part here is attention to each individual's ability to fulfill her own capacity to contribute.[18] And the source of that depends ultimately on her autonomy and integrity as a person. It's this that prevents my conviction of error from overriding my respect for another's autonomy. It follows that differences must be settled by full discussion where there is space for criticism and an openness to self-criticism with confidence that the confrontation of views will contribute to fuller knowledge and enhance the understanding, enthusiasm, and capability of everyone for common tasks.

Here's another story; this time not a parable but a small example from current history – a lesson drawn from the example of participatory budgeting as it was initially developed in Porto Alegre, Brazil (Menser 2005; see also Menser and Robinson 2008). When the Workers Party came to power some years ago, the new municipal administration found itself in somewhat fragile political circumstance and needed to secure its credibility by delivering real change. It did this in part by drawing poor sections of the community into the budget process and giving them a measure of control over a limited percentage of municipal expenditures. But this was not done in a purely formal way by allocating a set amount to each neighborhood. Instead, there was a democratic determination of the most pressing needs and a priority was placed on addressing the needs of those least well served under the circumstances then confronted. Moreover, so that residents could actually participate on the relevant committees there were training sessions to develop the skills necessary to understand the budget process – accounting, for example – and also skills in public speaking so folks could learn to intervene effectively in meetings. What is important here both with respect to defending and extending the right to communicate is recognition of the need to mobilize others so the views of all are known, and the recognition also that training is essential. If persons are to manage their affairs in common not only must there be a mania for meetings, there must be a mania for training. Here the lessons of Kimberle Crenshaw's (1989) attention to intersectionality as a political principle cannot be overemphasized – listen first to those who have historically been silenced by the burden of multiple oppressions.

The most essential constitutive uses of coercion in bourgeois society ensure the exploitation of labor by capital on the one hand and the separation of commodity producers on the other, and it is a measure of human advance that socialism looks past these to forms of expression and communication. For the coercive reproduction of the separation of self-seeking competitive enterprise, socialism proposes associated production coordinated and spurred by open and fraternal competition based on full publicity for the benefit of all; for the coercive subordination of working people to the alien will of a capitalist who functions as a mere personification of the dictatorship of things, socialism substitutes the conscious unity of will and action that results from the "turbulent, surging, overflowing its banks," public meeting democracy of working people (Lenin LCW 27: 271 ["On the Immediate Tasks of the Soviet Government"]).

In the *Critique of the Gotha Programme* Marx writes:

Right by its very nature can consist only in the application of an equal standard; but unequal individuals (and they would not be different individuals if they were not unequal) are measurable only by an equal standard in so far as they are brought under an equal point of view...

In a higher phase of communist society, after the enslaving subordination of the individual to the division of labor, and therewith the antithesis between mental and physical labor has vanished; after labour has become not only a means of life, but life's prime want, after the productive forces have also increased with the all round development of the individual, and all the springs of co-operative wealth flow more abundantly – only then can the narrow horizon of bourgeois right be crossed in its entirety and society inscribe on its banners: From each according to his ability, to each according to his needs.

(1989 MECW 24: 87)

The passage is familiar but for the pervasive assumptions bourgeois ideology makes about communism, it is easy to miss the radical implications here. Communism is supposed reduce everything to sameness, but it is the law of value that does that. For all its celebration of individuality, it's actually boundaries, not individuals, that the bourgeoisie celebrates. Rights are limited because rooted in and functioning to reproduce our separations. They're problematic not only because they rest on coercion but because they compel a homogenization of difference. Yet reaching beyond has nothing to do with surrendering what's been accomplished in their defense. Instead it means constructing a circumstance where social relations actually encourage the uniquely particular contribution any can make to the richness of social life – this at least is what it means for the full and free development of each individual to be society's ruling principle.

The horizon offered by the commodity formed individual is too narrow. The rights guarantees that have shaped her have secured important advance over precapitalist economic forms. These will persist as long as the material foundation that gives rise to them persists. But we can also point beyond to social arrangements where we learn to express ourselves freely and fully, surely, but think first of our attentive engagement with one another, listening as a normative imperative, and listen to mobilize for common action. We *need* the views of each other and this entails our respect for individual difference as we engage them, a respect grounded in the way we depend materially on the contribution each can make uniquely to our common tasks. It is essential to insist upon and defend personal liberty as a barrier to the reactionary brutalities of a decaying social form. At the same time if I view others not through the prism of limits that ratify our separation, but instead as persons gathered with me on a productively substantial ground where I am able to develop and realize fully my own capacities and powers because I am richly associated with them, and they with me, then together we not only defend, but extend those basic democratic liberties that now exist, and extend also, beyond them, the unexplored dimensions of our emancipation as fully individual social beings.

7 Conclusion

Winning the battle of democracy

> [T]he first step in the revolution by the working class is to raise the proletariat to the position of ruling class, to win the battle of democracy.
>
> *The Communist Manifesto.*[1]

"Overthrow capitalism and replace it with something nice!"

I recall a few years ago seeing a news photo of a May Day rally in London with a large banner spread boldly across the line of march proclaiming "Overthrow Capitalism And Replace It With Something Nice." Humor loves raw nerves. Sure that decaying capitalism destroys our humanity, many seem to have lost confidence, nonetheless, about what to put in its place. It's common to think the empty space identified only needs filling with a suitable model. If someone would spell out the specific features we could expect of a socialist future, people would get it.

But Marx was no fan of blueprints. How popular forces in motion determined to hammer out the shape of events to come he was willing to leave to people in struggle, and he studied the Paris Commune to draw lessons. On the other hand, in lieu of blueprints he was not timid about outlining tasks: seizing on capital's most fundamental characteristic – the separation of the laboring producer from the instruments of production – he argued that overthrowing capitalism meant restoring the unity originally presupposed in a new historical form. This passage from "Value, Price and Profit" (1984 MECW 20: 129) is not well enough known. Here it is again:

> We should find this so-called *Original Accumulation* means nothing but a series of historical processes, resulting in the *Decomposition of the Original Union* existing between the Labouring Man and his Instruments of Labour.... The *Separation* between the Man of Labour and the Instruments of Labour once established, such a state of things will maintain itself and reproduce itself upon a constantly increasing scale, until a new and fundamental revolution in the mode of production should again overturn it, and restore the original union in a new historical form.

I'd like to suggest the value of devoting attention to developing a method consistent with this insight. In the foregoing essays I've offered a definition of capital as rooted in two separations – (1) the separation of laboring producers from the conditions of production and (2) the separation of individuals or units or of production from one another. The intersection of these two separations, I've argued, is constitutive of capital and shapes the world in which we live – it forms the causal structure that must persist and be reproduced if capital and capitalism are to be maintained. It follows that the task of transforming capital means finding forms of action that overcome materially capital's double separation – it is as if you were to take the molecular structure of a carbon compound and modify it to create a different chemical substance. But notice – and this is the really crucial point – because capitalism has socialized the productive forces, overcoming capital's separations can only be accomplished by discovering democratic forms of association adequate to the task. As I previously suggested, restoring the original unity of the laboring producer to the means of production is not a matter of restoring the weaver to her loom or the shoemaker to his last. Instead the separations distinctively characterizing capitalism will be overcome by forging a unity between laboring producers and the means of production in such a way that associated workers acting in common themselves manage the sustainable appropriation of nature to need. The transition to socialism just is winning the battle of democracy!

There are some virtues to this approach. For one thing, we can start from where we are. Any action, now, anywhere, can be tested by the extent to which it furthers democratic forms that foster association rather than separation, and this both in an objective sense and in a subjective sense. That is, on the one hand measures that block or erode the consequences of capital's monopoly of the objective conditions of production are on the agenda; on the other hand, so too are measures that develop forms of consciousness and organization that build the conditions of popular unity. Existing social relations must be transformed so that access to the material elements of a decent life are never out of reach regardless of sickness, loss of work or other disability. Additionally, forms of organization and forms of consciousness must overcome the separation of laboring individuals from one another. Traditional union organizing, for example, works to overcome separation insofar as it substitutes collective organization and a collectively bargained agreement for a separate contract of employment that connects each worker individually to her employer. Thus, solidarity is a moral essential. Unions themselves, of course, can contribute to reinforcing capital's separations by ratifying divisions among workers or by insulating an enterprise or an industry from the broader community of which it is a part. Comparably, forms of worker self-management can bring the means of production under worker control, and this is an irrepressible demand, making a powerful contribution to raising the consciousness and competence of workers to manage production on their own. But this too, unless seen as a step in a more comprehensive process of transformation, can leave capital's separations stubbornly in place; on the one hand worker-owned enterprises can remain separated from one another and from their communities; on the other the representative forms through which control is exercised can remain merely formal so that passivity prevails and the subordination of workers to the machines and the management that personifies them is left intact.

Once again on separation and association

In *The Civil War in France*, drawing on the experience of the Paris Commune, Marx suggested that the communism that members of the ruling class found "impossible" – that the means of production might be turned into "mere instruments of free and associated labor" – was instead quite possible: "if united cooperative societies are to regulate national production upon a common plan, thus taking it under their own control … what else, gentlemen, would it be but Communism, 'possible' Communism?" (1986 MECW 22: 335). More broadly in *Capital* and the preparatory manuscripts for it he spoke often of associated workers taking production under their common control.

But in an influential book, *The Economics of Feasible Socialism*, Alec Nove (1991) challenges Marx's idea of associated workers taking control of production. He finds the idea, and very much of the legacy of Marx regarding the transition to socialism, to be utopian and romantic. Moreover, given the complexities of modern production, those who follow Marx by supposing that the participative democracy of associated workers can take production under common control are not only utopian and romantic but often irresponsible as well.

But there is a profound difference between Marx's "possible communism" and Alec Nove's idea of "feasible socialism." Sir Henry Maine is remembered for the claim that all progressive societies trace a movement from status to contract. Marx, virtually an exact contemporary (though without the title), more searchingly traced a trajectory from the separations that materially ground contract to association. In fact, Nove's project seems feasible to him, and to many others, precisely because he doesn't call into question either of capital's defining separations.

Importantly, Nove does not interrogate the distinction I introduced in the last chapter between, on the one hand, an underlying separation best given expression by a celebration of the material boundaries that surround an individual and, on the other, an association of persons engaged in a common project of social life. He appeals to the limits we confront in the complexities of modern economic life without questioning the underlying material relations that give shape to those complexities. That is, given that he leaves the assumptions of separation in place, his conclusion follows: the market and the centralized plan define the parameters of economic life; there is no third way. In that case the trick is to find a mix that is more humane than either market or plan pursued to the extreme. Still, since, as he acknowledges (1991: 262–263), the socialism he has in view may not differ much from capitalism with a human face, and since there is no evidence at all that this latter thing is feasible, there is reason to pause. Nor is there any reason to lament a missing path if a reproduction of capital's separations continues to define the narrow horizon available to us. It's Nove's assumptions that pose the problem; give those up and what opens is not a third way but a different world – another world is possible!

Here is Nove's claim (1991: 48):

> To recapitulate: in a complex industrial economy the interrelation between its parts can be based in principle either on freely chosen negotiated contracts (which means autonomy and a species of commodity production) or on a system of binding instructions from planning officials. *There is no third way.* What can exist, of course, is some *combination* of the two basic principles: that is, some kinds of decisions could be freely negotiated, others would be subject to binding administrative instruction. In fact, these principles *must* be combined, *must* coexist (do coexist under modern capitalism too) [emphasis in original].

He argues that there is a "centralizing logic" to a modern interconnected economy and adds that "if the sheer complexity of marketless planning generates both bureaucracy and inefficiency, it is really not very relevant to advocate 'democracy' as a cure" (1987: 99). Appeal to the "self-rule of associated producers" as a result is for him just sloganeering, resting on no serious analysis (1987: 104; 1991: 254). And though there is a place for planning in the mix that must exist, the autonomy of separate units of production must be preserved and "a species of commodity production" with it (1991: 48).

There is much to say here. First, democracy is not the cure for capital's separations; association is. Democracy, and the solidarity that must drive it, is the way to get from separation to association. Without doubt, democracy is an intrinsically defining feature of association itself, but if separation is left in place, democracy is formal, a bridge to nowhere. Think of the simple example of moving from an individual contract of employment to a collective agreement – employees joined in capitalist production exist as separate individuals, isolated individuals brought together only by the machines that govern their activities and capital would just as soon keep it that way. Solidarity is a bridge to their association and democracy a manifestation of it.

Second, attention to studies in the social shaping of technology surely caution that we should not be too quick to attribute too much to modern complexities. Marx is very clear these have been shaped by the capital relation. The industrial revolution was driven by the reproduction of the social relation of capital, and if socialism is itself to be more than a formal cover for the perpetuation of class, there will need to be a new socialist industrial revolution as well. Why not expect modern complexities that are a product of capital's dynamic, like the concentration and centralization of capital, for example, to give way as the machine's domination of living labor must certainly do?

Third, what is the magic of "freely chosen negotiated contracts" which loom so large in Nove's analysis? What after all is the magic of contract? We've had a chance to explore that. Contract is not required for individuals or units of production to negotiate freely with one another. What contract adds is coercion. That's the thing, whether Nove acknowledges it or not, that he finds so appealing. Contract is a bridge for resolving the contradictions of self-regarding separation and for reproducing them. Start with association and then there can be free negotiation still and disagreement and difference, but these can be resolved, as I suggested in Chapter 6, by persons who share a basis for action in common and start from a premise of unity; the challenge is to create a culture where they then struggle over difference with a view to achieving a new basis for unity. No doubt if separation remains in place the more or less decentralized exercise of coercion dispensed by the type of judicial system England pioneered has more appeal than Kafka-like coercive directives imposed by a remote and impersonal authority implementing a bureaucratic central plan. But the premise in each case is separation. Bettelheim (1975) has shown how the persistence of commodity categories leads to a plan that effectively perpetuates market phenomena as it dissimulates them. That is, for socialists the issue is not plan or market, but their material ground. If there is separation, then coercion is necessary to bind the self interest of one to the self interest of another and either a coercive plan or contracts of market exchange can serve this function. If there is association then coordination may be accomplished by free negotiation fully sensitive to the variety of different local or self interests without losing grasp of the common project that binds. Coercion, in that perspective, becomes more and more redundant in function of a more and more organic coordination with one another. Indeed we can find these tendencies played out today in the evolution of established forms of everyday contract. On the one hand, adhesion contracts, which are imposed by one party on another because of an imbalance in bargaining power and quite typically may be unilaterally modified at the discretion of the stronger party – employer-run health insurance plans are a classic example – can be a vehicle for dictatorial imposition far from freely negotiated and capable of bureaucratic outrage oppressive enough to rival examples from the command economies of countries of the East – BP, for example, made it a condition of participating in Gulf spill cleanup that workers not use respirators, even ones that were self-provided. On the other hand, relational contracts show how a longstanding association between contractual partners may allow for adjustment and realignment of expectations without the need for coercive judicial intervention. We can pursue a trajectory from separation through coordination to association rather than from separation rooted in an imbalance of power through coercion to oppression.

In spite of what history has suggested to some, the ambition to build a society where free and associated producers control the conditions of labor does not require that socialists genuflect to an all knowing central planner who, backed by a monopoly of state power, dispenses goods and justice with an unbending will. That idea, too, proposes socialism with capital's separations left intact. The claim instead is that associated workers can take conscious control of what they do as we want conscious control over our actions as individuals. But, simply, the market blocks that aspiration. Because labor cannot be directly compared, and is instead compared only through the intermediary of things on market display, no one can know, except after the fact, what the labor invested in a product will actually be worth. It's one thing to say no one can know the future, but neither do we willingly embrace blind forces of which we are ignorant if we can help it. We want to know how we produce and with what consequences, but the market blocks that. So we search for alternatives. There is no illusion here that the alternative we're after will be error free anymore than any of us individually goes through our days without mistake. But we can try to work together to govern consciously what we do, and it is only class interest attached to the persistence of the structures of capital that makes us think a dictatorship of value and its spontaneous laws better serve society.

There is good authority, of course, for taking the stereotype of central planning given life by the command economies of the East as a model of what socialism must mean. In *The Economic Problems of Socialism in the USSR*, Stalin (1972) claimed that the progress of socialism would lead to a central power controlling the whole of social production and entirely arranging for the distribution of it to social need. That was the image of a socialist future. For the present, he thought, commodity production persisted, not because of the pervasive separation of productive entities from one another, but because, in addition to foreign trade, there were two productive sectors, state enterprises and collective farms, and those features of the Soviet economy required these different units or sectors exchange commodities. But the time would certainly come, he claimed, when there will be only one all embracing production sector, with the right to dispose of all the consumer goods produced in the country [and at that point], commodity circulation, with its money economy will disappear, as being an unnecessary element in the national economy" (1972: 15–16). Thus Stalin claimed that commodity circulation will be replaced "by a system of production and exchange under which the central government or some other socio-economic center might control the whole product of social production in the interests of society (1972: 68–69).

But notice the sense in which in this vision capital's historic mission prevails. Track the image to its material ground. Rather than any tendency we might associate with a possible communism of free and associated producers, the concentration and centralization of capital better corresponds to such an exclusive accumulation of social power. Socialism is not the concentration and centralization of power, but a *centralized coordination of powers* – not power, singular, but the gathered powers, plural, of workers associated for a common task. There is not an emptying of autonomies on some one institutional other the way an employee surrenders autonomy to an employer, but instead social individuals empowered by their association. In fact, an exclusive institutional control of the whole product of society suggests nothing so much as separation taken to a fantastic extreme. A democratic coordination of individuals, organically linked in an aggregate of cooperative associations connected locally, regionally, nationally and globally in ways that reflect coherent social, economic and ecological priorities that reflect coherent social, economic, and ecological priorities will give fuller expression to the aspirations of socialists for a society of associated producers in common control of their productive resources and capacities.[2]

These examples suggest we look more carefully at the phenomenon of separation and Marx's lifetime of meditations on it. I mentioned in Chapter 3 his observation in preparatory materials for his Doctoral Dissertation, "Notebooks on Epicurean Philosophy" (1975 MECW 1: 493), that separation is always the separation of a unity, and I noted the significance this had for the definition of capital. If this emphasis on separation and the overcoming of it is missed in Marx, much of what he's after will be missed. For example, in addressing his call to transcend the existing division of labor, Nove (1991: 50) asks "[h]ow can the inescapable separateness of human productive activities be replaced and by what?" He goes on to suggest the absurdity of Marx's vision of overcoming the division of labor by thinking someone is going to fish in the morning, hunt in the afternoon, herd cattle in the evening and engage in criticism after dinner, all without becoming a fisherman, hunter, cattle herder or critic. (1975 MECW 5: 47 [*The German Ideology*]). Nove (1991: 51) underscores the silliness he finds by offering a more contemporary iteration. Mimicking the structure of Marx's passage he writes:

> Men will freely decide to repair aero-engines in the morning, fill teeth in the early afternoon, drive a heavy lorry in the early evening, and then go to cook dinner at a restaurant without being an aero-engine maintenance artificer, dentist, lorry-driver or cook.

Of course it is easy to attribute silliness to Marx or another and then on that basis find their ideas utopian or romantic or whatever.

But Nove has missed the thrust of Marx and Engel's small parable. Every separation is the separation of a unity. If we're going to investigate the separateness of human productive activities, we need to ask what unity the separation we consider is a separation of. Also, there is a distinction to be made between the separation of a unity and diversity or difference within a unity. As Aristotle observed a good while ago, an eye separated from the body is not an eye at all. So, too, a laborer separated from the conditions of production is not a laborer at all. Call that separation. On the other hand, if I clean in the morning, do dishes after lunch and farm in the afternoon, these are different activities in which are manifested the way I get through my day. Moreover, it's through developing my different capacities and powers that I grow in richness as a human being. If I add the study of mathematics or a musical instrument to my day, these are different activities but they are not divorced from me. But if I hire someone to cook or clean or farm or keep accounts, then these activities become separate, but not because they are different activities.

The point of Marx and Engel's example is that even activities as diverse as cattle herding and fishing and engaging in criticism are coherent expressions of difference within the unity of an individual life if they are not given proprietary significance so that they define a person in the marketplace. But now consider the lorry driver who supposes to do dentistry in the afternoon. What is the unity at issue in this case? This is not the unity of an individual taken for him or herself as the hunter/fisher/critic of the *German Ideology*. It is not the unity of a machinist or a scholar who learns to sing. The unity at issue is the unity of social labor and society's distribution of it, and there is no conceivable reason why differences within that unity would be given expression in the absurd form Nove proposes. Quite the contrary. Insofar as we are concerned with our unity as social individuals Marx suggests exploiting the diversity of our distinct, even unique abilities rather than making a mish mash of them so that everyone is reduced to being good at nothing and dissatisfied with everything – from each according to ability, is Marx's appeal.

The point is not trivial. If you work with ideological assumptions that have their source in the social relations of capital, an aspiration for a transition to socialism that includes overcoming those characteristics that distinctively define capital will seem implausible, utopian and romantic at best. In fact there is a small cottage industry devoted to chiding Marx for his hunter/critic remark and connecting this too with his having supposed to explain socialism by giving an account of Robinson Crusoe on a desert island.[3] But though Robinson Crusoe spells out pretty clearly what gives the example relevance, if a reader leaves in place the assumptions of separation as a defining feature of capital's material ground, then the fundamental difference I've suggested between the separation of a unity and diversity or difference within a unity will be missed. Emphasizing that Robinson's activities are only different forms of the activity of one individual, Marx (1990: 169 [I.1.4]) tells us that "Despite the diversity of his productive functions, he knows they are only different forms of the activity of one and the same Robinson." But later he refers to "an association of free men, working with the means of production held in common, and expending their many different forms of labour-power in full self-awareness as one single social labor force" (1990: 171 [I.1.4]). In the later case, the difference is a difference of individual forms of labor power within a single social unity that depends – the point cannot be missed – on association. Substitute separation for association and you get the free worker forced into a social role if she's lucky enough to have a job; except by permission of another she lives in a condition of separation from the means of production as fully as an eye rolled on the floor is separated from the body.[4]

From the perspective of things to the perspective of persons

Grasping the significance of the transition from capital's separations to the conditions of unity for socialist association is the first thing for it clarifies the material ground for the transition to socialism. But there are additional points of attention underemphasized or sometimes confused by the socialist tradition that warrant clarification. In his speech at Riverside Church a year before he was murdered, Martin Luther King argued that we must shift from a perspective of things to a perspective of persons.[5] The most rigorous source of such thinking is

Marx; it defined his project. But in this respect, Engels' argument in *Anti-Duhring* (1987 MECW 25: 268) that socialism means replacing the government of persons with the administration of things misleads. Relations of coercion associated with the exercise of government power will disappear, of course – recall Marx's observation that relations imposed by force are unjust – but arranging our social accommodation with nature in ways that maximize individual human flourishing is hardly a task that will wither away. We will want a fully scientific understanding of the structures and patterns of social behavior that make this possible, nor can we expect such structures, once in place, to be static and unchanging. Indeed, just as capitalism led to a flourishing of the sciences of nature above all because it was driven by a tendency to reduce necessary labor to zero, so too we can expect socialism to lead for the first time to a real flourishing of the social sciences. No longer compromised by mystifications required by the reproduction of hostile and antagonistic relations of class oppression, the social sciences can be freely enrolled in the project of coming to full understanding of the social dynamics that most suitably sustain our accommodation with nature.

The shift of perspective from things to persons also has consequences for what kind of social science it is we think we're about. Marx's work, remember, is not political economy but a *critique* of political economy. Political economy may well be defined, as it usually is, by the production and distribution of things. But for Marx this gets the order of priorities wrong: production as a "display of material wealth," he writes, is "in antithesis to the productive development of the human individual" (1994 MECW 34: 109). Now the development of human potential is always within nature and mediated always by the social arrangements within which we engage nature. As a consequence, our understanding of the transition to socialism may be better thought of as grounded in a comprehensive and inclusive science of social ecology, of which political economy is an important part.

On this score those formulations of Marx that suggest the domination or mastery of nature seem out of place. Certainly we can make good use of the forces of nature and the homeostatic relationship we are able to establish with the environment depends on our knowledge of them. How we choose to live in our natural environment depends on our knowledge of them. But who dominates the wind? We build a dam, and make good use of the gravity that pulls water over it, but we don't dominate gravity.

Suppose we imagine our own flourishing reflected and realized in our engagement and association with others rather than imagining our well being measured by material goods that in separation we own. If the association is socialist, then our engagement will not be achieved through relations of mastery and domination, but through respect for the contribution each can make to our common project. We might also then come to realize that we are ever in a relation of cooperation with nature, that our flourishing is plainly realized in and through it and that the wonder and respect it evokes are better capable of capturing the potential of our connection with it than pretensions to mastery. Mastery suggests separation of a unity, but we are one of nature's own forces, Marx reminds

(1990: 283 [I.7.1], a difference within the unity of nature. Suppose we come to act toward one another the way Aristotle understood the relation of friends – each wants what is best for the other, or, in Marx's gloss, the full and free development of each is a condition for the full and free development of all. Then we might imagine extending the same attention to all being out of a mix of humility for what we do not know and of self-interest for the place and occasion of our flourishing. Recall that the machine and the factory itself were transformed in the image of capital. We can imagine a socialist transformation of the productive forces in the image of our reciprocal respect for the astonishingly rich and richly different powers and capacities together we manifest and a transformation of our relation to nature corresponding to this. The idea of dominating nature, in other words, seems still the legacy of the long history of class society. Because oppression has always rested on mastery over people, mastery over nature seemed an ideal to follow. Sir Francis Bacon is thought to have compared scientific experiment to subjecting someone to torture. The point is disputed, and probably he held no such view (Pesic 1999), but the idea is worth attention, and there's a take-home message to draw: where our relations with one another are fully cooperative, where hierarchy and subjugation can be found described in history books, but no longer among us, we can expect, also, a new respect for the natural world on which we depend.

From formal ownership to real control

In the *Communist Manifesto*, Marx and Engels write that communism, its defining feature, could be summed up in a phrase: "Abolition of private property!" We've had some of that, and surely there are lessons to draw from the experience. For one, we've learned to read in *Capital* what many missed: there's a huge difference between the juridical forms of ownership that get expressed by a form of legal title and ownership that reflects an actual form of control over a distinctive appropriation of nature. Addressing himself to the transition from feudalism to capitalism Marx noticed that at first capitalism took over the labor process as it found it. The first introduction of the capital relation into production did not change the nature of the labor process. It changed the character of the participants and introduced into the process the compulsion to produce surplus value, but as a technical matter, labor went on as before. Marx calls this the formal subsumption of labor to capital. The real subsumption of labor to capital occurs as capital penetrates the labor process itself and transforms it technologically. In this respect, capital brought a dynamic of scale, the development of machinery, the machine's domination of the worker and the separation from the worker of science and its applications. It is only with these changes, he argues, that we can speak of a specifically capitalist mode of appropriation. Notice the meaning here: the separation of the laboring producer from the conditions of production as a premise of production makes capitalist production possible and establishes the conditions for the formal subsumption of labor to capital. But it is only once that separation has become a part of the process of production itself, only once the machine has become independent of the worker and the worker become an appendage of the machine that we can talk of the real subsumption of labor to capital.

What conclusions can we draw, then, that look to the real, not merely formal, abolition of private property? What tasks are posed for a transition to socialism that corresponds to a socialist appropriation of nature that is real, not one defined merely by rhetoric or legal title or stored up in dreams? We already have an answer, though details need spelling out in struggle: because the means of production have been made social by capital, in order for individuals to recover control over the means of production as their own, historically new forms of association must be found that are democratic.

On this score, Marx's study of the transition from feudalism to capitalism immediately carries two implications. First, in order to abolish private property in actuality, not merely formally, the new forms of association that characterize the transition to socialism must be forms of association capable of overcoming capital's separations in the actual process of labor. Second, given a socialist revolution, the social relations that reproduce capital, the patterns of behavior that do so, will initially persist and it is only through determined class struggle that they will be overcome.

Assef Bayat's (1991) study of the international experience of workers' control confirms this point. He concluded that the most important factor compromising efforts at workers' control as they have emerged in the history of the last century in a whole diversity of circumstances was the persistence of the traditional division of labor, including relations of hierarchy and authority, as well as the persistence of capitalist forms of the organization of production. He underscores the mistake involved in supposing the laws of technique inexorable or that science and technology can be thought of as ideologically neutral. He writes, "[if] the present direction of modern technology in the West (Taylorism, automation, fragmentation of work, specialization and computerization) tends to transfer control of living labour to machines and capital, the possibility of workers' control is restricted" (1991: 203). Bayat adds:

> The experiences of workers' control fail because they have to operate within the context of an inherited capitalist and authoritarian division of labor.
>
> An authoritarian division of labor in the workplace is one which involves a detailed division of tasks and their simple content, a separation of mental and manual labor, and an organization of work determined from above by the management structure in which the workers have little or no formal influence; the workers are not supposed to make sense of the total production of a commodity. An authoritarian division of labour deprives the mass of labourers of comprehensive technical knowledge, will and judgement; they therefore have no say in crucial matters such as investment priorities, choice of technology, choice of product, pricing and so on. The way in which work is organized in today's industrialized countries, for instance in car production, exemplifies such an arrangement. In such a work organiza-

tion, power resides in the hands of those who conventionally possess knowledge and power, that is, the elite of mental workers whose work ideology and social mentality is shaped by the prevailing capitalist worldview, and who have an interest in the existing social and technical structures.

(1991: 180)

To suppose that this catalogue of features that characterize the social kind capital as it has decisively penetrated the process of production can be overcome by a change in the bare legal form of ownership is a fatal error. Engels made the point in *Anti-Duhring*: "State ownership of the productive forces is not the solution of the conflict, but concealed within it are the technical conditions that form elements of that solution" (1987 MECW 25: 266). Social or public ownership of whatever form offers the possibility for the revolutionary transformation of capital's separations, but it does not in itself transform capital as a social kind: for that, the producer must actually control the organization of work and its product, not the reverse; living labor must actually dominate dead labor, not the reverse. Thus, Bayat concludes his analysis by observing that "Workers' control is a combination of ideology, practice and institutions that overrides such authoritarian work arrangements and the division of labor. A successful realization of workers' control therefore means, precisely, revolutionarization of the prevailing division of labour at work" (1991: 180).

In the former USSR the error of confusing the formal possibility offered by juridical forms of ownership with the consolidation of socialism obscured the magnitude of the task of transforming capital as a social kind. Thus, although the Stalin constitution of 1936 proclaimed socialist ownership, enterprise regulations codified the bureaucratic domination of one-man management and emphasis was placed on accelerating the growth of the productive forces within traditional forms rather than on transforming the organization of labor. In a particular conjuncture the development of the productive forces can be critical; still, placing all emphasis on this can amount to treating the productive forces, rather than class struggle, as the motor of history (Bettelheim 1974). The means and forces of production set limits, parameters for what is really possible, but it is changes in the social relations of labor that can reshape and develop and reproduce them in a new form, in that way creating new possibilities that open on altogether different limits. And it is class struggle that changes the distinctive forms of how individuals relate to one another as they work.

Mao Zedong challenged the Soviet approach by arguing that socialist relations of production could not but be imperfect in the early phases of the revolution and both that attention to their transformation and to the leading role of class struggle was required. He wrote: "It must not be assumed that the new system can be completely consolidated the moment it is established, for that is impossible. It has to be consolidated step by step" (1971: 481 ["1957 Conference on Propaganda Work"]). Thus, he explained in *On the Correct Handling of Contradictions Among the People* that while socialist relations of production were in harmony with the development of the productive forces, nonetheless, "they are still far from perfect, and this imperfection stands in contradiction to the growth of the productive forces" (1971: 445). But Mao's point too can be misunderstood if it is assumed that socialist relations are to be perfected while capitalist technology, technique and the organization of production are taken over intact. That capitalism has socialized the means of production should not be understood to mean that it has *fully* socialized them – both the separation of the worker from the conditions of production and the separation of productive entities from one another mark limits to this: means of production held apart from the laboring individuals needed to bring them to life are not fully socialized; productive units marked off by the boundary posts of enterprise autonomy, even though fully integrated into the social division of labor, are not fully socialized. If socialist relations of production are imperfect, this means they have not succeeded in bringing to full maturity a new social kind corresponding to the ambitions of a society of free and associated workers.[6]

The cooperative movement must also do more than make sure that legal title to every workplace is lodged in the workforce. Comprehensive cooperative ownership would be a tremendous achievement, of course, but if it is not coupled with aggressive steps to revolutionize relations and methods of work it will leave in place the basis for class differences and these will not take long to reassert themselves.[7] That is, like state ownership, cooperative ownership also offers possibilities only, not results. To own in association with others offers the possibility of democratic structures, but relations of hierarchy and authority reproduce themselves spontaneously in our ordinary lives and will do so also within cooperative structures unless persistently challenged by a struggle to transform established interests and patterns of behavior that are the legacy of class society. Moreover, even where formal structures of participation guarantee, for example, one person one vote, this also can remain a mere shadow of democracy if traditional patterns of the division of labor are not challenged and if there are not lively and effective processes for collective discussion, investigation and decision.[8]

Indeed, without being linked to revolutionary struggle that is national and global, the cooperative workplace sooner or later will tend to confront realities first given expression by the Fabian socialists Beatrice and Sydney Webb [Webb and Webb 1914]: democratic associations of producers must succumb, they thought, either to competitive pressures of the marketplace and learn to subordinate cooperative goals to profit seeking or they will succumb to the complexities of modern factory life and perpetuate traditional managerial hierarchies. This is the so-called "degeneration thesis." In *Capital* Marx noticed that under capitalism "the co-operation of wage-labourers is entirely brought about by the capital that employs them." [1990: 449 [I.13]. Suppose instead cooperation is brought about by a group of laborers themselves – like the first capitalists, cooperators have worked a change in the nature of relations in the workplace but have left the technical processes of production in place. In the end individual employees will still be brought together by the cooperative employer. A cooperative firm is still a firm, an autonomous producer, a legal personality which hires labor and provides work. The division of labor still exists, segmentation of the work force still exists, habits and structures of authority still exist. Control of work is still separated from the activity of work. Connections between individual functions of work may not be established by the participative collaboration of workers, nor the plan and methods of work, and so on. Nothing changes automatically with a change to cooperative ownership. As a technical matter, the task of coordination still constitutes a barrier to rank and file control. In fact, we have little experience in democratizing the work of directing, superintending and adjusting combined social labor, and it is a conceit of Western liberalism that it has amassed much expertise in democracy. As Maurice Bishop (1983), the former Prime Minister of Grenada, said at Hunter College the year he was killed, democracy reduced to pulling a lever in a booth once every four or five years is a limited achievement.[9] The challenge of democracy consists in actually mobilizing the participation of masses of citizens in women's, student, labor, cooperative, farmer and other popular organizations of production and social life.

To fashion collective mechanisms whereby the goals and processes of common labor are the result of willing cooperation is the product of years of transformation. But it is also the fundamental thread guiding an effort to remake the world of work in the image of associated labor: just as the separation of the worker from the means of production made capitalism possible, it is overcoming that separation by joining associated labor to its tools that makes cooperative labor possible.

A final note on this point for the sake of clarification. If capitalism moved from the formal subsumption of labor to capital to the real subsumption of labor to capital, there is a temptation to see the transition to socialism as simply reversing this in order to achieve the real subsumption of capital to labor. Now while it is certainly true that the transition to socialism will subordinate capital, dead labor, to living labor, the challenge of socialism is more than this. Instead, socialism is the much more expansive accommodation of human individuals in their flourishing to nature and to each other, and, through their social arrangements, the appropriation of nature to this. The transition to socialism refers to the move from the formal possibility of subordinating the appropriation of nature to human flourishing to the real activity of associated labor doing so.

Overview: winning the battle of democracy

In Chapter 3 I described capital's separation of the laboring producer from the conditions of production by breaking this down into four phases of the cycle of production. These were (1) premise, (2) starting point, (3) process, and (4) result. The first explained how the separation of the laboring producer from the conditions of production was a premise of capitalist production; the second explained how the contractual sale of labor power for a wage created the real possibility of production, but as a possibility of capital, not of labor; the third explained how the separation of labor from its conditions penetrated the activity of production itself so that living labor was subordinated to value's self-increase and to the domination of the machine; and the fourth showed how capital's appropriation of the entire product reproduced the cycle of separation. Moreover, because this cycle reflected a separation from the conditions of production as values, the analysis of Chapter 2 showed that it rested on the separation of productive units from one another: labor is subordinated to the blind operation of the law of value so that no one, and certainly not laboring producers, controls market forces and their consequences.

Given this understanding of the process of capitlist production, we can find an anchor for the tasks of transition as follows: winning the battle of democracy means overcoming the separation of units of production from one another and the separation of workers from the conditions of production in all the ways enumerated in the paragraph just above. That is, the transition to socialism means overcoming capital's double separation, and engaging this struggle means taking concrete steps to blunt the force of any aspect of capital's separations. It means also building conditions of unity that make it possible to do so.

First, plainly if separation is to be overcome, the direct producer cannot be found in a circumstance where labor has been reduced to mere abstract possibility so that the worker is without the objective means to labor or survive. As premise, the private monopoly of the conditions of production by a non-producing class must be overcome. Nature, Marx reminds, does not produce people possessing nothing but their labor power, and the wage relation has no basis in natural history. Neither does poverty on the scale we confront today – when Europe began its ravages of the globe over half a millennium ago it did not find nearly half of humanity without bare, reliable means of survival. Nature produces beings connected to an environment that, if they endure, sustains them, and it is our social history that has produced a class of persons – the overwhelming majority of humanity – divorced from access to the means of support except by permission of another. The social arrangements that account for this must be transformed.

Second, the laboring producer cannot be dependent on a wage contract for access to the means of production. The so-called free contract of employment is a relationship the worker is driven to coercively – lacking the means of labor, she must enter a contract of employment. Moreover, the terms of the contract subordinate her life activity to the command of another. Human flourishing is not consistent with the compromise of personal autonomy given expression by the employment contract.

Third – and this is the crux – regardless of the forms of juridical ownership adopted, abolishing the monopoly of non-producers over the conditions of production will remain merely formal unless working people in association actually are able to exercise control over the means of production in the labor process itself. Just as capital becomes distinctively what it is by the penetration of the separation of labor from its conditions into the very process of production, so too, overcoming capital as a social kind means the revolutionary transformation of its distinctive separations in the process of production. Formerly, there was the unity of labor and its tools under the possession and control of the laborer. In capitalist production this is inverted; the process of production divides work and disciplines the laborer according to the rhythms of the machine. Pretty clearly this is an inversion that needs inverting.

Nor can the laborer be subordinated to the reproduction of value and its increase. Labor must organize production according to its own rhythms, rather than those of value, and both the division of labor and the organization of production must be transformed so that labor, no longer a burden, is life's prime need. Plainly for these ambitions to be realized the enterprise form itself must be transformed so that the barriers that insulate it from the communities of which it is a part are dissolved. In effect, it is no more possible to imagine building socialism on the basis of the autonomous capitalist firm than it would have been to make the feudal manor the institutional basis for capitalism.

Fourth, the appropriation of labor's product and its use cannot be governed by non-laborers, and the social product must serve social need, not the increase of value in exchange. Determined and met democratically, social need must provide the minimum basic requirements for a decent life for all humanity and create also the conditions that make possible the full and free development of each individual as a condition for the full and free development of all. This in turn means that social production must further those social arrangements which most successfully reproduce our sustainable accommodation with nature.

Finally, even assuming common control of production within a firm, social labor still cannot be considered fully cooperative to the extent it is subject to the dictatorship of market caprice. By universalizing commodity production, capitalism deepens the division of labor in society and this extends the interconnected dependence of firms on one another; yet, given enterprise autonomy, their connections remain essentially spontaneous and uncoordinated. If associated workers are to gain control over their labor, therefore, they must gain participative control with others also over the market itself by establishing networks of cooperation connecting productive capabilities and needs. The separation of units of production from one another must be overcome.

It is not a matter here of abolishing the market. The market will no doubt survive for a relatively long historical period. It is a matter of overcoming step by step the social relations of separation that generate market exchange in the first place. It is also a matter of intervening politically in the market so that through the application of social, economic and ecological criteria the market can be subordinated to social need.

Democratic tasks

If I have no models of a socialist future, I have no model either for winning the battle of democracy. Still, I would like to suggest a few examples of democratic tasks many would put on the agenda both to suggest how struggles that people now engage or envision are intrinsically connected to the task of overcoming capital's separations and, by doing so, to suggest how these are connected to each other. My own experience is limited, as I'm quite aware. No doubt what is required here is a democracy battle clearing house, an electronic version of

Lenin's *Iskra* – a gathering of proposals, reports and applicable strategies from worker and democratic correspondents locally, regionally, nationally and globally.

Overcoming the separation of workers from the conditions of production as premise

Begin with this: no one can be without the opportunity to contribute to social production, or, where such contribution is suspended by sickness or disability or age, no one can be without the means to a decent life. Neither can contributions now often unrecognized like pregnancy or child rearing or caring for others compromise access to the means of a decent life. Justice Thurgood Marshall of the U.S. Supreme Court once suggested in dissent that anyone who applied for a government job was constitutionally entitled to one unless the government could give a reason for denial. The case focused on whether fair procedures required reasons, but can provoke an expansive reading that acknowledges just how perverse social arrangements are that withhold access to productive labor. Make the government an employer of last resort, full stop. Marshall argues both that access to work goes to the very essence of personal freedom protected by the Constitution and also that government cannot unfairly discriminate in the benefits it makes available.[10] As I write, the U.S. government has demonstrated an ability to provide hundreds of billions of dollars to bailout private citizens in the financial sector. The claim of the jobless is not less substantial or less momentous for national well being. And a bailout of the unemployed means jobs, not limited term unemployment relief, although a guaranteed basic income can provide a way to secure a decent living for periods of training, job change, injury, sabbatical, and so forth.[11] Interestingly, developments in information technology have given new bite to this call. User generated initiatives like the development of free software, the variety of wiki movements, and peer to peer production and design have created wealth globally and an enormous amount of it. Yet such contributions are very typically self-funded. This sets limits. It is not utopian to imagine an exponential growth in the contribution such self-motivated activities could make if underwritten by a basic guaranteed income for every human being and if coupled with the minimal resources required to put internet communication within reach of all.

Almost half of humanity remains peasants, small farmers or landless agricultural laborers and there is a continuing relevance to the call for equal access to land and credit, especially for women. Also, among the lessons of the Commune that bear remembering is the decree that provided for taking over abandoned factories so that they could be turned over to cooperatives of workers. The same applies to abandoned space, including urban space, that can be cultivated.

Overcoming the separation of workers from the conditions of production as a starting point of production

All matters regarding the right of individual workers to organize collectively in order to bargain over employment are democratic demands, including the right to organize and participate in union activities without being murdered. The right to be free from discrimination in employment and the right to union democracy are democratic demands. The right to bargain over all matters affecting enterprise concern – hiring and firing, allocation of work, conditions of work, what is produced, how it is produced, how it is sold – is a democratic demand, and to the extent that any such matters are blocked by labor law rules, then labor law reform is a relevant demand. The right to space and time for organizing at work, also often blocked by labor law, is a democratic demand, as is employment security: the still prevalent nineteenth-century rule that an employer has a right to fire for any reason or no reason – employment at will – is a bedrock of the separation of the working producer from the conditions of production and should survive nowhere. A community's right to support union campaigns is a democratic demand. Movements like the worker center organizing that has developed in the U.S. mobilize communities behind the employment concerns of unorganized workers and can also make a powerful contribution to democracy at work.

Actually, the most far reaching critique of the employment contract has its source in the separation of work and reward embodied in the call, "from each according to ability, to each according to need." From the perspective of communism's highest stage, work and material reward come apart. For the present, steps can be taken. The provision of transportation, health care, education and training, childcare, recreation and other benefits as public goods freely available to all divorces the satisfaction of social need from the wage bargain. In fact, the failure of efforts to rely on the employment contract to undergird a private welfare system could not be more dramatically demonstrated than by the callous and crabbed U.S. experience with health care.

Overcoming the separation of workers from the conditions of production in the labor process

I have emphasized that transforming capital as a social kind means transforming the activity of production. Winning the battle of democracy means transforming all forms of the organization of work that subordinate persons to things. For starters this means appreciating that the laboring producer is the most precious productive force, that her development is the goal of production, and that transforming production means looking first to mobilize popular initiative for work rather than mobilizing funds to be invested at a profit.

Two aspects to the transformation of work are fundamental. On the one hand, as Bayat argued, workers cannot take control of production by adopting without change the organization of labor inherited from capitalist production. This was a structural defect that repeatedly surfaced in the examples of workers' control he studied. On the other hand, every circumstance bottling up the volcano of initiative latent in the population of earth constitutes also a structural defect to add to his indictment. Workers must be free to modify and refashion the processes and instruments of work and to organize work in ways that make it more efficient, more democratic and more humane.

Marx thought transforming the division of labor was key. In his first description of the labor process in *Capital* (1990: 284 [I.7.1], he explained that what is distinctive about the way humans transform nature is that they form a conception of what is to be done and then discipline their activity in order to realize the plan they've conceived. Recall the distinction I made between separations of a unity and difference within a unity. Although a plan of work and its execution form a unity, capital severs this so that the worker executes the plans of another under the command of another:

> Hence the interconnection between their various labours confronts them, in the realm of ideas, as a plan drawn up by the capitalist, and, in practice, as his authority, as the powerful will of a being outside them, who subjects their activity to his purpose.
>
> (1990: 450 [I.13]

This is the first aspect of the division of labor to be overcome – the authoritarian separation that divorces the purpose and goal of production from its physical implementation.

In a later description of the labor process Marx recalls this theme but adds to it a precision; the tasks of mental and physical labor, once part of an intrinsic unity, are also severed:

> When an individual appropriates natural objects for his own livelihood, he alone supervises his own activity. Later on he is supervised by others. The solitary man cannot operate upon nature without calling his own muscles into play under the control of his own brain. Just as head and hand belong together in the system of nature, so in the labour process mental and physical labour are united. Later on they become separate; and this separation develops into a hostile antagonism.
>
> (1990: 643 [I. 16])

This, then, is a second aspect of the division of labor to be overcome.[12]

In their book describing the project of participatory economics, Albert and Hahnel (1991) argue that segregating workers by tasks makes a fully participative workplace impossible. Instead, they suggest the need for "balanced job complexes" throughout the economy. The idea here is that if 80 percent of all work is routine and 20 percent complex and creative, then the division should not be made among separate persons but instead each person should perform an 80/20 mix of tasks. This doesn't mean every person in a hospital should do brain surgery – from each according to ability remains a relevant constraint – but it does mean every brain surgeon should empty bed pans. Significantly, no technical impediment prevents this latter reform from being implemented anywhere now – executive or supervisory personnel of any sort can spend time each week at manual or routine labor – indeed there is nothing to prevent requiring that every public official do so.[13]

The philosopher Paul Gomberg (2007) has argued that ensuring everyone an opportunity for work that is meaningful is a basic requirement of social justice. From the premise that self-directed, self-chosen work is more satisfying than work under the supervision of another, and also that complex work is more satisfying than the performance of routine tasks, he draws the conclusion that racial opportunity cannot be made equal without equalizing the opportunity for meaningful work. "No society," he argues, "treats its members as equal unless it provides an equal opportunity to contribute" (152–153). Thus, whereas traditional conceptions of justice place attention on people's entitlement to the distribution of social benefits – *distributive justice* – Gomberg argues that justice should emphasize instead what people are able to contribute – *contributive justice*. In effect, "from each according to ability" is a richer source of inspiration for the justice of our social arrangements than traditional measures. It is the opportunity to contribute to social life that develops most profoundly a sense of well-being and that can maximize individual flourishing. As Andrew Sayer (2009: 13–14) argues, developing Gomberg's idea:

> the egalitarian themes of economic justice will never be very persuasive as long as they focus exclusively on distributive justice, ignoring contributive justice, for this omission allows people to believe that inequalities in distribution are a product of different contributions, as if individual contributions were simply a matter of individual motivation and effort, as if the distribution of work of different qualities were a reflection of generic differences in intelligence plus effort and aspiration.

That is, it is a democratic task to call for equal access to meaningful work. Everyone must have the opportunity to develop their skills and talents in the self-directed performance of complex tasks.

Ultimately, if the organization of work is to be transformed so that it is to fall under the control of free and associated producers, then working people must take control of the whole of production. Recall Bayat's observation that authoritarian forms of work organization assume that a workforce is not supposed to make sense of what is being produced. Actually Bayat's study of the international experience of workers control shows workers do not hesitate to take over production in its entirety whenever traditional forms collapse. The task is not easy and without the impetus of revolution, traditional patterns tend to reassert themselves. Nonetheless, his separate study of the factory council or *shura* movement that emerged spontaneously at the time of the Iranian revolution against the Shah, shows how far reaching such impulses can be (Bayat 1987).

With no substantial experience to draw on, council organizations in many workplaces assumed responsibility for the whole of production – all issues of pay, benefits, profit sharing, and so forth, as well as control over hiring and firing, conditions of work, management of production and distribution, allocation of tasks, finances, and other administrative matters fell within the jurisdiction taken over. As one *shura* member told him:

> Look, the reason why the Revolution was made at all, was because we wanted to become our own masters, to determine our own destiny. ... We did not want the situation where one or a few make decisions for two thousand. When we, 2,500 workers, are working around these walls, we want to know what is going on here...
>
> (1987: 123)

According to the constitution of one *shura*, "the task of this Committee is composed of complete oversight of the process of production, from the supply of raw material to its transformation into the saleable product" (126). Where corruption was uncovered another conducted a "proletarian tribunal" at a mass meeting of workers of the factory (123). Also, some of these councils assumed their responsibilities ran to the welfare of the country as a whole. A *shura* member told him: "Syndicates take only the workers' [economic] interests into consideration, not the social [total] interests, or the interests of the whole country. But the *shura* concerns itself with the whole social interests, the country's interests..." (149) [brackets in original].

I argued that transforming the organization of work requires active respect for the volcano of inventiveness latent in the population of earth. Traditional patterns of the division of labor are challenged where, either from necessity or opportunity, labor seizes the chance to modify and rework its tools and conditions. As Bettelheim (1974: 81) argues, emphasizing the attention given to practice in the Chinese Cultural Revolution and its significance for technical change, "Machines are no longer viewed as immutable objects, but as subject to modification by the workers themselves." In *Shock of the Old: Technology and Global History from 1900*, David Edgerton (2006: 187) underscores the significance of the point: "Most invention has taken place in the world of use (including many radical inventions) and furthermore has been under the direct control of users," and he traces grassroots innovation to places like Ghana's Suame-Magazine industrial cluster where for more than three quarters of a century an aggregation of auto repair, metal working and blacksmith workshops (today employing 200,000 people) have depended on artisanal ingenuity of great originality. The point is not to romanticize such developments; they are sorely compromised by lack of secure land tenure or access to credit or government attention or development assistance, and typically also they lack worker health or benefit protections, confront congested working conditions, and so on. Yet it is important nonetheless to signal the enormous inventiveness that exists and to emphasize the democratic importance of mobilizing this.

As for high end grassroots inventiveness, Eben Moglen, counsel for the Free Software Foundation, argues that because an information economy depends on the sharing of information, full and open access to all information by everyone and without property constraints is actually competitively superior.[14] No doubt he would support Edgerton's claim that what counts is use – free software is not only being widely used in everything from cell phones to servers, but because it is able to produce a superior product at a lesser cost, and, because this will be increasingly true the more the production of information depends on collaboration, he predicts it will come to prevail. In truth, it is hard to see a future for conventional ownership if production depends so intensively on the sharing of information. Moroever, it is hard to justify using metes and bounds rules of property to constrain ideas if the distribution of information has zero or virtually zero marginal costs.[15] This last consideration, Moglen suggests, confronts the twenty-first century with a fundamental moral problem – if after a first copy any kind of information can be made available to anyone on earth basically without cost, what is the moral justification for withholding it? Indeed. Yet those invested in fences and barbed wire want to save us from folly – without incentives, they insist, social production will come to a stop. Without labor, we could remind them, social production will come to a stop, and Moglen counters with a personally crafted corollary to Faraday's Law:

> We are witnessing a phenomenon first noticed by Michael Faraday at the beginning of the nineteenth century. Wrap a coil around a magnet, spin the magnet. Electrical current flows in the wire. One does not ask, "what is the incentive for the electrons to leave home?" It's an inherent, emergent property of the system.... Moglen's Corollary to Faraday's Law says, wrap the Internet around every brain on the planet, spin the planet. Software flows in the network. It is wrong to ask, "What is the incentive for people to create?" It's an emergent property of connected human minds that they do create.... We are a social species, and we create together; that's our nature. The question to ask is, 'What is the resistance of the network?' Moglen's Corollary to Ohm's Law states that the resistance of the network is directly proportional to the field strength of the intellectual property system. The conclusion is: Resist the resistance.
>
> (2003b)

It is a democratic task to challenge barriers to the free flow of information. Suppress information today and you suppress technology, a dramatic example of Marx's claim that "From forms of development of the productive forces these relations [property relations] turn into their fetters."[16] It is also hard to see how ownership can preserve traditional patterns of work when "the liberation of information from the control of ownership liberates the worker from his imposed role as custodian of the machine...." (Moglen 2003a)

In a review of Edgerton's book, the historian of technology Edward Tenner (2007) asks a question implicitly posed by Edgerton's account: what explains the pervasive persistence of older technologies; how can we explain "why the future is running behind schedule." Suppose new social relations of association were to release the reservoirs of inventiveness, low tech and high tech, that exist the world over. I think we would not be surprised by the fact of a new socialist industrial and technological revolution. I think we would be stunned only by the fact that it could have so far outrun our imaginations.

Overcoming the separation of workers from the conditions of production as result

All challenge to capital's control over the results of production is a democratic task whether this be the claim of a workforce to a share of the product or a community's claim to meet social need through taxation or otherwise. Here the most important democratic demand is for the socialization of finance – the finance system in its entirety must be brought under public control as a public utility in order to serve public need. National banks, for example, could be mandated to extend credit for infrastructure creation or repair or other job creation projects. In any case the call is not just for public ownership of financial institutions, but for their democratization. Albo, Gindin and Panitch (2010: 110) write:

> What is in fact needed is to turn the whole banking system into a public utility so that the distribution of credit and capital would be undertaken in conformity with democratically established priorities, rather than short term profit.... It is hard to see how anyone can be serious about converting our economy into a sustainable one without understanding that we need a democratic means of planning through new sets of public institutions that would enable us to take collective decisions about allocating resources for what we produce and how we produce and where we produce the things we need to sustain our lives and our relationship to our environment.

They quote from a former member of the Bank of England's Monetary Policy committee:

> There is a long standing argument that there is no real case for private ownership of deposit-taking banking institutions, because these cannot exist safely without a deposit guarantee and/or lender of last resort facilities that are ultimately underwritten by the taxpayer. ... The argument that financial intermediation cannot be entrusted to the private sector can now be extended to include the new transactions-oriented, capital-markets-based forms of financial capitalism.... From financialization of the economy to the socialization of finance. A small step for lawyers, a huge step for mankind.
>
> (112–113)

A comparable argument can be made for any institution so integral to the economy that it cannot be allowed to collapse: too big to fail means too big to be run for private profit.

Just as capitalist control of the product of capital is used to reproduce and extend the capital relation, so too socialist and democratic control of investment must be used to shape and expand democratic and socialist relations. A call for investments to repair historic inequalities in economic advantage can be made now, and Gomberg's point applies: it is opportunities for meaningful contribution that must be equalized. This suggests that targeted investment in education needs to be coupled with job creation strategies responsive to enhanced skills development. So too, investments that would offer alternatives to established patterns of the division of labor can be privileged, again by providing time and resources for training. Producer cooperatives can be favored, and also producer consumer alliances that open the opportunity for non-market collaboration as reflected, for instance, in the best examples of the community supported agriculture movement. Surely organic and local agriculture can make a claim for investment priority to rival long established subsidies to agribusiness. Also, as Albo, Gindin and Panitch suggest, investments that develop a sustainable relation to the environment are needed, and urgently. In general investments that support the solidarity economy are on the agenda.

Overcoming the separation of units of production

Finally, as I've explained, where the connections of units of production are marked by self-interested separation so that markets persist, associated workers do not fully control their conditions of production. No doubt transformation here will be over a long historical period, but steps can be taken to intrude questions of social need into ordinary market dynamics. Thus, pricing mechanisms are needed that take the full costs and benefits of social production into account. Sophisticated models of social cost benefit analysis or of ways to measure social return on investment exist, but these still rely on monetizing the bottom line – in effect if the results of production are to be compared against their social cost, forms of common measure are required and monetary evaluations are not only ubiquitous but also familiar even where clearly inadequate: what is the money equivalent of widespread health deterioration resulting from environmental pollution, for example? Bettelheim (1975) suggested years ago that theoretical space needs to be created where social utility and actual labor costs could be measured independent of the market in ways that do not reproduce commodity categories. Instead, alternative and politically relevant forms of measuring how goods and services are priced are required and also democratic forms of association that make it possible to arrive at these. Such alternatives envisioned would take into account existing economic realities, of course, but they would look also to assert the domination of social priorities. Bettelheim argued therefore for the need to develop a social and economic calculation, an SEC, distinct from a monetary calculation. Given Chernobyl, Bhopal, and the BP oil spill in the Gulf of Mexico, not to speak of global warming, today we would want to make explicit that this was a social, economic, and *ecological* calculation, an SEEC. But the goal remains the same: to measure democratically the effectiveness of social production in terms that do not reflect the operation of the law of value and the dominance of criteria of profitability first of all, but instead subordinate these to the satisfaction of social needs. That is, instead of methods of calculation that reproduce commodity categories more or less spontaneously, we want forms of evaluation that reflect, reproduce and extend democratic structures capable of transforming capital's separations.

Forms of production that move beyond enterprise autonomy are probably best given expression by networks of cooperation that emerge with a community's support and commitment to a vibrant and democratic cooperative movement. The beginnings of the Basque region's Mondragon cooperative project provide a model; the original Fagor cooperative, started by five graduates of a local vocational school begun by the parish priest, played an instrumental role in fostering the incubation of other democratic enterprises. From 1956 when it began to 1986, Mondragon provided the impetus for 103 new cooperatives of which only 3 failed. So, too, in Northern Italy a cooperative culture has developed that requires a portion of profits be reinvested in the growth of new cooperative employment. In North America in October 2009, the United Steelworkers entered into an agreement with the Mondragon Cooperative Corporation, now a multinational enterprise, for enterprise development according to cooperative principles.[17]

The point here is that an entirely different culture of democracy is fostered where producers form networks with each other and with consumers they serve. The New York City Cooperative Network which began in the winter of 2010 is a good example of how the support of community organizations providing educational, legal, economic development, and other assistance can join to help worker cooperatives in ways that not only facilitate connection but that are also calculated to blunt constraints the market would ordinarily be thought to impose. While fledgling development is fragile and often does not take hold, in the long run the impulse cannot be suppressed. As one participant in the NYC Network said:

> On the one hand there is the value of democracy. This is something we all want to promote, especially at this time. On the other hand, there is the intensely pragmatic need for people 1) to have access to good jobs and 2) to become the drivers in their economic lives. The worker co-operative model brings both of these together. A strong network can spread this opportunity to other impoverished and immigrant communities in New York City where people are locked out of meaningful access to work opportunities. And, the network can be a resource to anyone who is interested in learning how to start, implement and incubate a worker owned business.
>
> (Johnson 2010)

Close links between community organizations and worker cooperatives illustrate a point made in a different context by Diane Flaherty (1992: 94): "the locus of socialism is not the individual firm." Thus, Bettelheim (1975: 91) argued that there's a difference to be remembered, and a radical one, between the commune form of a cooperative network and the self-standing self-managed enterprise.[18] While the later is usually an exclusively economic unit of production, the former provides an umbrella under which social priorities reflecting the needs of democratic development trump exclusively economic considerations. Drawing inspiration from the Paris Commune, Marx appealed not to an autonomous enterprise, but to a community that works. On this model, production is organized inclusively by a community capable of taking into account political, social and ecological criteria in the objectives it sets for itself. Here too, though, there is no space to relax the battle for democracy; community representatives may not participate directly in production and may tend to identify with established hierarchies or come to act like separate strata so that by inadvertence or design worker efforts to revolutionize the social relations of work get ignored.

Conclusion

From the Bolshevik revolution to the collapse of the Berlin Wall to the streets of Cairo today, from resistance to Hitler to decolonization and national liberation, from the movements for the self determination of peoples to the movements for equal rights in every form, the last century has been a century of democratic struggle. It is the social movements for democracy that define our age, and it is the unity of these in a popular democratic front that can form the strategies required to confront global capital.

There seem to me basically three parts to this. First, the struggle for democracy at work is ultimately the decisive democratic struggle. Whatever you think about the word "proletariat," the employment relation is not yet yesterday's news – it characterizes capital. At the bottom, capital is a particular form of the activity of labor in production and meaningful social change means transforming this. Moreover the struggle for democracy at work is bourgeois society's weak link; there cannot be robust democracy in society where there is not democracy at work. Additionally, the struggle for democracy at work forms conditions of unity to join all who work. Whether a person produces surplus value for a capitalist, is self-employed, or works in a cooperative or commune engaged in the construction of socialism, or anything in between, the challenge of democracy at work is presented in each case. No one who relies on the market or who works for another is exempt; no one fully participates in the control of their conditions of work.

Particularly important here is the way the struggle for democracy at work has the potential to build revolutionary unity. In his writings on the factory council movement in Turin in the early years of the last century, Gramsci (1977) underscored the limits of trade union organizing insofar as it remained confined to bargaining over wages and hours and working conditions. Inevitably the consequence of such working class organizing was to divide people by sector, level of income and so forth, and also to isolate labor from the community. Instead, Gramsci wrote, organizing producers around taking control of the productive process itself has the capacity to unite all who participate, regardless of the role they play in production. Whether they are skilled, unskilled, administrative, clerical, technical, engineering or manual employees, everyone who participates is essential to the final result. Not only that – insofar as components are required from a parts supplier who is in the next town or state or nation or on another continent, links of solidarity are required with that workforce also. Thus, he saw the factory councils as a way to contest capital's control over the organization of labor on the shop-floor and in so doing to develop rank and file capacity to manage the whole of production – for Gramsci the council movement was a form of training and a way to bring to the awareness of working people that they were "creators of history and could learn to do without the intervention and domination of capital:"

> The worker can see himself as a producer only if he sees himself as an inseparable part of the whole labour system which is concentrated in the object being manufactured, and only if he experiences the unity of the industrial process which *in toto* demands collaboration between manual workers, skilled workers, administrative employees, engineers and technical directors.
>
> (1977: 110)

If working people are to claim the right to self-government in the workshop and thus to challenge the control of work, there is no alternative to surmounting division.

Second, the struggle for democracy cannot succeed unless the struggle for democracy at work is connected to the movement for democracy in society. Marx made the point in the Inaugural Address to the First International in 1864 when, in the course of celebrating victories of the cooperative movement in England, he argued that "[t]o save the industrious masses, co-operative labour ought to be developed to national dimensions, and consequently, to be fostered by national means. ... To conquer political power has therefore become the great duty of the working classes." (1985 MECW 20: 12 ["Inaugural Address of the Workingmen's International Association"]) He went on:

> [o]ne element of success they possess – numbers; but numbers weigh only in the balance, if united by combination and led by knowledge. Past experience has shown how disregard of that bond of brotherhood which ought to exist between the workmen of different countries, and incite them to stand firmly by each other in all their struggles for emancipation, will be chastised by the common discomfiture of their incoherent efforts.

It's important to read these comments today with a gloss as expansive as the spirit with which they were spoken: the conditions of revolutionary combination require working people "stand firmly by each other in *all* their struggles for emancipation" That is, the struggle against capital as a social kind can prevail only if it is joined to and succeeds in joining movements of women, of indigenous people, of people of color and others who work for sustainability, peace and social justice, and for respect, equal treatment and popular control in every form – *all* their struggles!

Third, not only is winning the battle of democracy the world over the key to the transition to socialism but the transition to socialism is the key to completing any struggle for democracy. That is, the democratic movements cannot reach successful conclusion as long as capital's separations remain in place. Democracy requires association. Democracy that ratifies and reproduces the walls that secure capital's self-regarding boundaries remains hollow and formal. Democracy that is substantive and real can only be achieved in association where there is full respect for the flowering of difference within a common unity.

CODA: social kinds, capital as a social kind, and winning the battle of democracy

These propositions summarize essential points I've made:

1 Social Kinds

1.1 Social arrangements that mediate the accommodation *homo sapiens* make with nature are causal structures of labor activity. These are distinctively characterized by the form of the relation individuals take to nature and to each other in the actual process of production. Such structures are manifest in patterns of social behavior that cause them to persist and be reproduced; we refer to them as the fundamental social kinds of life.

1.2 By knowing these structures we can develop strategies to transform them.

1.3 Transforming such structures involves transforming both the social relations of labor activity in which people engage and the material forces in which those relations are embedded. The material forces of production ultimately determine the parameters of real possibility within which the relations of production move; within those parameters social relations of labor activity shape and reshape the forces of production, not only transforming them but also transforming the real possibilities they offer.

1.4 The development of human production is the development of human potential; that is, the goal of production, wealth, properly conceived, is the development of human flourishing in nature. Our own age has learned indelibly that the development of human potential is possible only if the accommodation we establish with nature is sustainable.

2 Capital as a Social Kind

2.1 As a social kind, capital is characterized by the separation of laboring producers from their conditions of production and the separation of enterprise units from one another.

2.2 Divided from nature and each other by capital's separations, laboring individuals lose control of the products of their labor and these become a means of dominating them. In association they can take common control of their conditions of life in order to promote their reciprocal flourishing.

2.3 Because the means of production under capitalism have become social, overcoming capital's separations means discovering democratic forms of activity by which individuals participating in association with one another can surmount, step by step, all modes of activity that presuppose and reproduce their separations.

3 Winning the Battle of Democracy

3.1 It is transforming capital's separations democratically that gives unity to the global struggle against capital: the transition to socialism means winning the battle of democracy.

3.2 The struggle of working people to take control of their conditions of production forces a democratic struggle for the unity of labor in a way more limited forms of working class action do not.

3.3 The struggle of working people to take control of production cannot be sustained unless it is connected to a large democratic social movement, national and global, for the revolutionary transformation of political power.

3.4 Today's social movements for democracy can only be completed insofar as the self-regarding separations that define capital as a social kind are overcome. While separation may be thought of as the separation of a unity; diversity marks difference within a unity. Respect for difference requires unity in a common project of association to make the full and free development of each a condition for the full and free development of all.

Notes

1 Introduction: social kinds in social theory

1 "[C]onstantly keep in mind," Engels wrote in the Supplement to the Preface of 1870 for his pamphlet on *The Peasant War in Germany*, "that socialism, since it has become a science, demands that it be pursued as a science, that is, that it be studied" (1988 MECW 23: 631).

2 I have not said that mind is not a causal activity of the brain. My point is only that reference can take place without triggering the organism's causally engaged interaction with the world.

3 The larger passage from which this excerpt is taken is helpful:

> Let us now ask not what a general theory of objectivity would look like, but whether anything can be done to capture this underlying concern about objectivity. We need not require freedom from all value and bias in order to have objective inquiry if there nonetheless exist mechanisms that would operate to make one's factual presuppositions more factual over time, or that would shape values in such a way that the norms governing inquiry come to approximate norms that would, if followed, permit or encourage this sort of self-correction. That is, although we cannot, even in principle, have direct access to the objects of inquiry, there may yet exist mechanisms of belief formation that incorporate feedback from the object to the inquiring subject. This feedback would force us, if we are to realize our goals, to reexamine our theory and values in such a way that our beliefs are appropriately controlled over time by the object as well as by our subjectivity.
>
> This sort of objectivity is possible even though all perception of and inferences about the object are mediated by theory and norms because the object nonetheless has a direct way of affecting us: causally. To have no "conceptual niche" for a given phenomenon does not in general prevent that phenomenon from influencing our fate through all-too-familiar causal mechanisms.
>
> Feedback operates upon norms as well. For example, in twentieth-century science operationalist criteria for the admissibility of concepts have been relaxed and relaxed again as it proved impossible to reformulate scientific theories within operationalist confines while at the same time preserving their power to guide scientific practice and theory development. Something had to give, and in this case it was a methodological canon that had great initial intuitive appeal.
>
> To be most effective in achieving this sort of objectivity, we must regularly and ambitiously insert ourselves into the causal nexus, operating on the basis of our beliefs and norms. When anticipated outcomes are not realized, we may experiment with various different beliefs and norms to see if we fare better, shifting our allegiance toward beliefs and norms that let us do as much as possible as

successfully as possible. This process gives objects ample opportunity to affect us causally, and the fact that we find reversals frustrating, but continue to hold onto our ambitions, has been decisive in producing whatever degree of objectivity we have achieved. There is no guarantee that our readjustments, even when they lessen frustration while feeding ambition, will carry us away from error and toward truth. The most that can be said is that if we extend our ambitions and practical activity further and further, forcing ourselves upon the world in ways ever more removed from the commonsense world of ordinary needs and objects, and if we meet unprecedented success, then we are not simply reifying our beliefs when we suppose that their evolution has been shaped by the nature of things as well as by our preconceptions.

4 This point is elaborated briefly on p. 9
5 Railton is at p. 6 above. In the Preface I quoted Hilary Kornblith (1993: 6–7) as follows:

> Indeed it was the application of the causal theory of reference to natural kinds which allowed for the elaboration of a sophisticated scientific realism.... On the account of science which began to emerge..., it is the business of science to discover the real causal structure of the world; what this means, in a word, is the discovery of natural kinds and the causal relations among them ... natural kinds make inductive knowledge of the world possible because the clustering of properties characteristic of natural kinds makes inferences from the presence of some of these properties to the presence of others reliable.

6 The passage occurs in his critical notes on the disintegration of the Ricardian School written for the planned fourth volume of *Capital* – his historical survey and critique of the theories of surplus value (1989 MECW 32: 348). Samuel Bailey had argued that "Whatever circumstances ... act with assignable influence, whether mediately or immediately, on the *mind* in the interchange of commodities, may be considered as causes of value." Plainly it would be hard to make a social kind of the universe of factors that would fill such a bundle – we would have no stable causal structure to study because the cause of value would be a contingent product of the lunch meat that caused dyspepsia, the obligation to attend a daughter's afternoon piano recital, flattery or insult at the pub, and all manner of other incidents bearing on the mental life of market participants. Marx responds with the argument quoted on p. 12.
7 Of course because of the energy required this is not a practical proposition; nonetheless, Glenn Seaborg is reported to have accomplished the feat in 1980 (Browne 1999).
8 Features that are homologous reflect a common evolutionary origin like the wings of a bat and the flippers of a whale; features that are analogous are similar in function but have evolved differently such as the wings of insects and the wings of birds. In (2003: 540) Boyd gives a different example that may be used to make the same point: Renaissance scientists used the term 'acid' to refer to reagents with an acrid smell, sour taste, and so on without anything approximating theoretical understanding of the unobservable properties that account for these empirical features; today we would refer to substances that are electron pair acceptors. Nonetheless, though theoretically superficial, Renaissance usage referred and we may speak of referential continuity. Issues concerning the continuity of scientific reference surface in considering Marx's relation to Ricardo, and I take these up briefly in Chapter 2.
9 Roy Bhaskar uses the category "alethic truth" to distinguish reference that merely succeeds from reference that reflects our capacity to explain, fallibly, the real reason or ground of things (1994).
10 Marx understated his point. Because the power of abstraction is essential to grasping interconnection, it is an important complement to experiment and essential to all science.

11 Ian Hacking (1991) underscores that

> Debugging is not a matter of theoretically explaining or predicting what is going wrong. It is partly a matter of getting rid of "noise" in the apparatus.... The instrument must be able to isolate, physically, the properties of the entities that we wish to use, and *damp down all other effects* that might get in our way.
>
> (252; [emphasis added])

Some features of an experiment you physically abstract from so they do not interfere; others you take precautions to eliminate to prevent any possibility that they do. Hacking offers an example from the 1970s of an instrument called PEGGY II that made use of electron spin to focus magnetically a stream of polarized electrons. This required using a laser beam to kick electrons off a particular crystal. Potentially disruptive features of the experiment included (1) jitters of the laser beam itself, (2) backscattering of dislodged electrons, and (3) the potential for dust particles in the apparatus polarizing as well. All these had to be controlled so that they would not distort or falsify results and this was done by means of experimental design. Boyd (1985: 5; 8–9) shows how experiments that investigate electrical phenomena must shield off the electrical hum that occurs at 60 Hz as a result of alternating current used in electric wiring in order to avoid distorting experimental results. Sampling also suggests an analogy to abstraction insofar as steps must be taken to ensure that the experiment is designed so that it will generate relevantly representative data.

12 In the *Poverty of Theory* E. P. Thompson (1978: 96) offers a critique of Althusser's concept of 'relative autonomy' – the relative autonomy of law, for example – by arguing that, in the history with which he was familiar, law "was at *every* bloody level":

> I have, as it happens, been interested in this myself, in my historical practice: not, of course, in any grand way ... but in a very petty conjuncture: in an island on the edge of the Atlantic, very well supplied with lawyers, at a moment in the eighteenth century. So my evidence is highly marginal, as well as being seriously contaminated by empirical content. But what I discovered there would make *Le Structure a Dominante* boggle. For I found that law did not keep politely to a "level" but was at *every* bloody level; it was imbricated within the mode of production and productive relations themselves (as property-rights, definitions of agrarian practice) and it was simultaneously present in the philosophy of Locke; it intruded brusquely within alien categories, reappearing bewigged and gowned in the guise of ideology; it danced a cotillion with religion, moralising over the theatre of Tyburn; it was an arm of politics and politics was one of its arms; it was an academic discipline, subjected to the rigor of its own autonomous logic; it contributed to the definition of the self-identity of both rulers and of ruled; above all, it afforded an arena for class struggle, within which alternative notions of law were fought out.

There is nothing to disagree with here, of course – at the level of manifest behaviors. Nonetheless, Thompson misses something important: as he suggests the social reproduction of the capitalist moment he describes would not have been possible without relations of force to ensure that the social behaviors required by a muscular young capital do in fact reliably reoccur. But Thompson misses the capacity to isolate those relations by means of the power of abstraction – in the manner of a natural scientist, the social theorist can disregard law's pervasive empirical presence to particularize instead the constitutive relations that are necessarily associated with the capitalist mode of production. These are real causal structures we access by means of thought. By abstracting to them we can show their source and function. I offer an example in Chapter 5.

13 And Marx is clear on the point a paragraph before the quoted passage; after explaining that his dialectical method is exactly the opposite of Hegel's, he continues:

For Hegel, the process of thinking, which he even transforms into an independent subject, under the name of 'the Idea', is the creator of the real world, and the real world is only the external appearance of the idea. With me the reverse is true: the ideal is nothing but the material world reflected in the mind of man, and translated into forms of thought.

(1990: 102 [Postface to the Second (German) Edition])

2 Why is this labor value? Commodity-producing labor as a social kind

1 The German is as follows: "Sie hat niemals auch nur die Frage gestellt, warum, dieser Inhalt jene Form annimmt" (1970 MEW 23: 95).
2 I draw here on suggestions from D. K. Modrak (1985).
3 "Therefore, when Galiani said: Value is a relation between persons ('*La Ricchezza è una ragione tra due persone*') he ought to have added: a relation concealed beneath a material shell" (1990: 167 [I.1.4; emphasis in original]). The Moore and Aveling translation reads "between persons expressed as a relation between things" (Marx: 1967: 74).
4 "All commodities are non-use-values for their owners, and use-values for their non-owners. Consequently, they must all change hands" (1990: 179 [I.2]).
5 The characterization seems paradoxical because the social form to which it refers is a contradictory one – a producer produces independently but as part of a social division of labor on which she depends.
6 Searles makes this observation in his audio lectures on the Philosophy of Mind (1996).
7 Alan Nelson (1990), for example, takes commodities to be fundamental to the description of economic phenomena but concludes that they cannot be thought of as natural kinds in any society; see also Alexander Rosenberg (1983) who finds kinds lacking among the phenomena of the market.
8 See Groff (2004) for a critical realist discussion of Ellis's rejection of social kinds.
9 "Cornell Study Examines Surge in Self-Injury" (Lockard, *Ithaca Journal*, 6/10/06).
10 In an Appendix to Chapter 4 (see pp. 100–1) I explain how we may use either the expression "the social kind of commodity-producing labor" or the expression "value as a social kind" to refer to the same causal structure of labor activity.
11 "As the commodity-form is the most general and the most undeveloped form of bourgeois production, it makes its appearance at an early date, though not in the same predominant and therefore characteristic manner as nowadays" (1990: 176 [I.1.4]). See also "The Method of Political Economy" where Marx observes that "as a category exchange value leads an antediluvian existence" (1986 MECW 28: 38; 1973: 101).
12 "[A] material composite is not the same as its essence," (Code 1984a: 117), and thus we distinguish in Aristotle between substance as the subject of attributive predication and primary substance as a thing's constitutive or substantial form (1984b). Socrates is a man and a member of the human species because the matter of which he is compounded is constituted into a particular individual by that which organizes what it is to be human (1986).
13 Marx refers to considering things in their "pure form," but not because they are empty of content.
14 The text here, somewhat modified, is taken from Engelskirchen (2008).
15 The Moore and Aveling translation has it that this is "the pivot on which a clear comprehension of political economy turns" (Marx 1967: 41). I think I do not exaggerate the significance of the point by echoing Watson and Crick's (1953) wonderful one page paper announcing their discovery of the DNA double helix, "Molecular Structure of Nucleic Acids: A Structure for Deoxynucleic Acids." The paper ended with a sentence that for all history must stand as a preeminent model of understatement measured by any standards: "It has not escaped our attention that the specific pairing we have postulated immediately suggests a possible copying mechanism for the

genetic material." What counts as social science can escape the attention of the custodians of dominant orthodoxies, still I suspect Marx's characterization of the social form of the labor that accounts for the commodity form carries as rich a potential for social theory as the Watson-Crick model has had for biology, though it will take a large social revolution to open space enough for this to be widely realized.

16 Clausius' papers on kinetic energy, published in German in 1857 and 1858, were quickly translated into English and appeared in *The Philosophical Magazine* in 1857 and 1859. Maxwell's work on kinetic theory began with his reading of Clausius' second paper, "On the Mean Length of the Paths Described by the Separate Molecules of Gaseous Bodies," in 1859. Thereafter the two of them carried on what has been described as a "scientific correspondence" in print for the next 15 years and this contributed to the rapid advance of understanding (Purrington 1997: 135–136). Clausius' papers are reprinted in Brush (1965).

17 The abstraction does not hold for gases under either high pressure or as they approach temperatures cool enough to liquefy. As a gas cools, the forces of attraction and repulsion among molecules can no longer be disregarded nor at high pressure can we disregard the space occupied by the molecules. But where no such extremes are presented, deviations in the actual behavior of different gases are negligible.

18 In *The Contribution to the Critique of Political Economy* (MECW 29: 270) Marx writes that

> The exchange value of a palace can be expressed in a definite number of tins of boot polish ... Quite irrespective, therefore, of their natural form of existence, and without regard to the specific needs they satisfy as use values, commodities in definite quantities are congruent, they take one another's place in the exchange process, are regarded as equivalents ...

People render products equivalent by the act of exchanging them. In *Capital* (1990: 180 [I. 2]) Marx quotes Gothe's *Faust*, "In the beginning was the deed."

3 Separation and subordination: the real definition of capital as a social kind

1 Referring to Platts (1997), Olivier Rieppel (2004) writes: "[W]e would emphasize today that since 'to be significant, similarity needs to be causally grounded' ... therefore attention to kinds reflects an effort to reach out to the causal structure of the world." That is, our demand for causal explanation drives us to organize our understanding of the world by means of kinds. The definition of a natural kind is a 'real' definition, not a verbal one, because it picks out (fallibly, approximately, revisably) a causal structure that accounts for the existence and development of a thing.

2 The phrase "determinations of existence," "Existenzbestimmungen,", occurs in the "Introduction" to the *Grundrisse*:

> Just as generally in the case of any historical, social science, so also in examining the development of economic categories it is always necessary to remember that the subject, in this context modern bourgeois society, is given, both in reality and in the mind, and that therefore the categories express forms of being, determinations of existence – and sometimes only individual aspects – of this particular society, of this subject, and that *even from the scientific standpoint* it therefore by no means begins at the moment when it is first discussed *as such*. This has to be remembered because it provides the decisive criteria for the arrangement [of the material].
> (1986 MECW 28: 43; 1973: 106 [emphasis and brackets in original])

3 See note 11, Chapter 1, and the accompanying text.

4 It may be helpful to spell out the logical equivalence. According to the rules of deductive reasoning I can say "if every time I have p, I have q, then because in this case I

have p I can therefore conclude I must also have q" More briefly, "if p, then q; here p; therefore q." I have affirmed the argument's antecedent and my argument is valid. I will also give a valid argument if I deny the consequent: "if p, then q; in this case not-q; therefore necessarily not-p." If p is always followed by q and I don't have q, then it follows that I don't have p. So "if p, then q" is logically equivalent to "if not-q, then not-p," and I can demonstrate the equivalence by starting with either the one assertion or the other. From this it follows that all ravens are black is logically equivalent to all non-black things are non-ravens.

5 The term is taken from the philosopher Nelson Goodman. Because it has been tested, theoretically elaborated, put to use, or similarly developed, a "projectable category" is one on which you have reason to rely.

6 Given the separation of workers from their conditions of production, social reproduction depends on how this separation is overcome. For capital, access to labor is possible if laborers who are free have the capacity to labor. The capacity to labor depends on the material maintenance of the worker. Therefore the wage exchanges not for labor but for the value of goods that assure the worker's maintenance. The point is developed below in the discussion of the exchange of labor power for a wage as the starting point of capitalist production.

7 The passage reads as follows: "Moreover, in the analysis of economic forms neither microscopes nor chemical reagents are of assistance. The power of abstraction must replace both" (1990: 90).

8 Marx uses a footnote to explain the distinction found in Aristotle's *Politics* between the art of household management and *chrematistic*, the art of acquiring things where making money is the goal. A householder may use exchange, but the purpose will be to obtain things for use (and thus to participate in simple exchange, C-M-C); it follows that the impulse to exchange will be limited by need (1990: 253–54 [I.4]; see Aristotle 1958: §§ 1256, 1257). Where exchange is used for making money, then, Aristotle notes, currency is the starting point and goal (that is, M-C-M'); the objective in that case, wealth, is without limit. Moreover, Aristotle observes, people tend to turn other arts, which by nature serve other ends – as medicine, for example, produces health – and use them in ways not consonant with their intrinsic nature but instead for monetary gain.

9 A clarification is important. Three different things happen: (1) part of the new value that labor creates goes to replace the value represented by the wage given for it, (2) part of the new value is surplus, delta M, the animating goal of capitalist production, and, (3) in addition, labor preserves the value of the raw material and means of labor used in production. Machines that are not used rust and lose value. It is the touch of labor's fire that brings material to life and allows their value to be passed to the product.

10 Consider a yardstick. It is able to measure other lengths because it is long. But how long is a yardstick? 3 feet. But feet are just increments into which we divide a yard. How long is a foot? 12 inches. But an inch is just a portion into which we divide a foot. In fact, length is similar to value in that it is measured by a form of physical activity: a meter is defined as 1.65076373×10^6 times the wavelength of light emitted by a krypton laser. Labor time can measure value in products because products are objects on which labor has been expended and the expenditure of labor takes time. The value of labor power can be measured by the activity of labor for the same reason. But you can't measure the duration of the activity of labor by the duration of the activity of labor.

11 "Epicurus' true principle ... seeks to destroy the reality of nature which has become independent by an explanation according to abstract possibility: what is possible may also be otherwise, the opposite of what is possible is also possible" (1975 MECW 1: 72). Thus, for Epicurus all the senses are of equal validity and, since they cannot be refuted, are equally true. One can believe anything as long as it is consistent with

sense experience – the sun is about two feet in diameter because that is how large it seems.

12 "Every child knows that a nation which ceased to work, I will not say for a year, but even for a few weeks, would perish" (1988 MECW 43: 67 [Letter to Kugelmann, 7/11/1868]).

13 The chapter on "Buddhist Economics" from *Small is Beautiful: Economics as if People Mattered* by E. F. Schumacher (1989: 50–59), considers a human person without the chance of obtaining work to be in a "desperate position, not simply because he lacks an income, but because he lacks this nourishing and enlivening factor of disciplined work which nothing can replace." Like Marx, according to this account a Buddhist considers labor not only a way to provide for life's necessities, but a way to develop a person's capacities and a way to manifest human sociality by joining with others in work. Thus, from a Buddhist point of view to think unemployment acceptable as long as those without work are adequately provided for "is standing truth on its head.… It means shifting the emphasis from the worker to the product of work.…" What is the product of work, in other words, if it isn't human flourishing – and the idea that human flourishing could be found in the consumption of goods is one without appeal to either the Buddha or Aristotle or Marx. The Schumacher excerpt is online: www.schumachersociety.org/buddhist_economics/english.html (last accessed on 07/06/10).

14 See especially (1990: 1019–1038 [Results] and "Formal and Real Subsumption of Labour Under Capital. Transitional Forms," also "Formal and Real Subsumption of Labour Under Capital: Transitional Forms" in *Economic Manuscript of 1861–1863* (1994 MECW 34: 93–121).

15 In a *Grundrisse* section devoted explicitly to alienation, Marx concludes:

> The worker's propertylessness and the ownership of living labour by objectified labour, or the appropriation of alien labour by capital – both merely expressions of the same relation from opposite poles – are fundamental conditions of the bourgeois mode of production, in no way accidents irrelevant to it. These modes of distribution are the relations of production themselves.
>
> (1973: 832; 1987 MECW 29: 210)

16 Compare Marx (1986: 390; 1973: 463) where, as Lukes (1985: 51) points out, the word here translated as "an injustice" – "ein Unrecht" – appeared in the earlier *Grundrisse* manuscript as "ungehorig," that is, "improper."

17 *Paradise Lost*, Book II, lines 648–59 and 790–802. Milton's account is harrowing. Online: www.dartmouth.edu/~milton/reading_room/pl/book_2/index.shtml (last accessed July 27, 2010).

18 I take the translation from an epigraph to the chapter, "Karl Marx and Humanity; the Stuff of Hope," in *The Principle of Hope*, v. 3, by Ernst Bloch. The essay is collected as an Appendix to the Eric Bentley edition of Brecht's *Galileo* in a translation by Richard Winston. It appears online: http://forerunner.finearts.yorku.ca/~couroux/facs4934/texts/brecht.pdf (last accessed July 27, 2010).

4 The concept of capital in the *Grundrisse*

1 Hilary Kornblith (1993: 33) argues this was only Locke's "official" doctrine and that the "dialectic of his discussion" forced him "to a realist and nonskeptical account of real essence." Here is Locke claiming that we are incapable of knowing the real essence of the natural substances on which we depend:

> This, though it be all the *Essence* of natural Substances, that we know, or by which we distinguish them into Sorts, yet I call it by a peculiar name, the *nominal Essence*, to distinguish it from that real Constitution of Substances, upon which depends this *nominal Essence*, and all the Properties of that Sort; which therefore,

as has been said, may be called the *real Essence: v.g.* the *nominal Essence* of *Gold*, is that complex *Idea* the word *Gold* stands for, let it be, for instance, a Body yellow, of a certain weight, malleable, fusible, and fixed. But the *real Essence* is the constitution of the insensible parts of that Body, on which those Qualities, and all the other Properties of *Gold* depend.

(1975, p. 439 [III, vi, 2], quoted in Kornblith (1993: 23–24)

2 Referring to Gilbert Ryle, *The Concept of Mind*, H. L. A. Hart, *The Concept of Law*, and others.

3 Thus it's possible to explain the continuity of scientific reference without getting trapped by dilemmas of the sort Thomas Kuhn (1970) suggested – a new perspective in science must mean we are no longer referring to the same entities earlier scientists worked with. If reference is determined by the things to which we refer rather than stipulated to by our definitions, then continuity of reference is possible even if previous understandings are discarded. On this basis I argued in Chapter 2 (see pp. 43–5) that Marx and Ricardo were talking about the same thing when they referred to labor as the source of value; without subtracting in any way from the revolutionary character of Marx's theoretical advance, there is continuity of scientific reference.

4 A point of detail is worth making because of the importance of form determination to Marx's analysis. In an immediately preceding paragraph Martin Nicolaus translates "einfachen Bestimmungen," as "simple aspects" but the phrase is the same as that used in the "Method of Political Economy" where at p. 100 he translates "einfachsten Bestimmungen" as "simplest determinations:" compare 1986 MECW 28 at p. 35 with p. 190. Continuity of meaning is better carried by preserving the emphasis on "determination;" in particular, "aspects" does not capture the causal overtones "Bestimmungen" can carry.

5 Of course because of the energy required this is not a practical proposition; nonetheless, the nuclear physicist Glenn Seaborg is reported to have accomplished the feat in 1980 (Browne 1999).

5 Value and contract formation

1 The paragraph that introduces Chapter 2 "The Process of Exchange" of *Capital I* (1990: 178–179) reads in substantial part as follows:

Commodities cannot themselves go to market and perform exchanges in their own right. We must, therefore, have recourse to their guardians, who are the possessors of commodities. Commodities are things, and therefore lack the power to resist man. If they are unwilling, he can use force; in other words, he can take possession of them. In order that these objects may enter into relation with each other as commodities, their guardians must place themselves in relation to one another as persons whose will resides in those objects, and must behave in such a way that each does not appropriate the commodity of the other, and alienate his own, except through an act to which both parties consent. The guardians must therefore recognize each other as owners of private property. This juridical relation, whose form is the contract, whether as part of a developed legal system or not, is a relation between two wills which mirrors the economic relation. The content of this juridical relation (or relation of two wills) is itself determined by the economic relation.

In a footnote at this point Marx underscores the distinctiveness of his approach by challenging Prodhoun's more traditional approach; Marx's footnote reads in part as follows:

Prodhoun creates his ideal of justice, of *'justice éternelle'*, from the juridical relations that correspond to the production of commodities . . . . Then he turns round and seeks to reform the actual production of commodities, and the corresponding legal system, in accordance with this ideal.

The first footnote to Marx's passage is omitted.

2 Early works important to these developments are Bhaskar's *A Realist Theory of Science* (1997) in natural science (first published in 1975), and in social science, Bhaskar, *The Possibility of Naturalism* (1998), and Keat and Urry, *Social Theory as Science* (1982 [first edition 1975]).
3 In "Consideration as the Commitment to Relinquish Autonomy" (1997) I give a full legal analysis of the problem of consideration. Here I track that account in order to make explicit how it rests ultimately on Marx's analysis of value as a social kind.
4 In the appendix to Chapter 4, "Value as a Social Kind," I explain how we may use either the form of expression I used in Chapter 2, "the social kind of commodity producing labor," or "value as a social kind" to refer to the same underlying causal structure of labor activity.
5 In my 1997 discussion of consideration I referred to this as a social relation of "interdependent autonomy."
6 The well known case is *Ricketts* v. *Scothorn*, 57 Neb. 51, 77 N.W. 365 (1898).

6 What ought to be done: Marxism and normativity

1 Wolfgang and Christoph Lauenstein (1989). *Balance* is 8 minutes long and won an Oscar in 1990. Online: www.youtube.com/watch?v=91bNp7HJolE (last accessed July 29, 2010).
2 In a footnote to *Capital* devoted to a critique of Jeremy Bentham, Marx underscored the significance of considering both underlying biological or other features of human nature and also human nature as it occurs in any particular historical and social circumstance:

> "[I]n no time and in no country has the most homespun manufacturer of commonplaces ever strutted about in so self-satisfied a way. The principle of utility was no discovery made by Bentham. He simply reproduced in his dull way what Helvetius and other Frenchmen had said with wit and ingenuity in the eighteenth century. To know what is useful for a dog, one must investigate the nature of dogs. This nature is not itself deducible from the principle of utility. Applying this to man, he that would judge all human acts, movements, relations, etc. according to the principle of utility would first have to deal with human nature in general, and then with human nature as historically modified in each epoch. Bentham does not trouble himself with this. With the driest naiveté he assumes that the modern petty bourgeois, especially the English petty bourgeois, is the normal man. Whatever is useful to this peculiar kind of normal man, and to his world, is useful in and for itself. He applies this yardstick to the past, the present and the future."
>
> (1990: 758–759 [I. 24.5])

Philosophers looking to psychology will sometimes make a show of taking into account the effects of social relations so that how I feel and act toward you will affect how you feel and act toward me, and so forth. But there is naiveté also to suppose that we can start with the individual grasped as a social atom and then explore her interactions with others in her immediate environment without any effort first to understand how different social relations may vary in their explanatory weight or priority. Social kind analysis suggests the obvious point that in the intersection of structures that form us as social individuals, some social forms will be more important than others.

3 Norman Geras (1985) has an extensive bibliography of contributions to the original debate.
4 Marx explains: "[W]hen a man seeks to *accommodate* science to a viewpoint which is derived not from science itself (however erroneous it may be) but from *outside*, from *alien, external interests*, then I call him 'base'." (1989 MECW 31: 349).

5 Prompted again by Aristotle: I owe the story to a discussion with Tony Preus. In his book called *Problems*, Aristotle asked:

> Why do states honour courage more than anything else, though it is not the highest of the excellences? Is it because they are continually either making war or having war made against them, and courage is most useful in both these circumstances? They, therefore, honour not that which is best, but that which is best for themselves.
>
> (1984: 1489 [*Problems*, Bk 27, 948^{a}31])

That is, Aristotle suggests a distinction between what is really possible for human flourishing, on the one hand, and what a given set of social arrangements requires, on the other.

6 Ned Block and Phillip Kitcher (2010) present the basic idea of natural selection in their critical review of Fodor and Piatelli-Palmarini, *What Darwin Got Wrong*, as follows:

> Natural selection, soberly presented, is about differential success in leaving descendants. If a variant trait (say, a long neck or reduced forelimbs) causes its bearer to have a greater number of offspring, and if the variant is heritable, then the proportion of organisms with the variant trait will increase in subsequent generations. To say that there is "selection for" a trait is thus *to make a causal claim*: having the trait causes greater reproductive success.

7 By way of analogy, Darwin's theory of natural selection can also provoke attention to causal mechanisms of social selection. How might such mechanisms work to reproduce and transform social kinds like capital? This has nothing to do with Herbert Spencer's insistence that human behavior should mimic the drama he found in nature, a drama that in any event had little to do with interrogating the goodness of fit between an organism and the ecological niche it inhabits. Instead, consider how I noted in the previous chapter (the section "Final Remarks") that amidst the tremendous diversity of judicial decisions

> results which correspond to social reproduction have a staying power those that do not lack, and understanding a rule like consideration does make it possible to explain why the category has persisted and been expressed in pretty much the same form for 400 years.

In other words, given social variation provoked by the phenomena of dispute resolution in law, those resolutions tend to be selected for that work to reproduce the persistent separation of productive units as part of the social division of labor, that is, that tend to reproduce the commodity form. Here's another example: apparently there are more slaves in the world today than at any time in human history, yet because capital as a social kind lacks mechanisms to select for slavery, there is no risk of this functioning in any other way than parasitic, as crime, whether the activity be cruelly tolerated or not. Making explicit the mechanisms of social selection applicable to capital and its transformation is work that needs doing.

8 Marx continues (1991: 460–461 [III.21]),

> [t]he legal form in which these economic transactions appear as voluntary actions of the participants, as the expressions of their common will and as contracts that can be enforced on the parties concerned by the power of the state, are mere forms that cannot themselves determine this content. They simply express it. The content is just so long as it corresponds to the mode of production and is adequate to it. It is unjust as soon as it contradicts it. Slavery, on the basis of the capitalist mode of production, is unjust; so is cheating on the quality of commodities.

9 In his article "Serve the People" (1971: 310), surely a moral injunction, and one free from bourgeois notions of self-sacrifice at that, Mao Zedong commemorated the death

of a soldier who had been part of the Red Army and participated in the Long March; Chang Szu-teh was killed accidentally while making charcoal when a kiln collapsed:

> All men must die, but death can vary in its significance. The ancient Chinese writer Szuma Chien said, "Though death befalls all men alike, it may be weightier than Mount Tai or lighter than a feather." To die for the people is weightier than Mount Tai, but to work for the fascists and die for the exploiters and oppressors is lighter than a feather. Comrade Chang Szu-teh died for the people, and his death is indeed weightier than Mount Tai.

In her journal Rachel Corrie (Craig and Cindy Corrie 2008: 79) asked what she could contribute and ran through a list of grand achievements beyond her doing: "I can wash dishes," she wrote, and will be remembered for it.

10 Not the least of which was, at a later day, by Marx himself, who listed Spartacus as his hero.

11 The point noticed in endnote 16 of Chapter 3 where the "Knell to its Doom" passage is quoted in full is relevant here. As I explain there, the word first used in the *Grundrisse* to characterize the imposition of force that separates labor from its conditions of realization, "improper" (1986 MECW 28: 390; 1973: 463), gets changed when the passage is reused in a latter manuscript to a stronger and more explicit moral indictment: the coerced separation is "an injustice" (1994 MECW 34: 246).

12 The first pages of Marx's "Chapter on Capital" in the *Grundrisse* are a model of the way ideological forms may be derived from a material analysis of underlying social relations; Marx concludes:

> Thus, if the economic form, exchange, in every respect posits the equality of the subjects, the content, the material, both individual and objective, which impels them to exchange, posits *freedom.* Hence equality and freedom are not only respected in exchange which is based on exchange values, but the exchange of exchange values is the real productive basis of all *equality* and *freedom.* As pure ideas, equality and freedom are merely idealized expressions of this exchange; developed in juridical, political, and social relations, they are merely this basis at a higher level.
>
> (1986 MECW 28: 176; 1973: 245)

13 Jonathan Swift (1729) found a way to call out the corrosive indifference concealed behind a mask of supposed horror: "A Modest Proposal for Preventing the Children of the Poor People in Ireland from Being a Burden..." is online: http://art-bin.com/art/omodest.html (last accessed July 23, 2010).

14 Here is an excerpt from Marx's description of the labor process (1990: 284 [I.7.1]):

> At the end of every labour process, a result emerges which had already been conceived by the worker at the beginning, hence already existed ideally. Man not only effects a change of form in the materials of nature; he also realizes [*verwircklicht*] his own purpose in those materials. And this is a purpose he is conscious of, it determines the mode of his activity with the rigidity of a law, and he must subordinate his will to it. This subordination is no mere momentary act. Apart from the exertion of the working organs, a purposeful will is required for the entire duration of the work. This means close attention. The less he is attracted by the nature of the work and the way in which it has to be accomplished, and the less, therefore, he enjoys it as the free play of his own physical and mental powers, the closer his attention is forced to be.

The last sentence is interesting: the normative standard to which we bend our will can be externally imposed or self-determined. Marxism certainly looks to leave behind the dull and heavy moralizing moralities of externally imposed obligation, but that does not mean leaving behind the free play of the normative.

15 While I cannot argue the point now, I think the thrust of what Thompson says is right even for the decentralized structure of relations of force that constitutes international law. Samir Amin (2004: 16) has warned of a return of the fascist vision of contempt for international law and called for its defense not as a "nostalgic look toward the past but on the contrary as a reminder of what our future must be." Something more is required than the ambivalence toward the legality of the Iraq War some "newstream" scholars of international law found so wrenching (Craven, Marks, Simpson, and Wilde (2004)) and see David Kennedy quoted by China Mieville: "international law doesn't know what it is doing here folks" (Mieville 2005: 300). Also, I reject Mieville's own conclusion that struggle on the terrain of international law is "utopian and self-defeating" (2004: 302). All law, including international law, offers terrain where struggle is to be won, and consistent with Samir Amin's point, we can start by aggressively securing the prohibition against aggressive war, Nuremberg's "supreme international crime," not as a nostalgic look toward the past but exactly as a reminder for a necessary future.

16 To be fair, Lukes (1985: 32–33) adds other factors – scarcity and egoism and (assuming there were a consensus on how to live) lack of perfect information are also mentioned as jointly requiring justice and rights. Importantly, all of these characterize the human condition; that is to say, just as Ricardo and others thought bourgeois economic relations forever, on this view bourgeois justice and rights seem also destined inescapably to fill the future.

17 Attention to the virtue of respect in bourgeois society begins above all with Kant. As important as his account is, still, given a social system that depends on each person in each everyday exchange transaction relating to the other as a means to an end – buying a newspaper, coffee, etc. ("[e]ach serves the other in order to serve himself; and makes reciprocal use of the other as his means" [1986 MECW 28: 175; 1973: 243]) – and with a social system that, as we've seen, treats the worker not as the aim of production but as a means to produce things, there is some irony in the fact that Kant's theory should rest on treating the other always as an end, never as a means. Onora O'Neil (1986) suggests consent makes it okay, but each is inescapably a means for the other consent or no. So too, while in *Law's Empire* Ronald Dworkin (1988) argues that the principle of equal respect and concern represents the deepest characterization of law's integrity; nonetheless, given the disparities of wealth and poverty actually found within law's domain, and their accelerated increase, we seem forced to draw the startling and counterintuitive conclusion that law must play an immeasurably small role in the fashioning and reproducing of a society where its dominant principle has such slight and insignificant influence. Of course it is admittedly easy to argue that when it comes to irony Kantian approaches are outdone by the other dominant pillar of bourgeois moral theory: for a social system that has created magnitudes of misery undreamed of in human history, we are morally enjoined to seek the greatest happiness for the greatest number.

18 I discuss Paul Gomberg's (2007) provocative proposal for attention to "contributive justice" in Chapter 7.

7 Conclusion: winning the battle of democracy

1 The translation is as it appears in all standard versions; it is from the English version edited by Engels and published in London in 1888 (1976 MECW 6: 504). But it reads awkwardly; the word "the" before "ruling class" would help. Here is the German (Marx and Engels 1968: 44): "der erste Schritt in der Arbeiterrevolution die Erhebung des Proletariats zur herrschenden Klasse, die Erkämpfung der Demokratie ist." The meaning is clear: winning the battle for democracy is the first step in the workers revolution to transform the proletariat into a ruling class.

2 Immediately following the text in the *Communist Manifesto* explaining that the first step in the revolution is to win the battle of democracy, Marx and Engels continue:

The proletariat will use its political supremacy to wrest, by degrees, all capital from the bourgeoisie, to centralize all instruments of production in the hands of the State, i.e., of the proletariat organized as the ruling class; and to increase the total of the productive forces as rapidly as possible.

(1976 MECW 6: 504)

In an argument immediately below I will challenge those interpretations of the transition to socialism that place all emphasis on the development of the productive forces – emphases that always forget labor is the most important productive force. I argue also that wresting capital from the bourgeoisie is not a simple matter of transferring legal title, but instead that there must be an extended period of transforming precisely "by degrees" the social relations of work. In this perspective centralizing the instruments of production under the control of the proletariat organized as a ruling class cannot be separated from the question of winning the battle of democracy nor separated either from the actual forms of workable coordination, local, regional, national and global, that make the democratic organization of work really, not merely formally possible.

3 In an interesting book on the division of labor, J. B. Murphy (1993) makes a determined effort to misread Marx on this score. Thus he writes (1993: 216): "Anything that differentiates one person from another, in Marx's view, estranges man from his essence as a universal or species being." But the *Critique of the Gotha Programme* (discussed in the concluding pages of the previous chapter) shows Marx acutely sensitive to individual difference – "from each according to ability, to each according to need" is not a call for the homogenization of difference. Marx was after social arrangements that looked to the full and free development of each person's distinctive capacities and powers (see, for example, Marx 1973: 488; 1986 MECW 28: 411–412, quoted in the conclusion to Chapter Four above). Murphy's view also misses the distinction I've suggested between separation of a unity and difference within a unity. While the *Critique of the Gotha Programme* does look to a time when the division between mental and manual labor is overcome – this division pries apart features of our existence that, joined, are constitutive of our capacity to function coherently as causal beings – at the same time Marx recognizes how the distinctive development of individual ability and needs enhances rather than subtracts from the flourishing of *homo sapiens* individually and as a species.

4 Marx and Engel's (1975 MECW 5: 47) makes the distinction clearly enough in the hunter/critic passage also, but it is not usually considered in full:

And finally, the division of labour, offers us the first example of the fact that, as long as man remains in naturally evolved society, that is, as long as a cleavage exists between the particular and common interest, as long, therefore, as activity is not voluntarily, but naturally, divided, man's own deed becomes an alien power opposed to him, which enslaves him instead of being controlled by him. For as soon as the division of labour comes into being, each man has a particular, exclusive sphere of activity, which is forced upon him and from which he cannot escape. He is a hunter, a fisherman, a shepherd, or a critical critic, and must remain so if he does not want to lose his means of livelihood; whereas in communist society, where nobody has one exclusive sphere of activity but each can become accomplished in any branch he wishes, society regulates the general production and thus makes it possible for me to do one thing today and another tomorrow, to hunt in the morning, fish in the afternoon, rear cattle in the evening, criticize after dinner, just as I have a mind, without ever becoming hunter, fisherman, shepherd or critic.

If my participation in social activity is freely chosen, then I can develop my capacities according to my own self-determined priorities – the activities I choose will be differences within the unity of my own flourishing. If the division of labor in society is forced on me, then I fill a social role of society's making. I may try to bring my particular interest into harmony with the social interest, but I am still locked into a social role by my dependence on it for a livelihood. The unity here is social and I am separated from it because I am not in participative command of the distribution of social roles. By contrast, where society organizes production so that the contribution of each is according to ability, then what I make of myself is one thing and how society distributes tasks is another – my contributions will reflect those talents and capacities I can best offer others. That is I will contribute as a force of difference within a social unity in a way that fully respects my autonomy as a richly dimensioned individual.

5   I am convinced that if we are to get on the right side of world revolution, we as a nation must undergo a radical revolution of values. We must rapidly begin the shift from a thing-oriented society to a person-oriented society

Reverend Martin Luther King, April 4, 1967. The speech is widely available on the web: www.americanrhetoric.com/speeches/mlkatimetobreaksilence.htm (last accessed July 23, 2010).

6 Compare David Schweikart in *Against Capitalism* (1993: 342):

In essence, I have interpreted the transformation from socialism to communism, which Marx characterizes in terms of a shift in principles, as representing a shift in the general psychology of the population (related to a change in material conditions) rather than as some sort of structural transformation.

Like Nove, to whom he appeals, Schweikart does not really challenge the material conditions that reproduce either of capital's fundamental separations; moreover, Marx would not have thought of the revolutionary transformation of production as a "shift in principles;" still, there is no doubt people will learn to think very differently about themselves, about each other and about the natural world they engage. But this will not be done without profound structural transformation. The shift from socialism to communism is the completing and perfecting of a new social kind.

7 David Schweikart imagines a worker owned economy where after the revolution "most people could continue doing exactly what they were doing before" and that real change would occur gradually over a longer period "as workers began to exercise their newly acquired rights in the workplace." (1993: 282–83.) Rights in the workplace can play a role, but it is class struggle that will revolutionize patterns of work. Moreover, Schweikart's vision of real change has marked limits. In the following long passage from *Market Socialism: A Debate Among Socialists*, he describes the "higher stage of communism:"

Suppose our inner cities have been rebuilt, the health and educational opportunities of our citizens equalized and enhanced, and our communities stabilized. More and more we can expect that the new investments our enterprises make will be for the purpose of reducing work time (shorter workweek, longer vacations, employee sabbaticals) and for making jobs more creative and interesting, rather than enhancing income. Suppose we reach the point – and fifty years after the revolution we may be close to it – where almost everyone feels that their incomes are sufficient to free them from financial anxieties and to allow them to lead what on their own terms they would regard as a good life. Not many would say that they have *every-thing* they want. Tradeoffs would still have to be made. Some people would save to buy a bigger house; others would want to travel extensively; some would want to indulge in expensive hobbies; others would be content just to 'save for a rainy day'; some would like to throw big parties; others would like to give extensively to international relief efforts or help fund projects in areas of the world still struggling to overcome the legacy of neocolonial capitalism.

Let us suppose that not only do the vast majority feel financially secure, but most also feel that their main motivation for working is the satisfaction the job provides. It's not that work is play or that they wouldn't prefer even longer vacations, but all things considered they feel good about their jobs – and would want to work at these jobs even if they paid less than they do. That is to say, the size of the paycheck is not the principal motivation.

My question now is this: If we reached such a state, why would we want to reorganize the economy any further? Granted, it is still a market economy. Enterprises still sell their goods, and workers still receive incomes. There is still money, and even competition – though not of a cut-throat variety. The economy is solid and stable. It is not driven by capitalism's grow or die imperative. People can spend their lives without worrying much about economic matters.

I submit that such a society deserves to be called "the higher stage of communism." The society has left "the realm of necessity" and has entered "the realm of freedom." People really do, for the most part, work "according to ability," and consume "according to need." We have here the rational core of Marx's dream. The details may not be precisely what he had envisaged, but I don't think he would be terribly disappointed. In any event, were such a society to come to pass – and indeed become the attainable model for the rest of the world – I for one would argue that Marx's hopeful vision had been vindicated.

(1998: 175–176)

A half century of change to be fought for, without doubt. Yet, commenting on John Stuart Mill, Marx observed that "on a level plain simple mounds look like hills" (1990: 654 [I.16]). Call this version of "communism's higher phase" the storming of a simple mound school of revolution. Once was the task was to storm the heavens.

The references to working "according to ability" and consuming "according to need" recall the Gotha Programme passage I quoted in Chapter 6. The references to "the realm of necessity" and the "realm of freedom" evoke a well-known passage from the "Trinity Formula" chapter in *Capital III* where Marx observes that

> Freedom ... can consist only in this, that socialized man, the associated producers, govern the human metabolism with nature in a rational way, bringing it under their collective control instead of being dominated by it as a blind power; accomplishing it with the least expenditure of energy and in conditions most worthy and appropriate for their human nature. But this always remains a realm of necessity. The true realm of freedom, the development of human powers as an end in itself, begins beyond it, though it can only flourish with this realm of necessity as its basis.
>
> (1991: 959 [III.48.3])

But Marx did not think production could be brought under collective control as long as the blind powers that dominated a market society persisted. Nor, I will argue, can opportunity be equalized without winning the battle of democracy.

8 I briefly mention below Albert and Hahnel's (1991) concept of "balanced job complexes." Their argument, persuasive to me, is that where the distinction between simple and creative or between routine and empowering work remains, this will be reflected in patterns of democracy at work – those relegated to mundane tasks will tend to play a lesser role in workplace deliberations and this will finally be reflected in familiar forms of passivity even where opportunities for democratic participation exist.

9 The speech is online: www.thegrenadarevolutiononline.com/bishspkhunter.html (last accessed July 31, 2010).

10 Marshall's dissent was in *Board of Regents* v. *Roth*, 408 U.S. 564 (1972).

11 A global basic income guarantee is a sure way to attack the extremes of global poverty as they present themselves today. According to Thomas Pogge (2007)

42 percent of the world's population live below the World Bank's poverty line measure of $2 a day and have access to about 1 percent of the world's wealth. The richest 10 percent of the world's population claim 85 percent of global wealth.

12 In fact, Andrew Sayer (2009) recalls Adam Smith's judgment that without the opportunity to exert the understanding, simple repetitive tasks stultify (Smith 1976: v. 2, 302–303 [Bk. V, Ch. 1, Pt. III, Art. II, "Education of Youth"] and notices also Murphy's (1993) reference to contemporary research that confirms this. Murphy (7) observes that this research found "that the cognitive capacities of men with complex jobs developed through work whereas the cognitive capacities of men with simple and repetitive jobs deteriorated." Murphy pertinently adds: "we now attempt to protect workers from harm to their physical capacities: why should we not protect them from harm to their mental capacities?" Paul Gomberg (2007) also discusses these contemporary findings at 72–74.

13 Dongping Han (2008), who grew up in a rural Chinese village during the Chinese Cultural Revolution and who has given a fresh account of that period, reports that village leaders, formerly exempt from manual work, were required to work with farmers on a regular basis. By the end of the Cultural Revolution villagers had come to take the practice for granted, and this, he adds, contributed to a stronger public spirit than formerly existed. See also Chapter 3, "Transformations in the Social Division of Labor," in Bettelheim (1974) where he discusses steps taken during the Cultural Revolution to overcome the distinction between administrative tasks and performance tasks and also the distinction between mental and manual labor. His analysis is important: using the admittedly limited and anecdotal experience available to him, he drew far reaching theoretical insights that remain provocative for us.

14 [W]e have made a social network committed to the proposition that the central executable elements of human technology can be produced by sharing – without exclusionary property relations ... [and] the non-executable elements of culture – art, useful information, and so on – can be *distributed* without exclusionary property relations ... Thus we observe the new political economy of software.... [W]hen the marginal costs of goods is zero, any non-zero cost of barbed wire is too high.... My proposition ... is that for functional goods with zero marginal cost, production without property relations produces superior goods. And this is true the more that collaboration is necessary in order to produce.

Freeing the Mind: Free Software and the Death of Proprietary Culture
(June 29, 2003)

15 Thomas Jefferson's conviction that ideas are intrinsically free is needs remembering:

He who receives an idea from me, receives instruction himself without lessening mine; as he who lights his taper at mine, receives light without darkening me. That ideas should freely spread from one to another over the globe, for the moral and mutual instruction of man, and improvement of his condition, seems to have been peculiarly and benevolently designed by nature, when she made them, like fire, expansible over all space, without lessening their density in any point, and like the air in which we breathe, move, and have our physical being, incapable of confinement or exclusive appropriation.

(Letter to McPherson, August 13, 1813)

16 Moglen notes the example of a Presidential committee in the Clinton years that proposed (without irony) to require all K-12 institutions that received federal funds should devote a portion of their curriculum to teaching children that "sharing information is wrong" – noticing the irony, Moglen asks what the institution communicating that information would be called. The Marx quote is from the Preface to *The Contribution to the Critique of Political Economy* (MECW, v. 29: 263); Marx adds, "[t]hen begins an era of social revolution."

17 The agreement is online and provides in substance:

1 Increase participative "one class" employee ownership of businesses through understanding, adopting, and practicing the MONDRAGON Corp. cooperative model as it may apply in hybrid combinations for USW-represented companies.
2 Integrate collective bargaining with MONDRAGON Corp's cooperative practices and model, such as having the Union's Bargaining Committee also serve as the Social Council.
3 Further explore next generation hybrid approaches to collective bargaining that allow deeper worker participation and union/management collaboration.
4 Explore co-investing models and opportunities using successful precedents such as the USW's participation in the Quebec Solidarity Fund, which invests back into the greater Quebec community, and the MONDRAGON Corp. Eroski Foundation which has similar goals and a fully integrated community ownership structure.

Online: http://assets.usw.org/Releases/agree_usw_mondragon.pdf.

18 Addressing projects of self-administration, Bettelheim (1975: 91) writes: "These enterprises continue to be linked to the market and under these conditions the workers cannot really dominate either their means of production or their products, since this use is itself dominated by commodity relations."

Bibliography

Albert, M. and Hahnel, R. (1991) *The Political Economy of Participatory Economics.* Princeton: Princeton University Press.

Albo, G., Gindin, S., and Panitch, L. (2010) *In and Out of Crisis: The Global Financial Meltdown and Left Alternatives.* Oakland, CA: PM Press.

Althusser, L. (1990) "On the Materialist Dialectic," in Althusser, L., *For Marx*, London: Verso.

Althusser, L. and Balibar, E. (1979) *Reading Capital.* London: Verso.

American Law Institute (1981) *Restatement (Second) of Contracts.* St. Paul: American Law Institute.

Amin, Samir (2004) "U.S. Imperialism, Europe and the Middle East," *Monthly Review*, 56: 13–33.

Aristotle (1984) *The Complete Works of Aristotle*, J. Barnes, ed. Princeton: Princeton University Press (Bollingen).

Aristotle (1962) *The Nicomachean Ethics*, trans. M. Ostwald. Indianapolis: Bobbs-Merrill.

Aristotle (1960) *The Metaphysics*, trans. R. Hope. Ann Arbor: The University of Michigan Press.

Aristotle (1958) *The Politics of Aristotle*, trans. E. Barker. Oxford University Press: Oxford.

Arthur, C. J. (2002) *The New Dialectic and Marx's Capital.* Leiden, Boston, Koln: Brill.

Arthur, C. J. (1998) "Systematic Dialectic," *Science and Society* 62: 447.

Arthur, C. J. (1993) "Hegel's Logic and Marx's Capital," in Moseley, F. (Ed.), *Marx's Method in Capital: A Re-examination* (pp. 63–97). Atlantic Highlands, NJ: Humanities Press.

Arthur, C. J. (1979) "Dialectic of the Value Form," in D. Elson, ed., *Value: The Representation of Labour in Capitalism* (pp. 67–81). London: CSE Books.

Ashley, Clarence D. (1913) "The Doctrine of Consideration," *Harvard Law Review* 26: 429.

Backhaus, H.-G. (1992) "Between Philosophy and Science: Marxian Social Economy as Critical Theory," in W. Bonefeld, R. Gunn, and K. Psychopedis, eds., *Open Marxism v. 1: Dialectics and History.* London: Pluto Press.

Backhaus, H.-G. (1980) "On the Dialectics of the Value-Form," *Thesis Eleven* 1: 94–120. Originally written in 1969; published as "Zur Dialektik der Wertform," in A. Schmidt (ed.), *Beitraege zur marxistischen Erkenntnistheorie* Frankfurt a.M. (1980).

Barton, JL. (1969) "The Early History of Consideration," *Law Quarterly Review* 85: 872.

Bayat, A. (1991) *Work, Politics and Power: An International Perspective on Workers' Control and Self-Management.* New York: Monthly Review.

Bayat, A. (1987) *Revolution in Iran: A Third World Experience of Workers' Control.* London: Zed Books.

Bettelheim, C. (1976) *Class Struggles in the USSR: First Period 1917–1923.* New York: Monthly Review.

Bettelheim, C. (1975) *Economic Calculation and Forms of Property.* New York: Monthly Review.

Bettelheim, C. (1974) *Cultural Revolution and Industrial Organization in China: Changes in Management and the Division of Labor.* New York: Monthly Review.

Bhaskar, R. (1998) *The Possibility of Naturalism.* 3rd edn. (first published 1979). London: Routledge.

Bhaskar, R. (1997) *A Realist Theory of Science* (first published 1975). London, New York: Verso.

Bhaskar, R. (1989) *Reclaiming Reality.* London, New York: Verso.

Bloch, E. (1986) *The Principle of Hope.* Cambridge, MA: MIT Press.

Block, N. and Kitcher, P. (2010) "Misunderstanding Darwin," in *The Boston Review*, v. 35, no. 2 (March April 2010). Online: http://bostonreview.net/BR35.2/block_kitcher. php (last accessed July 27, 2010).

Bishop, M. (1983) Speech at Hunter College, June 5, 1983. Online: www.thegrenadarev- olutiononline.com/bishspkhunter.html (last accessed July 31, 2010).

Bishop, R. C. (2007) *The Philosophy of the Social Sciences: An Introduction.* New York: Continuum.

Boyd, R. (forthcoming) "What of Pragmatism with the World Here." Online: www. richard-boyd.net/home/papers (last accessed July 20, 2010).

Boyd, R. (2003) "Finite Beings, Finite Goods: The Semantics, Metaphysics and Ethics of Naturalist Consequentialism," *Philosophy and Phenomonological Research*, v. 66 (2003), pp. 505–564 and v. 67, pp. 27–47.

Boyd, R. (1999a) "Homeostasis, Species, and Higher Taxa," in RA. Wilson, ed., *Species: New Interdisciplinary.* Cambridge, MA: MIT Press.

Boyd, R. (1999b) "Kinds as the 'Workmanship of Men': Realism, Constructivism, and Natural Kinds," in J. Nida-Rumelin, ed., *Rationality, Realism, Revision, (Perspectives in Analytical Philosophy*, v. 23, pp. 52–89). Berlin: Walter de Gruyter.

Boyd, R. (1991) "Realism, Anti-Foundationalism, and the Enthusiasm for Natural Kinds." *Philosophical Studies*, 61: 127–148.

Boyd, R. (1988) "How to Be a Moral Realist," in G. Sayre-McCord, ed., *Moral Realism.* Ithaca: Cornell University Press.

Boyd, R. (1985) "*Lex Orandi est Lex* Credendi," in P. M. Churchland and C. A. Hooker, eds., *Images of Science.* Chicago: University of Chicago Press.

Boyd, Richard (1979) "Metaphor and Theory Change," in A. Ortony, ed., *Metaphor and Thought.* Cambridge: Cambridge University Press.

Brecht, B. (1966) "Writing the Truth: Five Difficulties." Online: http://forerunner.finearts. yorku.ca/~couroux/facs4934/texts/brecht.pdf (last accessed July 20, 2010). Also in E. Bentley, ed. *Galileo* (R. Winston trans). New York: Grove Press.

Browne, M. (1999) "Glenn Seaborg, Leader of the Team that found Plutonium, Dies at 86." in *The New York Times* (February 27, 1999; Section A, p. 1).

Brush, S. G. (1965) *Kinetic Theory, v. 1.* London: Pergamon Press.

Code, A. (1986) "Aristotle: Essence and Accident," in R. E. Grandy and R. Warner, eds., *Philosophical Grounds of Rationality: Intentions, Categories, Ends*, Oxford: Oxford University Press.

Code, A. (1984a) "On the Origins of Some Aristotelian Theses About Predication," in J. Bogen and J. E. McGuire, eds., *How Things Are*, pp. 101–131. Boston: D. Reidel.

Code, A. (1984b) "The Aporematic Approach to Primary Being in *Metaphysics Z.*" *Canadian Journal of Philosophy* (supp. 10: 1–20).

Collier, A. (1989) *Scientific Realism and Socialist Thought.* Hertfordshire: Wheatsheaf (Simon and Shuster International Group).

Collier, A. (1981) "Scientific Socialism and the Question of Socialist Values," in K. Nielsen and S. Patten, eds., *Marx and Morality (Canadian Journal of Philosophy Supplementary Volume VII)*, 121–154. Guelph, Ontario: Canadian Association for Publishing in Philosophy.

Corbin, A. L. (1963) *Corbin on Contracts*, v. 1, St. Paul: West Publishing.

Corrie, R. (2008) *Let Me Stand Alone: The Journals of Rachel Corrie*, C. Corrie and C. Corrie, eds. London: Granta.

Craven, M., Marks, S., Simpson, G. and Wilde, R. (2004) "We Are Teachers of International Law," *Leiden Journal of International Law*, 17 (2004), pp. 363–374.

Crenshaw, K. (1989) "Demarginalizing the Intersection of Race and Gender: A Black Feminist Critique of Antidiscrimination Doctrine, Feminist Theory, and Antiracist Politics." 1989 *Chicago Legal Forum*, pp. 139–167. Online: http://faculty.law.miami.edu/zfenton/documents/Crenshaw–DemarginalizingIntersection.pdf (last accessed July 21, 2010).

Cullenberg, S. (1999) "Overdetermination, Totality and Institutions: A Genealogy of a Marxist Institutional Economics." *Journal of Economic Institutions*, 33–4: 801–815.

Devitt, M. and Sterelny, K. (1987) *Language and Reality: An Introduction to the Philosophy of Language.* Cambridge, MA: MIT (Bradford Book).

Dworkin, R. (1988) *Law's Empire.* Cambridge, MA: Harvard (Belknap Press).

Edgerton, D. (2006) *The Shock of the Old: Technology and Global History Since 1900.* New York: Oxford University Press.

Eldred, M. and Hanlon, M. (1981) "Reconstructing Value-Form Analysis," *Capital and Class*, 13: 24–60.

Ellis, B. (2002) *The Philosophy of Nature: A Guide to the New Essentialism.* Montreal and Kingston: McGill-Queens University Press.

Ellis, B. (2001) *Scientific Essentialism.* Cambridge: Cambridge University Press.

Enc, B. (1976) "Reference of Theoretical Terms," *NOUS*, v. 10: 261–282.

Engels, F. (1988) "Supplement to the 1870 Preface for *The Peasant War in Germany*," in *Marx Engels Collected Works*, v. 23. New York: International Publishers.

Engels, F. (1987) *Herr Duhring's Revolution in Science (Anti Duhring)* in *Marx Engels Collected Works*, v. 25. New York: International Publishers.

Engelskirchen, H. (2008) "On the Clear Comprehension of Political Economy: Social Kinds and the Significance of §2 of Marx's *Capital*," in R. Groff, ed., *Revitalizing Causality: Realism about Causality in Philosophy and Social Science.* London: Routledge.

Engelskirchen, H. (1997) "Consideration as the Commitment to Relinquish Autonomy," *Seton Hall L. Rev.* 27: 490–573.

Fanon, F. (1968) *The Wretched of the Earth.* New York: Grove Weidenfeld.

Farnsworth, E. A. (1999) *Contracts.* 3rd ed. New York: Aspen.

Farrell, R. B. (1969) *A Dictionary of German Synonyms.* Cambridge: Cambridge University Press

Flaherty, D. (1992) "Self-Management and Socialism: Lessons from Yugoslavia," *Science and Society*, 56:1, pp. 92–107.

Foucault, M. (1990) *A History of Sexuality*, v. 1. New York: Vintage.

Freire, P. (2005) *The Pedagogy of the Oppressed*. (30th anniversary edn.) New York: Continuum International.

Frye, M. (1983) *Politics of Reality.* Trumansburg, NY: The Crossing Press.

Geras, N. (1985) "The Controversy about Marx and Justice," *New Left Review*, v. 150: 47–85; also in A. Callinicos, ed., (1989) *Marxist Theory.* Oxford: Oxford University Press.

Gomberg, P. (2007) *How to Make Opportunity Equal: Race and Contributive Justice.* Oxford: Blackwell.

Goosens, W. K. (1977) "Underlying Trait Terms," in S. Schwartz, ed., *Naming, Necessity, and Natural Kinds.* Ithaca, NY: Cornell.

Gordon, J. D. III (1991) "Consideration and the Commercial-Gift Dichotomy," *Vanderbilt Law Review*, 44: 283.

Gordon, J. D. III (1990) "A Dialogue About the Doctrine of Consideration," *Cornell Law Review* 75: 987.

Gramsci, A. (1977) *Selections from Political Writings: 1910–1920.* Minneapolis: University of Minnesota.

Groff, R. (2004) *Critical Realism, Post-positivism and the Problem of Knowledge.* London: Routledge.

Hacking, I. (1992) "Making Up People," in E. Stein, ed., *Forms of Desire: Sexual Orientation and the Social Constructionist Controversy.* New York: Routledge.

Hacking, I. (1991) "Experimentation and Scientific Realism. *Philosophic Topics*," 13: 77–87 (1982). Reprinted in Boyd, Gasper and Trout, eds., *The Philosophy of Science*, pp. 247–260. Cambridge, MA: MIT.

Han, D. (2008) *The Unknown Cultural Revolution: Life and Change in a Chinese Village.* New York: Monthly Review.

Heinrich, M. (2007) "Review Article: Karl Marx, *Das Kapital. Kritik der politischen Ökonomie, Dritter Band*, Hamburg 1894, in: Karl Marx, Friedrich Engels, *Gesamtausgabe* (*MEGA*). Zweite Abteilung, Band 15, hg. von der Internationalen Marx Engels Stiftung Amsterdam. Bearbeitet von Regina Roth," *Historical Materialism* 15: 195.

Heinrich, M. (1989) "Capital in General and the Structure of Marx's *Capital*," *Capital and Class*, 38: 63–79.

Hempel, C. (1945) "Studies in the Logic of Confirmation (I)," *Mind*, 54: 1–26.

Holmes, O. W. (2009) *The Common Law.* Cambridge, MA: Harvard (Belknap Press).

Hume, D. (1888) *A Treatise on Human Nature.* Oxford: Oxford University Press.

Jefferson, T. (1813) "Letter to Isaac McPherson, August 13, 1813." Online: http://people.csail.mit.edu/hqm/writings/jefferson/odur.let.rug.nl/usa/P/tj3/writings/brf/jefl220.htm (last accessed July 3, 2010).

Johnson, M. (2010) "A Network of Cooperatives Gets Organized in New York City: Low-income and immigrant workers well-represented." *Grassroots Economic Organizing (GEO)Newsletter*, v. II, no. 5. Online: http://geo.coop/node/435.

Keat, R. and Urry, J. (1982) *Social Theory As Science* (2d ed.), London: Routledge & Kegan Paul.

Keller, R., Boyd, R., and Wheeler, Q. (2003) "The Illogical Basis of Phylogenetic Nomenclature." *Bot. Rev.* 69(1): 93–110.

King, M. L. (1967) "Speech at Riverside Church, April 4, 1967." Online: www.americanrhetoric.com/speeches/mlkatimetobreaksilence.htm.

Kornblith, H. (2002) *Knowledge and its Place in Nature.* Oxford University Press.

Kornblith, H. (1993) *Inductive Inference and its Natural Ground: An Essay in Naturalistic Epistemology*. Cambridge, MA: MIT Press.

Kosman, A. (1994) "The Activity of Being in Aristotle's *Metaphysics*," in T. Scaltas, D. Charles, and M. L. Gill, eds., *Unity, Identity, and Explanation in Aristotle's Metaphysics*. Oxford: Clarendon Press.

Kripke, S. (1972) *Naming and Necessity*. Cambridge, MA: Harvard.

Kuhn, T. (1970) *The Structure of Scientific Revolutions*, 2d edn. Chicago: University of Chicago.

Lauenstein, W. and C. (1989) *Balance*. Online: www.youtube.com/watch?v=91bNp7HJolE (last accessed 21 July 2010).

Lear, J. (1988) *Aristotle: the Desire to Understand*. Cambridge: Cambridge University Press.

Lenin, V. I. (1965) "On the Immediate Tasks of the Soviet Government," in *V.I. Lenin Collected Works*, v. 27. Moscow: Progress Publishers.

Lenin, V. I. (1963) "Conspectus of Hegel's Book *The Science of Logic*," in *V. I. Lenin Collected Works*, v. 38. Moscow: Foreign Languages Publishing House.

Lockard, B. (2006) "Cornell Study Examines Surge in Self-Injury." *Ithaca Journal*, 6/10/06, pp. 1B–2B.

Locke, J. (1975) *An Essay Concerning Human Understanding*, P.H. Nidditch, ed. Oxford: Oxford University Press.

Lukes, S. (2008) *Moral Relativism*: New York: Picador.

Lukes, S. (1985) *Marxism and Morality*, Oxford: Oxford University Press.

MacCormick, N. (1972) "Voluntary Obligations and Normative Powers I," *Proceedings of the Aristotelian Society* 46: 59 (Supp. Vol. 1972).

MacIntyre, A. (2007) *After Virtue*. 3rd edn. Notre Dame, IN: University of Notre Dame Press.

Magdoff, F. and Foster, J.B. (2010) "What Every Environmentalist Needs to Know About Capitalism," *Monthly Review*, v. 61, #10. Online: www.monthlyreview.org/100301magdoff-foster.php (last accessed 20 July 2010).

Mao Tsetung [Mao Zedong] (1971) *Selected Readings from the Works of Mao Tsetung*. Peking: Foreign Languages Press.

Mao Zedong (1977) *Selected Works of Mao Zedong*, volume. V. Beijing: Foreign Languages Press.

Marcuse, H. (1941) "Some Social Implications of Technology," in *Studies in Philosophy and Social Sciences*, v. IX. Online: http://users.ipfw.edu/tankel/PDF/Marcuse.pdf (accessed, 20 July 2010).

Marx, K. (1994) *Economic Works 1861–1864*, in *Marx Engels Collected Works*, v. 34. New York: International Publishers.

Marx, K. (1992) *Economic Manuscript of 1861–63*, in *Marx Engels Collected Works*, v. 33. New York: International Publishers.

Marx, K. (1992) *Capital*, v. 2. London: Penguin Books.

Marx, K. (1991) *Capital*, v. 3. London: Penguin Books.

Marx, K. (1990) *Capital*, v. 1. London: Penguin Books.

Marx, K. (1989) *Economic Manuscripts of 1861–63*, in *Marx Engels Collected Works*, v. 32. New York: International Publishers.

Marx, K. (1989) *Economic Manuscript of 1861–63*, in *Marx Engels Collected Works*, v. 31. New York: International Publishers.

Marx, K. (1989) *Marx Engels Collected Works*, v. 24. New York: International Publishers.

Marx, K. (1988) *Economic Manuscripts of 1861–63: Capital in General (The Production*

Process of Capital), in *Marx Engels Collected Works,* v. 30. New York: International Publishers.

Marx, K. (1987) *The Grundrisse,* in *Marx Engels Collected Works,* v. 29. New York: International Publishers.

Marx, K. (1986) *Marx Engels Collected Works,* v. 22. New York: International Publishers.

Marx, K. (1986) *The Grundrisse,* in *Marx Engels Collected Works,* v. 28. New York: International Publishers.

Marx, K. (1985) *Marx Engels Collected Works,* v. 20. New York: International Publishers.

Marx, K. (1983) *Grundrisse der Kritik der politischen Ökonomie,* in *Marx Engels Werke,* Band 42. Berlin: Dietz Verlag.

Marx, K. (1976) *Marx Engels Collected Works,* v. 6. New York: International Publishers.

Marx, K. (1975) *Marx Engels Collected Works,* v. 3. New York: International Publishers.

Marx, K. (1975) *Doctoral Dissertation: Difference Between the Democritean the Epicurean Philosophy of Nature,* in *Marx Engels Collected Works,* v. 1. New York: International Publishers.

Marx, K. (1973) *Grundrisse* trans. M. Nicolaus. Harmondsworth: Penguin, NLB.

Marx, K. (1970) *Das Kapital,* Buch 1, in *Marx Engels Werke,* Band 23. Dietz Verlag: Berlin.

Marx, K. (1970) *Das Kapital,* Buch III, in *Marx Engels Werke,* Band 25. Dietz Verlag: Berlin.

Marx, K. (1967) *Capital I* (Moore and Aveling, trans.). New York: International Publishers.

Marx, K. and Engels, F. (1976) *The Communist Manifesto,* in *Marx Engels Collected Works,* v. 6. New York: International Publishers.

Marx, K. and Engels, F. (1975) *The German Ideology,* in *Marx Engels Collected Works,* v. 5. New York: International Publishers.

Marx, K. and Engels, F. (1968) "Manifest der Kommuniwstischen Partei," in *Ausgewahlte Schriften in Zwei Banden,* Band 1. Berlin: Dietz Verlag.

Meikle, S. (1991) "History of Philosophy: The Metaphysics of Substance in Marx," in T. Carver, T., ed., *Cambridge Companion to Marx* (pp. 296–313). Cambridge: Cambridge University Press.

Menser, M. (2005) "The Global Social Forum Movement, Porto Alegre's 'Participatory Budget,' and the Maximization of Democracy" *Situation: Project of the Radical Imagination,* v. 1, #1. Online: http://ojs.gc.cuny.edu/index.php/situations/article/view/8/9 (last accessed July 20, 2010).

Menser, M. and Robinson, J. (2008) "Participatory Budgeting: from Porto Alegre, Brazil to the U.S.," in J. Allard, C. Davidson, and J. Matthaei, eds., *Solidarity Economy: Building Alternatives for People and Planet.* Chicago: Changemaker Publications.

Mieville, C. (2005) *Between Equal Rights: A Marxist Theory of International Law.* Leiden: Brill.

Mieville, C. (2004) "Commodity Form Theory of International Law: An Introduction," *Leiden Journal of International Law,* v. 17, no. 2, pp. 271–302.

Milios, J., Dimoulis, D., and Economakis, G. (2002) *Karl Marx and the Classics.* Burlington, VT: Ashgate Publishing Co.

Modrak, D. K. (1985) "Forms and Compounds," in J. Bogen, and J. E. McGuire, eds., *How Things Are.* Dordrecht: D. Reidel Publishing Co.

Moglen, E. (2003a) "The dotCommunist Manifesto." Online: http://emoglen.law.columbia.edu/publications/dcm.pdf (last accessed July 21, 2010).

Moglen, E. (2003b) "Freeing the Mind: Free Software and the Death of Proprietary

Culture." Online: http://emoglen.law.columbia.edu/publications/maine-speech.html (last accessed July 21, 2010).

Moravcsik, J. M. (1991) "What Makes Reality Intelligible? Reflections on Aristotle's Theory of *Aitia*," in L. Judson, ed., *Aristotle's Physics: A Collection of Essays*. Oxford: Clarendon Press.

Murphy, J. B. (1993) *The Moral Economy of Labor: Aristotelian Themes in Economic Theory*. New Haven: Yale University Press.

Murray, P. (1997) "Redoubled Empiricism: The Place of Social Form and Formal Causality in Marxian Theory," in F. Moseley and M. Campbell, eds., *New Investigations of Marx's Method*. Atlantic Highlands, NJ: Humanities Press.

Murray, P. (1993) "The Necessity of Money: How Hegel Helped Marx Surpass Ricardo's Theory of Value," in F. Moseley, ed., *Marx's Method in Capital: A Reexamination*. Atlantic Highlands, NJ: Humanities Press.

Nelson, A. (1990) "Are Economic Kinds Natural?," in W. Savage, ed., *Scientific Theories* (Minnesota Studies in the Philosophy of Science, XIV. Minneapolis: University of Minnesota Press.

Nove, A. (1991) *The Economics of Feasible Socialism*. (2d. edn.). London: HarperCollins Academic.

Nove, A. (1987) "Markets and Socialism," *New Left Review*. I/161: 98–104.

O'Neil, O. (1986) "Perplexities of Famine and World Hunger," in T. Reagan, ed., *Matters of Life and Death: New Introductory Essays in Moral Philosophy*, 2nd edition, New York: Random House.

Peirce, C. S. (1992) "On a New List of Categories," in N. Houser and C. Kloesel, eds., *The Essential Peirce: Selected Philosophical Writings*, v. 1. Bloomington, Indianapolis: Indiana University Press

Pesic, P. (1999) "Wrestling with Proteus: Francis Bacon and the "Torture" of Nature," *Isis.*90: 81–94.

Pinker, S. (1999) *How The Mind Works*. New York: Norton.

Plato. (1961) *Phaedrus*, in E. Hamilton and H. Cairns, eds., *Collected Dialogues of Plato*. New York: Bollingen.

Platts, M. (1997) *Ways of Meaning: An Introduction to the Philosophy of Langugage* (2d ed.), Cambridge MA: MIT.

Pogge, T. (2007) "Poverty and Human Rights." Online: http://www2.ohchr.org/english/issues/poverty/expert/docs/Thomas_Pogge_Summary.pdf.

Pollock, F. (1914) *Law Quarterly Review* 30: 128 (unsigned review).

Pound, Roscoe (1945) "Individual Interests of Substance – Promised Advantages," *Harvard Law Review* 59: 1.

Psillos, S. (1999) *Scientific Realism: How Science Tracks Truth*. London: Routledge.

Purrington, R. (1997) *Physics in the Nineteenth Century*. New Brunswick, NJ: Rutgers University Press.

Putnam, H. (1996) "The Meaning of Meaning," in Pessin, A. and Goldberg, S., eds., *The Twin Earth Chronicles*. Armonk, NY: M. E. Sharpe.

Putnam, H. (1991) "Explanation and Reference," in R. Boyd, P. Gasper, and J. D. Trout, eds., *The Philosophy of Science*. Cambridge, MA: MIT.

Quine, W. V. (1991) "Natural Kinds," in R. Boyd, P. Gasper, and J.D. Trout, J. D., eds., *The Philosophy of Science*. Cambridge, MA: MIT.

Railton, P. (1991) "Marx and the Objectivity of Science," in R. Boyd, P. Gasper, and J. D. Trout, eds., *The Philosophy of Science*. Cambridge, MA: MIT.

Rawls, J. (1971) *The Theory of Justice*. Cambridge, MA: Harvard.

Raz, J. (1977) "Promises and Obligations," in P. Hacker and J. Raz, eds., *Law, Morality and Society*, Oxford: Oxford University Press.

Reale, G. (1980) *The Concept of First Philosophy and the Unity of the Metaphysics of Aristotle*. Albany: State University of New York.

Resnick, S. and Wolff, R. (2004) "Dialectics and Class in Marxian Economics: David Harvey and Beyond," *New School Economic Review*, 1:1 (91–114).

Reuten, G. (1993) "The Difficult Labor of a Theory of Social Value: Metaphors and Systematic Dialectics at the Beginning of Marx's *Capita*," in F. Moseley, ed., *Marx's Method in Capital: A Reexamination*. Atlantic Highlands, NJ: Humanities Press.

Reuten, G. and Williams, M. (1989) *Value-Form and the State*, London: Routledge.

Rieppel, O. (2005) "Modules, Kinds, and Homology." *J. of Experimental Zoology*, 304B: 18–27.

Rieppel, O. (2004) "Monophyly, Paraphyly, and Natural Kinds." *Bio. and Phil.*, 19:1–23.

Robinson, J. (1962) *Economic Philosophy*. Harmondsworth: Penguin.

Rosdolsky, R. (1977) The Making of Marx's 'Capital'. V. 1. London: Pluto

Rosenberg, A. (1983) "If Economics Isn't Science, What Is It?' *The Philosophical Forum*, v. XIV, Nos. 3–4, pp. 296–314.

Sayer, A. (2009) "Contributive Justice and Meaningful Work," *Res Publica* 15: 1–16.

Schumacher, E. (1989) "Buddhist Economics," in *Small is Beautiful: Economics As If People Mattered.* New York: Harper. Online: www.schumachersociety.org/buddhist_economics/english.html (last accessed on 07/06/10).

Schweikart, D. (1993) *Against Capitalism.* Cambridge: Cambridge University Press.

Searles, J. (1996) *The Philosophy of Mind.* Springfield, VA: The Teaching Company.

Smith, A. (1976)   *The Wealth of Nations,* E. Cannan, ed. Chicago: University of Chicago Press.

Smith, T. (1993) "Marx's *Capital* and Hegelian Dialectical Logic," in F. Moseley, ed., *Marx's Method in Capital: A Reexamination.* Atlantic Highlands, NJ: Humanities Press.

Stace, W. T. (1955) *The Philosophy of Hegel: A Systematic Exposition*, London: Dover.

Stalin, J. (1972) *The Economic Problems of Socialism in the USSR.* Beijing: Foreign Languages Press.

Taylor, Nicola (2000) "Abstract Labour and Social Mediation in Marxian Value Theory," unpublished Bachelor's thesis, Murdoch University School of Economics, Western Australia.

Tenner, E. (2007) "A Place for Hype." *London Review of Books*, May 10, 2007. v. 29, no. 9: 33–34.

Thompson, E. P. (1978) *The Poverty of Theory and Other Essays.* New York: Monthly Review.

Thompson, E. P. (1975) *Whigs and Hunters.* Pantheon: New York.

Wagner, G. (2001) *The Character Concept in Evolutionary Biology.* London: Academic Press.

Watson, A. (1991) *Roman Law and Comparative Law*, Athens, GA: University of Georgia Press.

Watson, J. and Crick, F. (1953) "Molecular Structure of Nucliec Acids: A Structure fpr Deoxynucleic Acids. *Nature* 171: 737–738.

Webb, B. and Webb, S. (1914) "Co-operative Production and Profit Sharing," *New Statesman: Special Supplement.*

Wendt, A. (1999) *Social Theory of International Politics.* Cambridge, New York: Cambridge University Press.

Wessman, M. B. (1996) "Retraining the Gatekeeper: Further Reflections on the Doctrine of Consideration," *Loyola of Los Angeles Law Review*, 29: 713.

Wessman, M. B. (1993) "Should We Fire the Gatekeeper? An Examination of the Doctrine of Consideration," *University of Miami Law Review* 48: 45.

Wilde, Lawrence (1998) *Ethical Marxism and its Radical Critics.* New York: Palgrave MacMillan.

Williams, B. (1996) "History, Morality, and the Test of Reflection," in C. M. Korsgaard, *The Sources of Normativity.* Cambridge: Cambridge University Press.

Williams, M. (1988) *Value, Social Form and the State.* New York: St. Martin's.

Williston, S. (1894) "Successive Promises of the Same Performance," *Harvard Law Review* 8: 27.

Williston, S. (1936) *Treatise on the Law of Contracts*, v. 1, New York: Baker, Voorhis.

Wilson, R. A. (1999) *Species: New Interdisciplinary Essays.* Cambridge, MA: MIT.

Wood, A. (1991) "Marx Against Morality," in P. Singer, ed., *A Companion to Ethics.* Oxford: Blackwell.

Wood, A. (1981a) "The Marxian Critique of Justice," in M. Cohen, T. Nagel, and T. Scanlon, eds., *Marx, Justice and History: A Philosophy and Public Affairs Reader* (pp. 3–41); reprinted from *Philosophy and Public Affairs*, v. 1, no. 3 (Spring 1972). Princeton: Princeton University Press.

Wood, A. (1981b) "Marx on Right and Justice: A Reply to Husami," in M. Cohen, T. Nagel, and T. Scanlon, eds., *Marx, Justice and History: A Philosophy and Public Affairs Reader* (pp. 106–134); reprinted from *Philosophy and Public Affairs*, v. 8, no. 3 (Spring 1979). Princeton: Princeton University Press. Reprinted from *Philosophy and Public Affairs*.

Wood, E. M. (1998) "The Agrarian Origins of Capitalism," *Monthly Review* 50: 14. Online: http://monthlyreview.org/798wood.htm (last accessed July 22, 2010).

Wolff, R. (1996) "Althusser and Hegel: Making Marxist Explanations Anti-Essentialist and Dialectical," in, A. Callari and D. F. Ruccio, eds., *Postmodern Materialism and the Future of Marxist Theory: Essays in the Althusserian Tradition*, Hanover and London: Wesleyan University Press.

Volosinov, V. N. (1986) *Marxism and the Philosophy of Language*, trans. L. Matejka and I. R. Titunik. Cambridge, MA: Harvard.

Young, I. M. (2002) *Inclusion and Democracy.* Oxford: Oxford University Press.

Index

abstract labor 52–4, 69–70
abstract possibility 67, 68–71, 160; *see also* real possibility
abstraction: "abstraction of object" (Althusser) 22–3; to distinctive specificity 13, 34, 51, 53, 56–62, 108–9; power of 20–1, 56, 62, 176n10, 180n7; rational abstraction 114; real abstraction 51; and scientific experiment 20–1, 108, 177n11; thinner or more tenuous forms of 61–2, 108–9
accommodation thesis 15
Albert, M. and Hahnel, R. 164
Albo,G., Gindin, S. and Panitch, L. 160, 168
alienation 26, 53, 55, 82–4, 94–5, 134, 140
Althusser, L. 19, 21–4, 27
Anglo-American law 105–6, 117, 130
appropriation of living labor by objectified labor 26, 78, 82, 93, 97, 101
Aristotle: actuality and process 124; aetiology 32; constitutive and attributive causes 8, 89; efficient, material, formal, and final causes 80, 91; Marx's study of 9, 28, 30–3, 35, 49, 62, 89, 124; matter-form composites (hylomorphism) 9–10, 28, 32–3, 35, 91, 95; Milo and the wrestler's diet 127–8; substance and primary substance (*ousia*) 32–3, 45, 178n12; theory of natural place 43
Arthur, C. 31, 46–7, 53, 110
associated workers' control of production 98, 139, 141, 147–8, 150–3, 158–61, 169, 173–4
association: as a condition for flourishing 103, 145, 154–5; cooperative association 98, 152, 158, 170–2; new historical and democratic forms of 138,

147–50, 156, 168, 173; *see also* separation (and association)
autonomy: and capital 71, 82, 101, 151, 160; juridical relations of 101; respect for personal autonomy 143–4; surrender or relinquishment of 25, 71, 83, 94–5, 101, 117–18, 120–1, 151, 160; and value 71, 111–13, 115–22, 135, 149; *see also* interdependent autonomy

Backhaus, H.G. 22, 45, 47–54, 90
Balance 125–6, 137
balanced job complexes 164, 189n8
bargain: Adam Smith's explanation of 106; collective bargaining 163, 171; enforcement of 117–20; meaning clarified 115, 118; and social reproduction of the commodity form 105, 120; and value 115–16, 119, 123; wage bargain 61; *see also* consideration (legal doctrine of); promise
base and superstructure 23, 105, 123, 177n12
Bayat, A. 156–7, 163, 165
Bettelheim, C: class struggle 157; commune and self-managed enterprise distinguished 170; double separation 25, 55, 92; modifying work and tools 166; persistence of commodity categories 42, 46, 150; real definition 63, 92; social and economic calculation (SEC) 169
Bhaskar, R. 5, 7, 10, 19, 39–40, 114, 122
Bishop, Maurice 159
Boyd, R.: accommodation thesis 15; central core conception of natural kinds 42–3; homeostatic property cluster kinds 8, 36; indeterminacy of classification 38; metaphysical innocence 5, 23, 35, 40, 42; natural kinds 7, 18, 38, 42, 56;